HISTORICAL ARCHAEOLOGY OF ARKANSAS

HISTORICAL ARCHAEOLOGY
OF ARKANSAS

A Hidden Diversity

Edited by Carl G. Drexler

The University of Tennessee Press / Knoxville

Library of Congress Cataloging-in-Publication Data

Historical archaeology of Arkansas : a hidden diversity / edited by Carl G. Drexler. — First
edition.
    pages cm
  Includes bibliographical references and index.
  ISBN 978-1-62190-182-2 (hardcover : alkaline paper)
  1. Archaeology and history—Arkansas. 2. Historic sites—Arkansas. 3. Social archaeology—
Arkansas. 4. Arkansas—Antiquities. 5. Arkansas—History, Local. 6. Archaeology—Research—
Arkansas. I. Drexler, Carl G.
  F413.H57 2016
  976.7'01—dc23
        2015000058

CONTENTS

Introduction. Arkansas Historical Archaeology through Time ix

1. Colonel Mustard and the Dog with the Crock in the
   Basement: The Power of Things in Places in
   Antebellum Arkansas 1
   Leslie C. Stewart-Abernathy
2. Archaeology of Kinship at Treat, Arkansas: Intersections
   of Past Lives, Memory, and Identity on the Landscape 23
   Mary Z. Brennan
3. A Symbolic and Sacred Landscape: The Confederate
   Cemetery in Fayetteville, Arkansas 45
   Duncan P. McKinnon
4. The Howe Pottery (3SA340): A Traditional Stoneware
   Manufacturing Site on Military Road in Benton, Arkansas 57
   C. Andrew Buchner
5. The Spread of Technology to a Rural Arkansas
   Blacksmith Shop 87
   Alicia B. Valentino
6. Zachary Taylor and the Sisters of Mercy: An Archaeology
   of Memory, Landscape, Gender, and Faith on Arkansas's
   Western Frontier 111
   Jamie C. Brandon and Jerry E. Hilliard
7. Uncovering the Past: The Lewis Log Home and Its Place
   in Ozark History 129
   Eric Proebsting
8. Thunder in the Hollow: The Archaeology of Missouri
   State Guard Artillery at the Battle of Pea Ridge 163
   Carl G. Drexler

9. The Archaeology of Judaism, Slavery and Assimilation
    on the Antebellum Frontier   191
        David M. Markus

    Contributors   219
    Index   223

ILLUSTRATIONS

Figures

Figure 0.1. Sites Discussed in the Text   xiv

Figure 1.1. Map of Arkansas Showing Selected Locations
Discussed in the Text   2

Figure 1.2. Upper and Lower Surfaces of a "Rose" Pattern
Red Transfer Printed Saucer   4

Figure 1.3. Skeleton of a Dog   8

Figure 1.4. East Half of the Foundations and Features of
the Ashley Mansion   11

Figure 1.5. Ms. McKicia Henry, Interpreter   15

Figure 2.1. Treat, Arkansas   24

Figure 2.2. Page Family Farmsteads along Moccasin Creek   37

Figure 3.1. Iron Gate and Stone Pillars at the Entrance to
the Confederate Cemetery   46

Figure 3.2. The Octagonal Shape of the Confederate Cemetery   50

Figure 3.3. Evidence of the "Slumping" of Recent Burials   52

Figure 3.4. Profile of Ground-Penetrating Radar Data   53

Figure 3.5. Plan View (Time-Slice) Showing Individual Burial
Shafts at the Confederate Cemetery   54

Figure 4.1. Site Plan View Map   58

Figure 4.2. Photo of the Exposed Kiln Feature; View West   68

Figure 4.3. Plan View Drawing of the Exposed Kiln Feature
at 3SA340   69

Figure 4.4. Detailed Plan and Profile Drawing of Feature 1   70

Figure 4.5. Drawings of Representative Howe Pottery Vessels   73

Figure 5.1. Van Winkle Features   90

Figure 5.2. Delineation of Blacksmith Shop Excavations   93

Figure 5.3. Stratigraphy of Van Winkle Forge Box   94

Figure 5.4. Van Winkle Blacksmith Shop Layout   95

Figure 6.1. Chimney Standing behind the Immaculate
Conception Church, Fort Smith   112

Figure 6.2. Postcard Showing the Chimney as Converted into   117
a Grotto

Figures 6.3a–d. Sanborn Maps Showing the Sisters of
Mercy Complex   118

Figure 6.4. Unit 2, West Profile   121

Figure 6.5. Artifacts Recovered from the Sisters of   123
Mercy Complex

Figure 7.1. Overview of Northwest Arkansas   134

Figure 7.2. Drawings of Front, Back, and Sides of the   139
Lewis House

Figure 7.3. An Early 20th Century Image of the   141
Saddlebag-Style Home Built

Figure 7.4. Ruth Morris and Elizabeth Mcgarrah Reed   150

Figure 7.5. Map of The Shiloh Museum Grounds   151

Figure 8.1. Pea Ridge National Military Park   175

Figure 8.2. 24-Pounder Canister Ball   179

Figure 8.3. 24-Pounder Canister Case Shot Fragment   179

Figure 9.1. Abraham Block and Fanny Block   195

Figure 9.2. 1982 Excavations at the Block Family House   203

Figure 9.3. Chimney Feature From 1999 Excavations at the   204
Block Family House

Figure 9.4. Second Hand Memory Map from Informant   206
Moss Rowe

Tables

Table 2.1. Population Returns for Allen Township   25

Table 2.2. Archaeological Sites   26

Table 4.1. Howe Pottery Artifact Recovery Summary   71

Table 4.2. Howe Pottery Stoneware Surface Treatment
Frequencies   72

ARKANSAS HISTORICAL ARCHAEOLOGY THROUGH TIME

Carl G. Drexler

> . . . Arkansas during these years was, to be sure, on the far fringe
> of national life. Its remoteness gave it a special character that
> seemed most obvious to transient observers. . . Yet Arkansas
> could also be understood not as a backwater but as a confluence
> of several streams of national development during the first half
> of the [19th] century.
>
> —Elliott West, foreword to *Bolton's Arkansas,*
> *1800–1860: Remote and Restless*

Early one warm, still morning in June of 2005, a small crowd of park
officials, academics, and interested members of the public gathered deep
inside Hobbes State Park, a wilderness area situated in the far northwest
corner of Arkansas. They were there to mark the opening of a walking trail and set of interpretive signs at the site of Van Winkle's Mill,
a sawmill community that had been the focus of a decade's worth of
archaeological investigation. The site was one of the early industrial
facilities of the Arkansas Ozarks, opening in the 1850s and lasting until
the early 20th Century (Jamie Brandon, personal communication, 2011).

The State Parks staff stretched a small banner behind the micro-
phone before the start of the ceremony. In addition to the park's name,
the banner bore the words "The Hidden Diversity." Hobbes staffers
originally created the slogan to reference the rich ecological diversity of
the mountainous terrain surrounding the site (Jamie Brandon, personal
communication, 2011), but the archaeological research at Van Winkle's

Mill showed that it was equally applicable to the cultural diversity of the site, in particular, and the state. The mill was an industrial center in what is usually thought of as an overwhelmingly agrarian state; it used enslaved African Americans as laborers in the years before the Civil War, though the mountain south is usually thought of as being home to only white yeoman farmers; and, finally, the site's namesake, Peter Marselis Van Winkle, was a New York City-born scion to a Dutch family that traced its history in the Empire State back as far as 1625, and therefore one of the few Northerners to emigrate to the region before the Civil War.

I chose to recycle the title for this volume because I see it as emblematic of the too-frequently unappreciated complexity of Arkansas's past. Historian Elliott West (1998) suggests that this very complexity may account for the inattention to the Natural State, as its "remarkable diversity within a relatively small area may have frustrated the search for the grand unifying themes that historians love." For most Americans, Arkansas' place in history is marked by two different events, the 1957 desegregation of Little Rock's Central High School and the emergence of Bill Clinton and Wal-Mart towards the end of the 20th century (West 1998).

These points in our state history are interspersed with a general negative perception of the state as a cultural and intellectual backwater, an image that has haunted Arkansas since its inception (Blevins 2009). This image masks a rich, diverse, and complex state history and, for our purposes, a rich history of historical archaeology. Several Arkansans, both native and immigrant, have been influential scholars within historical archaeology, and several of our sites have acquired national renown. Amongst these nodes of repute grow a network of less well-known projects that cover great spatial, topical, and temporal territory, from the colonial period through the Civil War and more recent periods. French, Native American, Spanish, African American, and European American sites, including battlefields, residences, forts, convents, trading posts, farms, boat wrecks, and myriad other kinds of sites have been (and continue to be) investigated.

This book is the first edited volume on historical archaeology in Arkansas, and we see this as an opportunity to showcase an illustrious history and current richness. That richness springs from strong traditions of research at the state and federal level, a function of the multitude of parks in a state that prides itself on its natural beauty, several contract firms that have worked in the state through the years, and by the Arkansas Archeological Survey, one of the earliest public archaeological programs in the country. To these are added the long history of public support through the Arkansas Archeological Society, and research from various state institutions of higher education. The work in this volume is a testament to the work that can come from unusually strong collaborations and cross-fertilizations of the various branches of archaeology. We also hope it be a useful resource for current and future archaeologists, historical and prehistoric in orientation, professional and avocational, and for the people of Arkansas whose interest is in the material traces of the recent past. We hope that the reader finds in these pages a window onto the rich, complex, and engaging history of the Natural State and its people.

I hope many of my fellow Arkansans find this an illuminating look at the state's recent archaeological past. I also intend the work to stand as a contemporary answer to a question often put to me by colleagues not from this state, namely, "why should I be interested in Arkansas?" Putting aside the regional parochialism inherent in this question, my standard answer pivots around the idea that closer scrutiny of Arkansas's past is necessary to tie together many of the major themes of America's past. Rather than the backwater our state get painted as, Arkansas is inescapably a historical nexus; a crossroads, if you will. This state is where the Southeast abuts the Southwest, and where the lower reaches of the Midwest meets both of the preceding. Part of the antebellum Deep South, it is also the roots of the great westward push of American settlement in the 19th century, and was our national border with Mexico for several generations. We cannot properly understand these phenomena, as well as Indian removal, the development of the military-industrial complex, and a hundred other topics on a national level without reckoning Arkansas's place in them. Our centrality is why "you" need "us."

Growing a lush understanding of these topics requires archaeological analysis in addition to the work of Arkansas's committed cohort of historians, both professional and avocational. Historical archaeologists frequently point out how archaeologists reach the least-documented people in society (typically women, non-whites, and the poor), an observation that I believe makes historical archaeology crucial to understanding Arkansas's past; as many of our historical complexities cannot be understood without fuller analyses of these marginalized groups. Additionally, archaeology traditionally works with longer time scales and across greater regions than historians, particularly local historians. This elasticity of scope and range serves as a bridge between locally-oriented historical research and wider historical and archaeological studies.

Setting the Stage

While numerous definitions of historical archaeology exist, from the methodological (Andrén 1998) to the thematic (Orser 1996), for the purposes of this chapter, we will follow Orser and Hall and Silliman (2006), among others, in viewing historical archaeology as being the archaeology of the origin and expansion of the modern world, a specific historical phenomenon born in Europe and typified by colonialism, modernity, capitalism, and Eurocentrism. For Arkansas, this would cover any site associated with the De Soto Expedition in the 1540s up through today. Additionally, we adopt the understanding of archaeology as man's material engagement with the world, a definition popular in archaeological studies of the recent past and materialist epistemologies. It is important to note that we do not require subject materials to have been excavated for their study to be considered "archaeological;" this is a deliberate stance taken to open archaeological research to topics and questions we are uniquely well-equipped to study.

To place the subsequent chapters in context, we use this opening chapter as an overview of the history of historical archaeology in Arkansas. This is not the first such effort (see below), but builds on those prior efforts and adds emphasis on the place of Arkansas in the formative debates of historical archaeology as a field, among other topics.

The first summary of historical archaeology in the region was Stewart-Abernathy's (1999) "From Famous Forts to Forgotten Farmsteads," a chapter in Mainfort and Jeter's (1999) *Arkansas Archaeology*. Though paying significant attention to Arkansas, Stewart-Abernathy did not cover the entire state, focusing instead on historical archaeology in the mid-South, an area roughly centered on Memphis, Tennessee, and extending south to Natchez, Mississippi, north to the mouth of the Ohio River, west as far as Little Rock, and east to the Tennessee River (Stewart-Abernathy 1999). Archaeologists interested in the wider mid-South area are directed to this work in particular, as Stewart-Abernathy, in addition to assessing the history of mid-South historical archaeology, also offered an extensive bibliography that contains more references than those cited, and is a valuable resource and guide for further reading.

South and Deagan (2002) offer an overview of historical archaeology in the U.S. Southeast as a whole, and include several references to research in Arkansas. They note, and it bears repetition here, that historical archaeologists working in the U.S. Southeast have traditionally been more intellectually aligned with colleagues outside of the region than with peers in the Southeast. They link this to the global nature of the subject under scrutiny (see the above-employed definition of the field). Truly regionalized historical archaeology, they assert, has appeared only in the past few decades (South and Deagan 2002:35). The recent upswing in historical archaeological research in Arkansas, including the recent *Arkansas Historical Quarterly* issue (see below) and this volume, are then stepping stones on the path to a self-contained Arkansas historical archaeology.

Most recently, Kwas (2009a) provided a history of historical archaeology in Arkansas to foreword an edition of the *Arkansas Historical Quarterly* (AHQ), which focused on historical archaeology. Her article is arranged topically, following different threads of research (farming, human remains, Old Davidsonville, Historic Washington, etc.) through their respective histories. Kwas was writing to an audience of primarily historians, and her overview is a valuable introduction and ambassador work for non-archaeologists. The history presented here builds on Kwas's and Stewart-Abernathy's by adopting a statewide focus and being organized both chronologically and delving deeply into certain areas of interest to historical archaeologists.

Several themes emerge in preceding accounts that appear here as well. Among them is the importance, as noted above, of several institutions that were instrumental in building historical archaeology in Arkansas. State and federal agencies, particularly the National Park Service and Arkansas State Parks, were instrumental in spurring the first studies and supporting decades of research at places like Arkansas Post, Old Davidsonville, and Pea Ridge. The Arkansas Archeological Survey has carried forward numerous research projects at various sites, including some state parks, which has helped it grow into a model public archaeology system. It has always received strong support and enjoyed close ties with the Arkansas Archeological Society, the state's avocational group who, in addition to providing research topics have made many research projects, such as those at Historic Washington and Old Davidsonville state parks, possible through providing expertise and labor. Finally, the contract side of archaeology, conducted by in-state firms such as Mid-Continental Research Associates and Spears as well as out-of-state companies such as Panamerican Consultants (see Buchner, this volume) has also been an active area of research. The chapters in this book reflect these roots. Research emerging from state and federal parks, the Survey, the Society, and contract archaeology all grace the following pages, and these different sectors have cross-fed each other

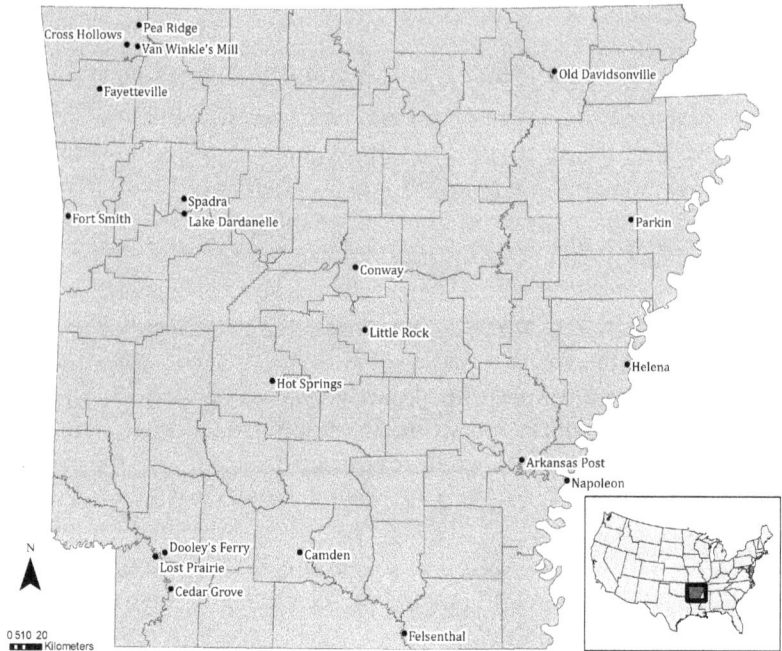

Figure 0.1. Sites discussed in the text.

by providing personnel, research questions, and support through the decades. While this can be said of many states, Arkansas's tightly-knit archaeological community, which frequently places avocational and professional archaeologists together, makes for an uncommonly strong partnership, and one that has helped keep archaeological research in this state truly focused on public service. The state's motto, *Regnat Populus*, means "the people rule;" and the history of archaeological research in this state very much reflects that ethos.

Arkansas Historical Archaeology in the Early Years (to 1960)

Previous discussions of the history of Arkansas historical archaeology start with the observations of an adventurer or antiquarian who, in traversing the state noted the existence of a historic site during his (it is invariably a man) prevarications. Kwas (2009a, 333–334) cites both William Stevenson, who documented Spanish forts on the Saline River and at Cane Hill in 1842, and Edward Palmer, who happened upon one of the various iterations of Arkansas Post (see below), the

17th century French and Spanish colonial site in eastern Arkansas, in 1882. Stewart-Abernathy, writing about historical archaeology in the mid-South, starts with Friedrich Gerstäcker, a German explorer who, in 1843, wrote of finding the remains of a fight between a Native American and a bear (neither of whom survived the fight) while exploring a cave in Newton County, in the northern part of the state. A rifle and a knife, "thickly corroded with rust" (Gerstäcker 1968; cited in Stewart-Abernathy 1999), lay at the man's side. Though these are all historical archaeological observations, they are far from the systematic sort of historical archaeology practiced today. The roots of that scholarship are traceable to the early 20th century in the United States, and branched widely into Arkansas in the 1950s.

Historical archaeology in the U.S. southeast dates to the 1920s, and was given a boost by the Works Progress Administration and Tennessee Valley Authority relief programs in the 1930s and 1940s (Lyon 1996). South and Deagan (2002) also note that for much of its early decades, historical archaeology was dedicated to Native American sites that contained historic period (European) materials. J. C. Harrington, one of the first true historical archaeologists in the United States, recalled that contact period sites like Jamestown, Virginia, and St. Augustine, Florida, were among the first to be studied because they at least were a bridge to the prehistoric period, and thus garnered the first generation of historical archaeologists less calumny from their peers at conferences and more professional respect than, for instance, Civil War battlefields (Lyon 1996).

While these early steps were taking place outside of Arkansas, local scholars were considering what historical archaeology could bring to the study of the state's past. Dr. T. L. and Mrs. Charlotte Hodges published "Possibilities for the Archaeologist and Historian in Eastern Arkansas" in the *Arkansas Historical Quarterly* in 1943. The Hodges identified Arkansas Post, historic Native American settlements (including tribes displaced during the Removal Period who had paused in Arkansas on their way west), the sites of De Soto and La Salle, and the submerged town of Napoleon (Hodges and Hodges 1943) as sites that would benefit greatly from archaeological exploration. Their prospectus identified several sites that were among the first subjects of historical archaeological inquiry in Arkansas.

As was the case elsewhere in the country, later European American and African American historical sites were largely overlooked in the early years of professional archaeological research. For example, when archaeologists from the River Basin Survey office in Lincoln, Nebraska, the forerunner of the National Park Service's Midwest Archeological Center (MWAC), sur-veyed the area to be inundated by the Dardanelle Reservoir in the 1950s, they utterly ignored historic sites. Davis (1987; 2002) notes that this was an unfortunate loss of an opportunity to study historic Cherokee sites dating to the early stages of the Removal Period, between the 1780s and the 1820s, as well as Dwight Mission and Spadra Factory, which supplied those communities. The same shortcoming haunts the Lower Mississippi Valley Survey, which explored the drainages for Bayou Bartholomew, the White River, and the Arkansas River as high as Little Rock (Phillips et al. 2003:Figure 1).

The Search for Arkansas Post

True, systematic, historical archaeology in Arkansas began, fittingly, at some of the earliest historic sites in the state, including the afore-mentioned Arkansas Post, a series of French and Spanish colonial sites dating from 1686 to the late 19th century. Arkansas Post was the first European settlement in what would become the Louisiana Purchase, and was intended to funnel the riches of the early fur trade in the west into French pockets (Arnold 1991:5–7). Through a succession of attempts at settlement, Arkansas Post remained a complex, multi-ethnic community that was both a site of administrative power and an important entrepôt between indigenous and colonial societies at the dawn of the fur trade era.

One must say "sites" in reference to Arkansas Post, as there were five incarnations of the same entity at three distinct locations occupied at various points from the 17th–19th centuries. Edward Palmer, of the Smithsonian Institution's Bureau of Ethnology was the first to excavate at one of these forts. Palmer crisscrossed eastern Arkansas in the 1880s, investigating numerous mound sites. During the course of his work, he conducted limited excavations on the "remains of [an] Old Fortification on [the] Arkansas river." Jeter (1990:230, 240–241) believes Palmer's notes to cover the Arkansas Post sited in eastern Desha County, which was oc-cupied between 1756 and 1779. Palmer's notes speak of a fort measuring 150 yards on a side with a causeway leading down to the Arkansas River. A local resident, Mr. Oliver Bizzell, claimed "numerous thimbles, pipes, broken dishes, parts of revolvers, gun, & pieces of silver coin... and Chinese and other coins were found with broken articles of Indian origin" (Jeter 1990:240; Kwas 2009a:334), suggesting a historic, multi-ethnic site. This first spate of fieldwork, occurring by happenstance during the course of a project focusing on prehistoric sites, did not lead to immediate further inquiry or into efforts to explore, preserve, or interpret the site.

Arkansans, themselves, took up the mantle of preserving Arkansas Post in the 1920s. Fletcher Chenault, a reporter for the *Arkansas Gazette*, penned articles clamoring for its protection in 1926. Dr. T. L. and Mrs. Charlotte Hodges purchased the land containing the Menard site in 1940, and played host to Phillip Phillips the following year. Phillips conducted some excavations there, but focused only on the prehistoric component of the site. The National Park Service began evaluating the site for inclusion in its system as early as 1939, though World War II delayed major research efforts (Coleman 1987:121; House 2002:257).

In 1957, the NPS dispatched Preston Holder to Arkansas, tasking him with locating the various Arkansas Posts. Aware that the work of Palmer and that of C.B. Moore (1908) and Phillip Phillips (1941), as well as recent historical research by Mattison (1957), Holder selected the Menard site as a starting point, assuming it to be the best candidate for being the original Arkansas Post, dating to 1686. Unfortunately, Holder was denied access to the bulk of the Menard site by Charlotte Hodges, though he was able to sample enough of the surrounding property to suggest that the site contained the stockade of either Fort Carlos III (1779–1792) or Fort Esteban (1792–1812), both iterations of Arkansas Post.[1]

Holder was soon thereafter shifted elsewhere to focus on other projects, so J. C. Harrington, Director of Interpretation for Region 1 of the National Park Service and one of the early dons of historical archaeology, contracted with the American Museum to send James A. Ford to work more extensively at Menard in 1958 (Ford 1961:1). His research led him to determine that the site was the village of Osotouy, a Quapaw village mentioned by French chroniclers (Davis 2002; Ford 1961) that was a contemporary to the late-18th century version of Arkansas Post.

Curiously enough, archaeological research intended to locate and aid in Arkansas Post's preservation actually worked against the effort to turn the site into a national park. Since the work of Holder and Ford located either later iterations of the Post or associated Native American villages, and not the 1686 Post proper, the National Park Service decided to mark the site as a National Memorial, not a National Park, in 1964 (Carrera 1976:4). The National Memorial today contains three of the known sites of the Franco-Spanish-American-Native American village that were Arkansas Post. These it interprets along with the Confederate presence of Arkansas Post during the Civil War and the January, 1863, battle that resulted in its capture by federal troops. The main fortification for this late engagement, known as Fort Hindman, has since eroded into the river.

The 1960s

Arkansas Post provided the background against which Arkansas historical archaeology in the 1960s would develop. Ford's work at the Menard-Hodges site was published at the beginning of the decade (Ford 1961), which would see several national and state-level developments that would dramatically increase the number of historical archaeologists working in the state and expand the breadth of historical projects conducted here. Significantly, the creation of several more federal parks beyond Arkansas Post, the passage of the National Historic Preservation Act, and the foundation and growth of both the Arkansas Archeological Society and Arkansas Archeological Survey all played key roles in this upsurge of work and interest.

Federal Historical Archaeology in Arkansas during the 1960s

Much of the historical archaeology in Arkansas in the 1960s took place under the auspices of the National Park Service. The move to establish Pea Ridge National Military Park, near Bentonville in the extreme northwest part of the state, involved the efforts of Rex Wilson, who dug at the site of Leetown. Wilson's work identified the footprint of several buildings at Leetown, one of the foci of the March 1862, battle; perhaps the most significant battle of the war fought west of the Mississippi River. Wilson also identified what appeared to be the graves of Union soldiers who passed away in the field hospitals during and after the battle. Those burials were subsequently removed to the National Cemetery in Fayetteville (Wilson 1965). Wilson did further excavations at Arkansas Post the following year, finding several early 19th century structures (Wilson 1966).

At the same time, the National Park Service began work at Fort Smith. The digs built upon the efforts of Clyde Dollar, who in 1958 used convict labor to locate the original fort on Belle Point, dating to 1817 (Coleman and Scott 2003:5–1, 5–2; Dollar 1960; Moore 1962). Between 1958 and 1966, Dollar and NPS archaeologist Jackson Moore delineated the walls of the early fort buildings, establishing details of the fort's construction, and determining the functions of some of the identified rooms (Coleman and Scott 2003; Dollar 1960; Dollar 1966; Moore 1962; Moore 1963). These were the last large-scale investigations at Fort Smith, as almost all excavations done since then have been done as mitigation or monitoring, not research (Coleman and Scott 2003:5–2–5–4).

Somewhat out of step with other national park projects of that period, the excavations did not lead to the reconstruction of Fort Smith. NPS Chief Historian Robert Utley, convinced that the reconstructions at Fort Union, North Dakota, Bent's Fort, Colorado, and others did not accurately represent the past to the public, persuaded Arkansas's senatorial delegation (including John McClellan, then chair of the Senate Appropriations Committee) to forego any reconstruction of the installation (Matzko 2001:78).

Like Arkansas Post, Fort Smith and Pea Ridge were both places whose significance ramified well beyond Arkansas. The Union victory at Pea Ridge essentially confirmed St. Louis in U.S. hands throughout the balance of the Civil War, allowing for federal expeditions down the Mississippi River that both split the Confederacy in two and established the reputations and expertise of U.S. commanders including U.S. Grant and William T. Sherman. Units from Iowa, Indiana, Illinois, Missouri, Louisiana, Texas, the Indian Territory, and Ohio all fought and died at Pea Ridge.

Fort Smith was the Army's major installation on the southern plains during the early stages of the Removal period, and the point of reference for establishing Arkansas's western border (and, by extension, the eastern border of the Indian Territory) in 1828. Like Arkansas Post, the sites' historical significance, just mentioned, twins with their archaeological significance. This is particularly true for the work done at Fort Smith, as Clyde Dollar's research there lay the base for one of the great debates in the formation of historical archaeology, the Dollar Exchange.

The Dollar Exchange

The 1960s were a crucial period for historical archaeology as a discipline. Stanley South initiated the Conference on Historic Sites Archaeology (CHSA) in 1960, a one-day conference that endured until 1982 and published 15 volumes of proceedings (South and Deagan 2002:41). The Society for Historical Archaeology formed in Dallas in 1967, providing an additional venue for the discussion of topics relevant to the field. It also began publishing a journal, Historical Archaeology, which together with the CHSA Papers afforded historical archaeologists places to publish and share research that would help shape the field over subsequent generations. With the folding of the CHSA in the 1980s, the SHA became the preeminent national conference on historical archaeology.

Arkansas's presence in this period revolves around the work of Clyde Dollar, an Arkansas native who excavated extensively at Fort Smith (see above). Dollar asserted that "historical archaeology must be architectural in orientation and reconstructive in both purpose and scope" (Dollar 1968:220). Even if the site was not to be reconstructed, Dollar wrote, the site should be excavated with an eye towards providing architectural information that could facilitate it. He believed that historical archaeologists should be well versed in historic construction techniques to be able to interpret sites. Dollar even saw architectural considerations as providing the salient difference between prehistoric and historical archaeology, in that the latter's sites were constructed in accordance with cultural patterns influenced by the physics of construction ("thrusts, loadings, and stresses") and used prepared foundations, commonly used units of measurement, distinct building styles, and architectural traits such as porches and cellars unique to historic sites (Dollar 1968:221). Dollar specifically referenced his work at Fort Smith several times to illustrate his points and observations.

Dollar's ideas are not widely followed in modern day historical archaeology, but the forum he initiated with his article, referred to as the "Dollar Exchange," was a crucial discussion to have at that point in the discipline's development (South and Deagan 2002:41). Practitioners of historical archaeology in the 1950s and 1960s came from a diversity of backgrounds, with few to none being steeped in a tradition of historical archaeology. Historians, architects, and prehistorians all made inroads into the field, bringing with them their specific approaches to historic sites research (South and Deagan 2002, 41). Dollar's assertion that 1) historical archaeology should be architectural in orientation and reconstructive in purpose and that 2) historical archaeology was a distinct discipline from history, anthropology, and prehistoric anthropology forced historical archaeologists to ponder what they thought the focus of the emerging discipline, and what its relationship to other areas of inquiry, should be.

Dollar's views were not completely original, as some of the founders of historical archaeology saw reconstruction as one of the important foci of the field's early history. Harrington (1955), in an analysis of the objects of contemporary historical archaeological investigations, concluded that "[b]y far the majority of archaeological projects undertaken at historic sites have had as their primary, and often sole, purpose the securing of data for use in interpreting the site to visitors. In a few cases the goal has been a full-scale reconstruction of the entire scene." He specifically points out Colonial Williamsburg, Yorktown, and Appomattox Courthouse in Virginia, Hopewell Village and Fort Necessity in Pennsylvania, and Sonoma Mission in California, among others, as places where Dollar's vision of the orientation, purpose, and scope of historical archaeology would ring true. Unlike Dollar, however, Harrington saw historical archaeology as an auxiliary science to history, not its own discipline.

Others had more grave doubts about Dollar's positions on these subjects, and it is these reactions to his work that have had the more enduring legacy within historical archaeology. Bernard Fontana (1978) strenuously objected to his architectural focus, noting that trash pits, privies, cemeteries, can scatters, and voyageur cargo lost in a riverbed all lack an architectural element, but are numerous and valuable historical sites. Cleland and Fitting (1978) provided a more extensive critique that has endured as an important part of historical archaeology's canon. They take issue with Dollar's stance that historical archaeology is a discipline unto itself. Rather than stress what they see as isolationism, they encourage interdisciplinarity, encouraging historical archaeologists to connect with prehistorians, cultural anthropologists, and historians intellectually to further historical archaeology. They also worry that Dollar's view of historical archaeology, which they lump together with Hume's (1961) and Walker's (1967), tends toward an overweight emphasis on method that sacrifices theoretical sophistication.

As the scholarly debates of the 1960s played out, and as historical archaeology grew and flowered as a discipline, Dollar's ideas did not endure. He did, however, ask important questions at a critical point in the development of the discipline that caused his peers to examine their positions on central epistemological questions (Lees 2001). Though Dollar is only rarely cited today, the responses that he evokes, particularly from Cleland and Fitting, still speak to historical archaeologists, suggesting that the debates initiated by Dollar's writings, based largely on his experience at Fort Smith, have not yet been entirely laid to rest.

The Foundation of the Society and Survey

In addition to the federal archaeological research just mentioned, the 1960s were a crucial period in the development of historical archaeology in Arkansas due to the foundation of two statewide groups, the Arkansas Archeological Survey and Arkansas Archeological Society. Of these, the Society formed first, in 1960, as Arkansans with an interest in archaeology sought community and the opportunity to participate in research. McGimsey and Davis (1992:10–11) point to growing public awareness of federal projects in Arkansas (presumably including that at Arkansas Post) and archaeologists at the University of Arkansas Museum as helping to build public interest in archaeology. In the winter of 1959–1960, avocational archaeologists worked with University of Arkansas Museum personnel to draft a constitution for the Society, which began in the latter year.

The early members of the Society were instrumental in advocating to the state legislature for the formation of a state archaeological program. The Survey was the fruit of their efforts. In addition to the work of Society members, Charles R. "Bob" McGimsey and Hester Davis, of the University of Arkansas Museum, were key to the Survey's founding, and worked with several heritage-minded state legislators over the course of nearly a decade to write and pass legislation that established the Survey (McGimsey and Davis 1992; White 1999).

The Survey opened in 1967 with three stations (Jonesboro, Arkadelphia, and Pine Bluff) in addition to the main office in Fayetteville. It now numbers 11 stations based at universities, state parks, and other institutions, with Arkansas's 75 counties divvied up between eight of them as territories for which the resident archaeologists are responsible for both research and public outreach (McGimsey and Davis 1992). McGimsey (1972) published his ideas of what a model program such as the Survey should be in *Public Archaeology*, hoping to provide a template for archaeologists in other states who sought to follow Arkansas's model. He specifically held up Arkansas's program as a model that other states could, and should, follow. More than just a bureaucratic document, McGimsey stressed the importance of knowledge of our collective past as a human birthright, one that must be both safeguarded and disseminated by effective and active public archaeological research.

Fagette (1994) correctly points out one crucial aspect of the ongoing relationship between the Society and the Survey. Not only were Society members fundamental to the founding of the Survey, allowing the people of Arkansas to have an influential voice in the process, the two organizations remain in a reciprocal relationship. For instance, Society members constitute review and advisory boards for each Survey station that annually assess the performance of the Survey staff in terms of fulfilling their public outreach and research missions, while Survey staff provide instruction during the annual Training Program dig, giving professional instruction to Society members. This relationship keeps the interested public and Survey staff in close contact, and encourages the development of research in response to public interest, as well as facilitating the dissemination of research findings through both Survey and Society channels.

Both organizations maintain publication series that have been inestimable in their value in terms of advancing our knowledge of Arkansas's past. The Society offers both *The Arkansas Archeologist* and *Field Notes*, a newsletter, that provide a record of archaeological work in the state, much of which was done by Survey archaeologists. Amongst the busy pages of these journals appeared one of the first stock-takings of Arkansas archaeology, written by State Archeologist Hester Davis (1969). It is clear that, at this point, historical archaeology was not a major concern within the Survey system. Davis twice equated archaeology with research on Native Americans, and mentioned Ford's work at Menard, but not his work at Arkansas Post proper (or that of Holder, Neitzel, or others, for that matter). This is, in part, due to where American archaeology as a whole was at epistemologically when the Survey opened its doors (the Society for Historical Archaeology was founded that same year), and the composition of the Survey staff, who were primarily prehistorians.

Though the Survey and Society would increase dramatically the amount of archaeological research done in the state, including historical archaeological research, it did not do so at the outset. At its inception, the Survey and Society dealt with historic sites only when their excavations encountered historic components. McGimsey, for instance, uncovered the African American men's dorm at the Parkin Lumber Company during excavations at the Parkin site, a Mississippian village, in the late 1960s (Stewart-Abernathy, personal communication, 2012), but McGimsey never pursued this aspect of the site as a topic worthy of study. The creation of the Society and Survey put in place the mechanisms by which historical archaeology in Arkansas would grow dramatically in the 1970s. One other historical development that would have great influence on the development of historical archaeology in Arkansas remains to be explored.

Federal Legislation

Several pieces of federal legislation in the 1960s and 1970s greatly spurred the development of historical archaeology. The passage of the Reservoir Salvage Act in 1960, and particularly the National Historic Preservation Act (NHPA) in 1966, increased the amount of archaeological research being done nationwide, including on historic sites (King 2004; Little 2007:13–14). Though other federal legislation both predates and postdates the issuance of the 1960s legislation, these acts established major regulatory driver that would put many archaeologists in the field and result in the exploration of thousands of archaeological sites in Arkansas alone. Highway construction, dam construction, military training, and a host of other federal actions now came with the legal requirement avoid or minimize damage to significant pieces of America's heritage (King 2004).

Querying the Survey's digital database, AMASDA, for references to historical archaeological literature shows the massive effect that federal legislation had on research in the state. AMASDA contains only two entries published during the 1940s. All of the seven from the 1950s relate to sites that would become federal parks. The 1960s saw marked uptick, to 17 publications, followed by a leap to nearly 200 in the 1970s, then another jump to nearly 400 for the 1980s. The numbers peak around 900 in the 1990s before dropping back down to the neighborhood of 400 in the first decade of this century. The federal legislation of the 1960s grew archaeological research by an order of magnitude almost immediately.

While clearly a boon to historical archaeology on a state and national level, we should bear in mind the observation by Stewart-Abernathy (1999:238–239), who, while acknowledging a major increase in the number of sites excavated, noted that the tendency for these reports to remain obscured in gray literature has minimized their scholarly utility. Though thousands of sites have been surveyed and, in some cases, extensively investigated, much of what has been learned about Arkansas heritage as a result remains siloed in agency files or in limited-distribution reports, keeping it from being adequately mined by contemporary practitioners. This situation may change in future, as recent initiatives, such as the Digital Archaeological Record (tDAR), which attempts to catalog gray literature in a topically and geographically-searchable online database, hold out some promise of making gray literature more accessible in the coming years. It remains to be seen, however, how thoroughly such efforts will be in cataloging past research.

Fluorescence in the 1970s

By the early 1970s, as the Survey continued to develop and the number of federally-mandated projects increased (see above), the Department of Anthropology at the University of Arkansas began to admit and train increasingly large numbers of graduate students. The formation of the Conference on Historic Sites Archaeology and Society for Historical

Archaeology in the preceding decade had brought attention to historical archaeology as a research area, and some of the new students were
interested in historic sites.

Among the first historical archaeological students were Patrick
Martin, David Stahle, and David Jurney, all of whom would leave an
imprint on various archaeological traditions. David Stahle's research on
dendrochronology, which he developed through his master's research
on Arkansas log buildings, would eventually extend across the country.
Jurney investigated the Ridge House, in Fayetteville, for his master's
thesis. Jurney's collaborator on the Ridge House was Patrick Martin,
whose publications would do much to bring historical archaeology to
Arkansans in the Survey and Society.

Martin had earlier worked with Stanley South at Charles Town
Landing, South Carolina, and in Ohio on several historic sites, and
thus came to the state primed with a background in the subject. He
was one of the field assistants during the University of Arkansas's 1971
field school at Arkansas Post, which focused on Jacob Bright's Trading
House (1804–1807) and William Montgomery's Tavern (1819–1821).
Directed by Michael Hoffman of the University of Arkansas, the dig
identified at least one structure built in French colonial style. Artifacts
consistent with the site's use as both a trading post (profusion of trade
goods) and a tavern (numerous alcohol bottles) were recovered, leading Martin (1977) to conclude that the site of the two enterprises had,
indeed, been discovered.

Martin (1971) also wrote the earliest assessment of historical archaeology in Arkansas, in the form of a short article written for the
Arkansas Academy of Science. Martin highlighted previous work by the
National Park Service (NPS) at Arkansas Post and Fort Smith, as well
as William Westbury's investigations of the fur trade posts at Spadra
and the Blanton Estate on the Red River. He also detailed some ongoing
projects at Arkansas Post and his own research at the JD Wilbur Pottery
site (3WA208), done under the auspices of the Survey.

Martin's expertise brought him to the attention of Survey director Bob
McGimsey, who hired him to work as a graduate assistant. McGimsey
wanted Martin to help fill a gap in the Survey's skill set and advocate
for historical archaeology (Martin, personal communication, 2011;
McGimsey and Davis 1992, 63). Martin's work and publications helped
build awareness of historical archaeology within the state's archaeological community during his student years at the University. He went on
to work at Fort Michilimackinac, on Michigan's Upper Peninsula, with

Michigan State University, studying under Lyle Stone and Arkansas alumnus Charles Cleland. He would later found one of the nation's premier programs in industrial archaeology at Michigan Technological University at Houghton. He collaborated with Robert Mainfort on a coal mining site in Threemile Creek, Logan County (Martin and Mainfort 1998), and consulted on Jamie Brandon and James Davidson's field school at Van Winkle's Mill in 2001.

During this same period, the Survey hired its first full-time historical archaeologist Sam Smith, who served as a station assistant at the Arkansas State University station in Jonesboro, under Dan Morse. In late 1973, Smith led a four week project focusing on the Cadron Settlement, a pioneer village near Conway (McGimsey and Davis 1992, 64). Smith later initiated research at Old Davidsonville State Park. Clyde Dollar picked the work up when Smith left for Tennessee soon thereafter. The work was later handed off to Leslie Stewart-Abernathy, though it was Shawn Bonath who oversaw the actual excavations (Bonath 1980).

The first historical archaeologist to serve as a Survey station archaeologist arrived in 1977. When Burney McClurkan left his position at the Pine Bluff station to work for the Arkansas Highway and Transportation Department, he was replaced by Leslie C. Stewart-Abernathy (née Abernathy), universally known as "Skip" (McGimsey and Davis 1992). Though based in Pine Bluff, Skip advised the rest of the Survey staff on historic sites issues and research around the state (McGimsey and Davis 1992, 67). From Pine Bluff (1977–1987) and later (1987 to present) the Russellville area,[2] Skip worked wherever he was needed in the state, often saying that his territory was "75 counties," meaning the entire state. Amongst his many projects, Skip would work on four rounds of the annual Arkansas Archeological Society Training Programs at Old Washington State Park, now Historic Washington State Park, and provide preliminary excavations that helped guide a fifth at Old Davidsonville State Park (see below) (Bonath 1980:3; McGimsey and Davis 1992:72–73).

Though not focused on historical archaeology to the extent that Skip was and remains, George Sabo arrived in 1979 with training in the field, which he quickly put to use at the Walker-Stone House in Fayetteville, on which he collaborated with Gayle Fritz. After two passing archaeologists noticed that ground-stripping activities had exposed historic and prehistoric artifacts, Sabo and Fritz excavated a historic midden dating to the 1875–1925 period (Sabo 1979).

Finally the 1970s saw a massive growth in the contract sector, as mentioned above. Much of this work took place under the aegis of the Survey and its Sponsored Research Program, though contract divisions from Southwest Missouri State University, Southern Methodist University, Texas Tech University, and the University of Missouri, along with Iroquois Research Institute and other private firms conducted research in the state. Of these projects, Lawrence Santeford and William Martin's (1980) work for the Survey overseeing a large-scale contract project for U.S. Army Corps of Engineers during the preparation for developments in the water supply system for the city of Conway, in Faulkner County, stands out as remarkable. Most of the Survey's projects were surveys or inventories, but the Conway Water System project was both a large-scale survey and intensive excavation project, which Santeford made a point of using oral historical information, gathered from descendants of the site inhabitants, who still lived in the area, to interpret. This work presages both Brennan's (this volume) recent research in Arkansas's mountains and an expanding research tool within historical archaeology.

Beyond this, Santeford and Martin critically analyzed cultural forms distributed throughout the upland South, focusing on the layout and notching of log cabins constructed from the eastern seaboard to east Texas. In addition, Santeford cited the continued use and creation of log houses as an index of isolation for residents of the mountains of central Arkansas, offering a parallel to Adams's (1976) research on market access at roughly the same time.

Where the 1950s saw the first sparks of historical archaeology catch at the state's nationally-significant sites through federal research, and the 1960s saw the development of several organizations that would be immensely beneficial to archaeology, the 1970s is the period when those developments gelled. Before, most of the professional work was done by federal staffers, brought in from out of state, to conduct their appointed projects. In the 1970s, trained, professional archaeologists, most of whom made Arkansas their home, conducted the bulk of the research in the state.

The growth of historical archaeology during this period, and the refinements in both techniques employed and questions asked of the archaeological record, mean that this is also a period when the body of historical archaeological literature goes from being focused solely on a few major sites to focusing on numerous smaller sites. To take only a single example, it is during the 1970s that we begin to see a profusion of small Ozark and Ouachita Mountain farmsteads being subjected to investigation. This began an expanding dataset on the archaeological record of Upland South settlement in the historic era, tying work done here to a research area that stretches to the eastern seaboard. Santeford and Martin make this case explicitly, showing ties between architectural styles in Faulkner County and analogues to the east. The ensuing decades would see a number of other projects take place that both added to our knowledge of Natural State history as well as carrying importance for historical archaeology on a regional and national scale.

The 1980s and 1990s

In April of 1980, Mr. Jerry Thomas, U.S. Army Corps of Engineers, and police officers from Lafayette County (southwest Arkansas) and the Arkansas State Police responded to reports of the discovery of a skeleton on the bank of the Red River. An initial inspection by Sandra Blaylock and subsequent testing by Frank Schambach and Neil Trubowitz, all of the Survey, identified a multi-component site, an African American cemetery overlying a Caddo farmstead. The testing phase yielded sufficient data to suggest that the Caddo component, named the Cedar Grove site, was eligible for listing on the National Register of Historic Places, and it was deemed necessary to move the cemetery to safeguard it during the Corps' efforts to stabilize the levy. Those involved initially believed it to be small, numbering perhaps five graves. By the time the project ended, archaeologists had discovered 125 (Limp and Rose 1985:2–3; Trubowitz 1984). The project was also remarkable for the speed at which the analysis took place. Members of the Cedar Grove Baptist Church requested reburial within 24 hours of exhumation, a condition which investigators strove to meet, largely with success (Davidson et al. 2002; Limp and Rose 1985:4–5).

The Cedar Grove project's historic component provides us with more than an example of an extensive cemetery relocation. It provided bioarchaeologists with one of the largest datasets on demography, health and disease, infection, trauma, and other aspects of rural life in the American West from the period (Boudreaux 1999; Davidson et al. 2002; Rose 1985).

That year was also the opening of a series of five straight years in which the Arkansas Archeological Society's Annual Training Program would focus on historic sites. The first of these was held at Old Davidsonville (northeast Arkansas Ozarks) in 1980, and organized by Shawn Bonath, a Minnesotan who studied historical archaeology at Florida

State University before coming to work for the Survey (Arkansas Archeological Society 1980). Old Davidsonville State Park marks one of
the first American communities in Arkansas, dating to between 1815 and
1830. Society members contributed over 1,600 person-hours of labor
in two weeks, identifying numerous structures across two city blocks
(Bonath 1980).

The later four Training Program digs (1981–1984) shifted to Historic Washington State Park, in southwest Arkansas. These were jointly-
organized by Skip Stewart-Abernathy and Frank Schambach, the Survey
archaeologist in southwest Arkansas, and were split efforts, with Skip
leading digs on historic features and Frank and John Miller working on
nearby prehistoric sites. The historic components were well-preserved,
being located in the park, which is an outdoor walking museum, offering a frontier Arkansas analog to Colonial Williamsburg. Like its east
coast counterpart, Historic Washington was planned to have significant
reconstruction of historic buildings, and the early 1980s digs were done
in no small part to characterize those structures before they were rebuilt
(Stewart-Abernathy 1981).

The historic component of the 1981 dig focused on the Sanders
House, home to the antebellum county clerk, Simon T. Sanders. Excavations uncovered architectural details of a detached kitchen which
were substantially different from what was then known about the site.
It also uncovered a piece of slate with the name of Sanders' daughter,
Sarah, scratched in it; a relic of her childhood in the 1840s (Davis
1981). Satisfied with the results at Sanders, the 1982 digs (still split
between prehistoric and historic foci) shifted to the rear yard the Block-
Catts House. At the close of the Society Dig that year, Society members found the edge of a large trash pit, which was further explored
in 1983. This was termed Feature 14, and is one of the largest and
best-documented middens from the region's early-19th century period,
one that informs our understanding of both frontier Arkansas and the
process of westward expansion (Arkansas Archeological Society 1983;
Stewart-Abernathy 1985).

These digs had important diasporic dimensions. Both the Sanders and
Block kitchens were abodes for enslaved and free African Americans who
lived and cooked in them. The Block-Catts House was also the home of
Abraham Block, an early immigrant to the area and one of southwest
Arkansas's first merchants. The Block family were some of the first Jewish immigrants to the Old Southwest, and their lives in Washington as
members of the Jewish diaspora has been more thoroughly explored by

David Markus in recent research that builds on the Society Dig excavations of the 1980s (Markus 2011).

The 1980s Society Digs in Historic Washington (then Old Washington State Park) also were the agar from which Skip grew the "urban farmstead" concept. The urban farmstead consisted of the house and associated outbuildings and other productive features, such as chicken coops and gardens that provided for household needs within a specifically non-farming, urbanized context (Stewart-Abernathy 1986a:6–7). This concept has been employed repeatedly since, in Maryland (Kimmel 1993), New Hampshire (Ford 2008), Michigan (Rotman and Nassaney 1997), and many other places.

In 1981, Stewart-Abernathy also worked to document and interpret the Sawdust Hill community, a group of people, mostly associated with the lumber industry in eastern Arkansas, who once lived in a small collection of homes that once stood on the Parkin site, now Parkin Archeological State Park. Acting as "project humanist," Stewart-Abernathy collected oral interviews, photographs, and maps of the former community to pull together a display that emphasized the history of the site from its settlement by Native Americans, through the De Soto Expedition, and to the 19th century, when lumber towns like Parkin and Earle helped convert a boggy forest into excellent agricultural land. Sawdust Hill was a place where African Americans and European Americans worked together as skilled laborers in relative harmony, a point Stewart-Abernathy was careful to make (Stewart-Abernathy 1982).

The Survey, which until 1981 had steadily grown and undertaken many projects on its own accord, such as Cedar Grove, found itself unable to compete for such work following the issuance of the Small Business Set Aside program, which redirected contracts away from state agencies such as the Survey and to small, private cultural resources management (CRM) companies. Though the Survey continued to do some contract-based work through its Sponsored Research Program, from that point forward, archaeological research in Arkansas, both historic and prehistoric, shifted increasingly towards the private sector (McGimsey and Davis 1992).

The survey of the Felsenthal region along the Ouachita River in southern Arkansas included an analysis of 15 historic sites identified during the fieldwork. Hemmings (1982) states that the relatively small number of sites identified, including none dating to the early historic (pre-1780) period was indicative of the difficulty of settling the oft-flooded landscape and evidence of the selection of more reliably accessible land for historic farmsteads. The Felsenthal study is instructive for similar riverine environments in the Deep South and Trans-Mississippi. Watkins (1982) provided the historical overview in the report, focusing on settlement, the Civil War, and the changes that infrastructural development brought to the area and the Felsenthal community.

Stewart-Abernathy also spearheaded excavations at the Moser Farmstead in the Ozarks, near Rogers, in 1982. Done as part of the Section 106 review for the construction of I-540, running between Fort Smith and Fayetteville, Stewart-Abernathy took it as an opportunity to confront stereotypes about the cultural isolation of the Ozarks by analyzing the consumption patterns of the former occupants through their material culture. His research deflates images of the Ozarks as the home to isolated, backwards people, but buttresses the image of the area's residents as valuing and practicing independence, self-sufficiency, and family pride (Stewart-Abernathy 1986b; Stewart-Abernathy 1987).

To better organize and give direction to archaeological research, the Survey issued a State Plan in 1982. Though largely regionally-organized, Stewart-Abernathy and Watkins wrote a statewide historical archaeological context that split the state's recent history into a number of different study units, settlement patterns, statewide research problems, constraints on research, and research priorities. They highlighted Anglo American settlement ("pioneer"), the influx of farmers in the late antebellum to early Great Depression eras ("maximum occupation), river-oriented terrestrial and marine sites ("riverine"), small-scale manufacturing ("localized industry"), and growth of 20th century Arkansas cities ("urbanization") as study units particularly worthy of study (Stewart-Abernathy and Watkins 1982).

While I (who does a substantial amount of Civil War research) disagree with their ranking my chosen subject lowest on their scale of importance, Stewart-Abernathy and Watkins' context for historical archaeology in Arkansas plays up the state's diverse and complex history. After thirty years, the document could do with an update, but it provides a strong basis from which to build. It is also somewhat disturbing to note how few of the chosen subjects have been extensively explored in the thirty years since its publication.

As mentioned at the outset, Arkansas has been typified as a very rural state, caricatured as being full of rusticated Lil' Abners (Blevins 2009; Brandon 2004). In contradiction to this image, we have had a measure of urban archaeology conducted here, beyond that of the Historic Washington Society Digs of the 1980s. For instance, Stewart-Abernathy headed a team of volunteers that salvaged a two-story cellar from the Ashley Mansion in downtown Little Rock in 1984 and 1985 (Katherine Cleek, personal communication, 2012). This massive collection of material, including parts of the plaster and brick columns that stood at the front of the house when it was used as the headquarters for Major General Frederick Steele during the Civil War, were recovered. Much of this work remains unreported, though Ernest (1994) used some of the material to study the shifts in urban residence pattern in late-19th century Little Rock, using the portion of the assemblage associated with when the structure was known as the Oakleaf Hotel. William McAlexander wrote his master's thesis on the phase of the site when it was home to Chester Ashley, a socially-prominent lawyer in territorial and antebellum Arkansas (McAlexander 1999).

Admittedly, Arkansas does not have an extensive history of maritime archaeological research, which is remarkable given the centrality of Arkansas's numerous rivers to its development and modern economy. Long bereft of quality roads and railroads, it was the state's river system that provided for its early settlement and commerce, and hundreds of shipwrecks sleep in our state's riverbeds. Some of these are quite notable, such as the Sultana, which exploded in 1865 while jammed with Union soldiers recently released from Confederate prison camps, killing 1,500. The Homer, a Confederate transport and erstwhile warship, lies along the banks of the Ouachita River near Camden. Our major inquiry into the state's shipping history came in 1988, when the Mississippi River fell dramatically during a nationwide drought, bottoming out at ten feet below the zero mark on the Memphis flood gauge. This drop exposed large swaths of the riverbed, including the hulls of six late-19th or early-20th century wooden boats. In a period of rushed salvage-oriented work, Stewart-Abernathy supervised excavations and recording projects on these "ghost boats of the Mississippi" before the water rose again. Though a rapid project, the project succeeded in documenting many construction and equipment-oriented details from a kind of ship for which we lack any surviving examples (Stewart-Abernathy 2002).

Arkansas archaeologists made some headway into the question of historic Native American settlement in the state during this period. While some tribes were resident at the time of the establishment of Arkansas Post in 1686, others arrived or passed through in the late 1700s, during the earliest stages of the Removal Period. Research on this subject in the 1980s and 1990s focused on two distinct areas, northwest Arkansas and the Great Bend region in the Southwest.

George Sabo (1990) and others produced a summary of knowledge on archaeological research in the Ozark Mountain-Arkansas River valley-Ouachita Mountain region, an area spanning northwest Arkansas and the adjacent corners of Missouri, Kansas, and Oklahoma. Sabo et al considered both the aforementioned historically-indigenous groups (Osage and Quapaw) and immigrant Native American peoples (Cherokee, Shawnee, Delaware, Kickapoo, Creek, and Choctaw) who fled the Southeast before being forced into the Indian Territory in the 1820s. They lay out the difficulties of doing research on early historic Native American sites, noting the similarities between individual sites in terms of basic artifacts and house construction types. Differences come in with "agricultural organization, in settlement patterns, in social organization, in traditional ceremonies and ritual practices that were retained, in newly adopted ceremonies, in other social activities, in the retention of traditional material culture, and in the adoption of Euroamerican goods" (Sabo et al. 1990). The authors encourage further inquiry on the regional scale, noting that such differences will not always be recognizable within the context of a single site, and historic Native Americans in the Ozarks and Ouachitas remain a subject much in need of further exploration.

In the southwest, Claude McCrocklin explored several sites on the west bank of the Red River near Garland City, known as Tara I-V. These were all sites with early 19th-century British ceramics, large quantities of animal bone and small arms ammunition, but virtually no evidence for agricultural activities (McCrocklin 1985; McCrocklin 1990a; McCrocklin 1990b). McCrocklin interpreted these sites to be the homes of the "Lost Prairie Cherokee," a band that followed Duwali (also known as Bowl or Chief Bowl) from the early reservations in the Arkansas River valley to the Red River instead of into the Indian Territory in 1828. The Lost Prairie Cherokee remained resident until 1830, when neighboring whites attacked their villages and forced them west, taking their fertile river valley lands for farms.

Stewart-Abernathy (1998) drew on McCrocklin's work in considering a wider research project on Arkansas Cherokee sites. Writing in the aftermath of the 1997 Trail of Tears conference, he was particularly interested in better understanding how Cherokee families made lives in Arkansas during the brief few decades of their presence, and how succeeding waves of white and black immigrants from the east compelled them further west. The work of Stewart-Abernathy, McCrocklin, and Sabo et al provide the basis upon which a truly crucial piece of intensive research could be founded. Such a contribution to the literature on the Removal Period would be of great scholarly value, and help to understand the negotiation of cultural boundaries during this period.

Some forty years on from the excavations that started historical archaeology in Arkansas, archaeologists returned to the quest for Arkansas Post. Two of the Arkansas Archeological Society's summer training program digs were held at sites associated with the post. In 1997 and 1998, Society members dug at the Menard-Hodges site in Wallace Bottom, building on the work of Holder, Ford, and others from forty years before (House 2002). The site survey class from the 1998 Training Program, under the direction of David Jeane, located a scatter of colonial ceramics and other artifacts at the Wallace Bottom No. 2 site on the shores of Lake Dumond. This was later determined to be the remains of a portion of Osotouy, a 17th century Quapaw site connected to the first location of Arkansas Post, occupied between 1686 and 1749. House (2002) summarized the results of these excavations, and Jeane, Starr, Weymouth, and Stewart-Abernathy presented on it and several associated contact period sites in the immediate vicinity at the 2000 meeting of the Society for Historical Archaeology in Quebec, Canada.

Three series of fieldwork focused on Arkansas Post, spread over some forty years, have succeeded in identifying several sites associated with this earliest European presence in Arkansas, indeed in the trans-Mississippi United States. Together, they point out the heavily French influence in the region, and the importance of the fur trade in bringing Europeans to the area and how that presence affected Native American communities throughout the Mississippi River valley (Stewart-Abernathy 2000). It also points out a tremendous research need, in that while we know something of the various Arkansas Posts, both archaeologically and historically, the French colonial period in the Trans-Mississippi South, which spanned a full century and extended into modern day Oklahoma, is currently woefully understudied. In Arkansas, a plethora of French town names, such as Champagnolle and Camden (formerly *Ecore Fabre* [Fabre's Bluff]), endure or are part of recent memory, have histories that stretch back to this colonial period, yet we know little beyond the fact of their association.

During this period, contract archaeology continued apace through various institutions. Several archaeologists, such as Roger Coleman with the National Park Service, John Riggs with the Corps of Engineers, Meeks Etchieson, Gary Knudsen, and Michael Pfeiffer with the U.S. Forest Service, John Miller with Arkansas Highways and Transportation

Department, and contract firms headed by Carol Spears and Robert Lafferty, in particular, produced masses of important research on hundreds of sites throughout the state (see above). Many of these focus on single or a few historic sites, many of them farmsteads, which, while determined to be of little significance on their own, together represent a storehouse of information on Arkansas, Upland South, Deep South, westward expansion, and other expansive historical and anthropological questions that remain ready for further inquiry.

The 1980s and 1990s saw tremendous growth in the amount of historical archaeological research done in the state, with well over 1,000 reports, journal articles, volume chapters, and other works going to press during this period. This expansive growth did not endure into the new millennium, though several key projects began in the Arkansas's state and national parks.

To the Present

Since 2000, contract archaeology has remained an active area of research in the state, though somewhat diminished in frequency (see above) as compared with the preceding decade. The Survey and Society remained active proponents of historical work, as will be detailed shortly. During the first decade of the 21st century, however, a number of federal projects took place that stood outside of the usual compliance-related work.

For starters, Douglas Scott led archaeological investigations at Pea Ridge National Military Park in Washington County under the auspices of the NPS's Systemwide Archeological Inventory Program (SAIP). Using techniques honed at the Little Bighorn (Scott and Fox 1987; Scott et al. 1989), Scott, fellow NPS archaeologists, and a crew of volunteers recovered around 2,700 battle-related artifacts that assisted the park in refining their interpretation of the battle and even adding to debates about the roles different units played in the engagement (Carlson-Drexler et al. 2008). Such work counters assertions by a past generation of archaeologists that little of value can be gained by the archaeological study of battlefields or that they simply lack below-ground remains (Hume 1976). Volf (2003) and Herrmann (2005) added to Rex Wilson's (1965) early research at the Leetown site at Pea Ridge during this period as well. This research, was one of the largest-scale surveys of an American battlefield conducted to date. In addition to assisting the park in interpreting the battle to the public, it provided the basis for several theses (Drexler 2004) and other studies (Caporaso et al. 2008; Coles 2003; Coles 2004;

Drexler and Coles 2004) that have expanded archaeologists' abilities to extract historical information from battlefield finds and to question the historical understanding of the battle and its participants (Drexler, this volume).

During this same period, Hunt (2008) completed research on Bathhouse Row, in downtown Hot Springs. Set aside for preservation in 1832, the Hot Springs have long been a haven for the tired and unwell, who sought solace in its waters. Hunt's work, remarkable if only for the novelty of working in the basements of several standing bathhouses, adds an important page to the growing body of literature focused on the archaeology of tourism. It also looks at the late-19th and early 20th century period, when Hot Springs was a resort, medical facility, and home to spring training activities for several major league baseball teams.

The Ozarks were another area focus of research during this period, as Jamie Brandon and others expanded on early fieldwork at an antebellum sawmill site deep in the hollows. Over several years, he and several collaborators worked with Arkansas State Parks to explore several sites at Van Winkle's Mill. The work served as the basis for Brandon's (2004) dissertation, along with those of Alicia Valentino (2006) and Robin Bowers (2003), and several other publications (Brandon and Davidson 2003; Brandon and Davidson 2005; Brandon et al. 2000). Collectively, these works challenge the image of the Ozark region as one dominated by yeoman farmers in that Van Winkle's Mill was very much an industrial facility run by a northern-born magnate. As a site operated primarily by slave labor before the war, it also directly confronts and deflates the notion that slavery in the South was confined to the plantation-heavy lowland regions, leaving the Upland South largely devoid of the peculiar institution (Brandon 2004).

The Ozark region bred more research on atypical sites. While the excavations at Van Winkle's Mill were ongoing, Jerry Hilliard started working at Mount Comfort Church, near Fayetteville. Mount Comfort Church was one of a few sites that had served as a "post colony" during the Civil War (Hilliard 2004). Post colonies were an effort sparked by Colonel LaRue Harrison of the 3rd Arkansas Cavalry (US) to defend loyal citizens from Secessionist depredations. Lacking troops to defend the multitudinous farmsteads scattered throughout the hills, Col. Harrison instead opted to nucleate the people in agrarian communities that could be, to some extent, self-defending. Hilliard's research identified a Civil War component to the site as well as documenting evidence of the building's burning at the close of the war. The story of Mount Comfort and the war in the Ozarks that provide its historical context graphically underscore the complexity of a community in wartime, and the lengths that belligerents may go in attempt to maintain control and counteract insurgency.

Hilliard also worked on the site of Camp Benjamin, a Confederate winter quarters situated in Cross Hollows, near Rogers, that dates to an earlier, more stable period of the Civil War. The camp had been occupied during the winter of 1861–1862, serving as the home for the entirety of General Benjamin McCulloch's division, and was burned and abandoned immediately before the battle of Pea Ridge (Hilliard et al. 2008). Though much obscured by the later impoundment of Beaver Lake, the site remains an important part of the landscape of the Civil War Ozarks.

Jamie Brandon replaced Frank Schambach at the Survey's station in Magnolia in 2006, upon Schambach's retirement. Brandon reinvigorated research at Historic Washington State Park, focusing on the Royston House (Brandon and Samuelsen 2008), returning to the Block-Catts House with David Markus (Markus 2011), and building upon Stewart-Abernathy's work from the 1980s. Kwas (2009b) also completed a survey of research at the park, showing in gorgeous color the fruits of decades' worth of work. Brandon also hosted the Society Dig there, focusing on Block Six, in 2011 and 2012. Block Six was the merchant district from the time of the city's founding until it burned in the late-19th century. Stewart-Abernathy had directed a portion of the 1984 Society Dig there, conducting surface collections, metal detector surveys, and mapping. Brandon's digs explored the area much more extensively. At the time of writing, the artifact analysis is underway, and will eventually serve as a major source of information on early frontier mercantile activity.

In one more return to sites studied a generation before, Kathleen Cande conducted excavations at Old Davidsonville, expanding on Smith's, Dollar's, Bonath's, and Stewart-Abernathy's from the early 1970s and 1980s, when the Society Dig was held at the site. Though antedated by Arkansas Post, Old Davidsonville was the American settlement in Arkansas planned and plotted as a county seat, featuring a courthouse, post office, and other buildings dating to the 1815–1830 period. Cande's work located these structures along with a cellar possibly linked to an inn or tavern (Cande 2008). Going beyond simple documentation, Cande linked the layout of Davidsonville to antecedents in Virginia and England (Price 1968; Reps 1969), which represented a break with the French and Spanish layouts seen in Arkansas before that point and playing up the cultural variability of European American immigrants to the lands of the Louisiana Purchase.

To close with a self-aggrandizing note, my own research at the site of Dooley's Ferry (Drexler 2013), on the Red River in southwest Arkansas, is one of the first in historical archaeology to specifically focus on the archaeology of a civilian community in wartime. As a node in the commodity chain that tied southwest Arkansas to the Atlantic World, Dooley's Ferry offers the opportunity to study how civilians endured periods of conflict and how we might recognize the marks of that endurance in the archaeological record. This is an understudied topic within historical and, more specifically, conflict archaeology.

Conclusion

This volume comes at a crucial time in the history of archaeology in Arkansas. Like the rest of the country, Arkansas experienced the economic downturn of 2008 and 2009, though perhaps felt it less sharply than some states. Concerns for the preservation of sites, loss of institutional memory through layoffs, and threats to the development of the field through decreased access to research funding have been a huge concern for a discipline that has a lot to bring to many tables. We see this period as one of both richness and instability. From Pea Ridge to Van Winkle's Mill to the Howe Kiln, this volume encompasses a vast range of topics that displays the richness of Arkansas's historical and archaeological records, a legacy for the people of this state that is a wellspring of insight and fascination.

We have imparted here a brief list of work done in the state, essentially hitting the main reference points in the history of this research. Unmentioned are the hundreds of small projects, student thesis research, and contract reports that fill out the canon. Like so many historiographies of established disciplines, this history is, of necessity, only a taste. It is my hope that it will whet the taste of fellow historical archaeologists, devotees of U.S., Southern, and Arkansas history as well as those curious about historic ceramic production, military history, oral historical techniques, public memory, and a host of other topics.

This book is dedicated to Skip Stewart-Abernathy because of his long and storied career as the Survey's de facto state historical archaeologist and his tireless advocacy for quality historical archaeology in Arkansas.

Though not the only historical archaeologist to serve or work in the state, Skip's focus on and passion for the subject warrant him special recognition here.

NOTES

1. Westbury (1976:51) later countered this interpretation, but did not offer expansive comments or an alternative interpretation of Holder's findings.
2. Skip's station was originally located at Arkansas Tech University, but is, since 2005, at the Winthrop Rockefeller Institute on Petit Jean Mountain.

REFERENCES

Adams, William H.
1976   Trade Networks and Interaction Spheres: A View from Silcott. *Historical Archaeology* 10: 99–112.
Andrén, Anders
1998   *Between Artifacts and Texts: Historical Archaeology in Global Perspective.* Plenum Press, New York.
Arkansas Archeological Society
1980   Introducing Shawn Bonath. *Field Notes: Newsletter of the Arkansas Archeological Society* 174: 8.
1983   The Best Ever! *Field Notes: Newsletter of the Arkansas Archeological Society* 193: 9–11.
Arnold, Morris S.
1991   *Colonial Arkansas, 1686–1804: A Social and Cultural History.* University of Arkansas Press, Fayetteville.
Blevins, Brooks
2009   *Arkansas/Arkansaw: How Bear Hunters, Hillbillies, and Good ol' Boys Defined a State.* University of Arkansas Press, Fayetteville.
Bonath, Shawn
1980   1980 Society Dig: Old Davidsonville. *Field Notes: Newsletter of the Arkansas Archeological Society* 175: 3–8.
Boudreaux, Jennifer R.
1999   Another Look at Cedar Grove: A Re-Analysis of a Historic African-American Cemetery. Master's thesis, University of Arkansas.
Bowers, Robin F.
2003   Ozark Industry: The Van Winkle Saw Mill, 1857–1882. Master's thesis, University of Arkansas.
Brandon, Jamie C.
2004   Van Winkle's Mill: Mountain Modernity, Cultural Memory and Historical Archaeology in the Arkansas Ozarks. Doctoral dissertation, University of Texas.
Brandon, Jamie C., and James M. Davidson
2003   *Archeological Inventory and Testing of Cultural Resources at Van Winkle's Mill (3BE413) and Little Clifty Creek Shelter (3BE412), Beaver Lake,*

Benton County, Arkansas. Unpublished report. Arkansas Archeological Survey, Fayetteville.

2005   The Landscape of Van Winkle's Mill: Identity, Myth, and Modernity in the Ozark Upland South. *Historical Archaeology* 39(3): 113–131.

Brandon, Jamie C., James M. Davidson, and Jerry E. Hilliard

2000   *Preliminary Archeological Investigations at Van Winkle's Mill (3BE413), Beaver Lake State Park, Benton County, Arkansas: 1997–1999.* Arkansas Archeological Survey, Fayetteville.

Brandon, Jamie C., and John R. Samuelsen

2008   *Preliminary Report: Royston House Test Investigations, 2007–2008.* Arkansas Archeological Survey, Fayetteville.

Caporaso, Alicia L., Carl G. Carlson-Drexler, and Joel Masters

2008   Metallurgical Analysis of Shell and Case Shot Artillery from the Civil War Battles of Pea Ridge and Wilson's Creek. *Technical Briefs in Historical Archaeology* 3: 15–24.

Carlson-Drexler, Carl G., Douglas D. Scott, and Harold Roeker

2008   *"The Battle Raged. . . With Terrible Fury:" Battlefield Archaeology of Pea Ridge National Military Park.* Technical Report No. 112. USDI/NPS Midwest Archeological Center, Lincoln, NE.

Carrera, Gregorio S. A.

1976   *Arkansas Post National Memorial: Administrative History.* USDI/NPS/ Arkansas Post National Memorial, Gillett, AR.

Cleland, Charles E., and James E. Fitting

1978   The Crisis of Identity: Theory in Historic Sites Archaeology. In *Historical Archaeology: A Guide to Substantive and Theoretical Contributions,* edited by Robert L. Schuyler, pp. 124–138. Baywood Publishing Company, Farmingdale, NY.

Coleman, Roger E.

1987   *The Arkansas Post Story: Arkansas Post National Memorial.* Professional Papers No. 12. USDI/NPS/Southwest Cultural Resources Center, Santa Fe, NM.

Coleman, Roger E., and Douglas D. Scott

2003   *An Archaeological Overview and Assessment of Fort Smith National Historic Site.* USDI/NPS/Midwest Archeological Center, Lincoln, NE.

Coles, Alicia L.

2003   Metallurgical Analysis of Shell and Case Shot Artillery from the Civil War Battles of Pea Ridge and Wilson's Creek (PERI and WICR). Lincoln, NE.

2004   Fracture Mechanics: Analysis of Shell and Case Shot Artillery from the Civil War Battles of Pea Ridge and Wilson's Creek. Paper presented at the 37th Annual Conference of the Society for Historical Archaeology, St. Louis, Missouri.

Davidson, James M., Jerome C. Rose, Myron P. Gutmann, Michael R. Haines, Keith Condon, and Cindy Condon

2002   The Quality of African-American Life in the Old Southwest near the Turn of the Twentieth Century. In *The Backbone of History: Health and Nutrition in the Western Hemisphere,* edited by Richard H. Steckel and Jerome C. Rose, pp. 226–277. Cambridge University Press, New York.

Davis, Hester A.
1969   A Brief History of Archaeological Work in Arkansas Up to 1967. *The Arkansas Archeologist: Bulletin of the Arkansas Archeological Society* 10(1–3): 2–8.

Davis, Hester A.
1981   A Great Time at Old Washington. *Field Notes: Newsletter of the Arkansas Archeological Society* 181: 9–14.

1987   The Cherokee in Arkansas: An Invisible Archaeological Resource. In *Visions and Revisions: Ethnohistoric Perspectives on Southern Cultures*, edited by George Sabo and William Schneider, pp. 48–58. Southern Anthropological Society Proceedings No. 20. University of Georgia Press, Athens.

2002   Pot Hunters, Salvage, and Science in Arkansas. In *Histories of Southeastern Archaeology*, edited by Shannon Tushingham, Jane Hill, and Charles H. McNutt, pp. 77–87. University of Alabama Press, Tuscaloosa.

Dollar, Clyde D.
1960   *Interim Report, Old Fort Smith Project.* Fort Smith National Historic Site, Fort Smith, AR.

1966   *The First Fort Smith Report.* Fort Smith National Historic Site, Fort Smith, AR.

1968   Some Thoughts on Theory and Method in Historical Archaeology. *The Conference on Historic Site Archaeology Papers* 2(2): 1–30.

Drexler, Carl G.
2004   Identifying Culturally-Based Variability in Artillery Ammunition Fragments Recovered from the Battlefield of Pea Ridge, Arkansas. Master's thesis, Department of Anthropology, University of Nebraska, Lincoln.

2013   Dooley's Ferry: The Archaeology of a Civilian Community in Wartime. Doctoral dissertation, Department of Anthropology, The College of William & Mary, Williamsburg, VA.

Drexler, Carl G., and Alicia L. Coles
2004   Thunder in the Trans-Mississippi. Paper presented at the 69th Annual Meeting of the Society for American Archaeology. Montreal, PQ.

Ernest, David M.
1994   *The Oakleaf Hotel: A Study of Urban Dynamics in Late 19th and Early 20th Century Little Rock, Arkansas.* University of Arkansas, Fayetteville.

Fagette, Paul H., Jr.
1994   The Founding of the Arkansas Archeological Survey. *The Arkansas Historical Quarterly* 53: 290–311.

Fontana, Bernard L.
1978   A Reply to "Some Thoughts on Theory and Method in Historical Archaeology. In *Historical Archaeology: A Guide to Substantive and Theoretical Contributions*, edited by Robert L. Schuyler, pp. 240–241. Baywood Publishing Company, Farmingdale, NY.

Ford, Ben
2008   The Presentation of Self in Rural Life: The Use of Space at a Connected Farmstead. *Historical Archaeology* 42(4): 59–75.

Ford, James A.
1961   *Menard Site: The Quapaw Village of Osotouy on the Arkansas River*. Papers of the American Museum of Natural History, Volume 48, Part 2. American Museum of Natural History, New York, NY.

Gerstäcker, Friedrich
1968   *Wild Sports in the Far West*. Duke University Press, Durham, NC.

Hall, Martin, and Stephen W. Silliman
2006   Introduction: Archaeology of the Modern World. In *Historical Archaeology*, edited by Martin Hall and Stephen W. Silliman, pp. 1–22. Blackwell, Malden, MA.

Harrington, J. C.
1955   Archeology as an Auxiliary Science to American History. *American Anthropologist* 57(6): 1121–1130.

Hemmings, E. Thomas
1982   *Human Adaptation in the Grand Marais Lowland*. Arkansas Archeological Survey Research Series No. 17. Arkansas Archeological Survey, Fayetteville.

Herrmann, Jason T.
2005   Non-invasive Survey Techniques in Cultural Landscape Investigation. University of Arkansas.

Hilliard, Jerry E.
2004   *An Antebellum Ozark Community and the Civil War: The Archaeology of the Second Mount Comfort Church (3WA880), Washington County, Arkansas (1840–ca. 1865)*. Arkansas Archeological Survey, Fayetteville.

Hilliard, Jerry E., Mike Evans, Jared Pebworth, and Carl G. Carlson-Drexler
2008   A Confederate Encampment at Cross Hollow, Benton County, Arkansas. *The Arkansas Historical Quarterly* 67(4): 359–374.

Hodges, T. L., and Mrs. T. L. Hodges
1943   Possibilities for the Archaeologist and Historian in Eastern Arkansas. *The Arkansas Historical Quarterly* 2(2): 141–163.

House, John H.
2002   Wallace Bottom: A Colonial-Era Archaeological Site in the Menard Locality, Eastern Arkansas. *Southeastern Archaeology* 21(2): 257–268.

Hume, Ivor Noël
1961   Preservation of English and Colonial American Sites. *Archaeology* 14(4): 250–260.
1976   *Historical Archaeology*. Alfred A. Knopf, New York.

Hunt, William J.
2008   *More Than Meets the Eye: The Archeology of Bathhouse Row, Hot Springs National Park, Arkansas*. Technical Report No. 102. Midwest Archeological Center, Lincoln, NE.

Jeter, Marvin D. (editor)
1990   *Edward Palmer's Arkansaw Mounds*. University of Arkansas Press, Fayetteville.

Kimmel, Richard H.
1993   Notes on the Cultural Origins and Functions of Sub-Floor Pits. *Historical Archaeology* 27(3): 102–113.

King, Thomas F.
2004   Cultural Resource Laws and Practice: An Introductory Guide. 2nd ed. Heritage
        Resources Management Series v. 1. AltaMira Press, Walnut Creek, Calif.
Kwas, Mary L.
2009a   The Growth of Historical Archaeology and Its Impact in Arkansas. The
        Arkansas Historical Quarterly 67(4): 329–341.
2009b   Digging for History at Old Washington. University of Arkansas Press,
        Fayetteville.
Lees, William B.
2001   The Impact of the River Basins Surveys Program in Historical Archaeology.
        In 66th Annual Conference of the Society for American Archaeology. New
        Orleans, LA.
Limp, W. Fredrick, and Jerome C. Rose
1985   Introduction. In Gone to a Better Land: A Biohistory of a Rural Black
        Cemetery in the Post-Reconstruction South, edited by Jerome C. Rose,
        pp. 1–5. Arkansas Archeological Survey Research Series No. 25. Arkansas
        Archeological Survey, Fayetteville.
Little, Barbara J.
2007   Topical Convergence: Historical Archaeologists and Historians on Common
        Ground. Historical Archaeology 41(2): 10–20.
Lyon, Edwin A.
1996   A New Deal for Southeastern Archaeology. University of Alabama Press,
        Tuscaloosa.
Mainfort, Robert C., and Marvin D. Jeter (editors).
1999   Arkansas Archaeology: Essays in Honor of Dan and Phyllis Morse.
        University of Arkansas Press, Fayetteville.
Markus, David M.
2011   "Of the House of Israel in America:" The Archaeology of Judaism, Slavery,
        and Assimilation on the Arkansas Frontier. Master's thesis, University of
        Arkansas, Fayetteville.
Martin, Patrick E.
1971   Historical Archaeology in Arkansas. Arkansas Academy of Science
        Proceedings 25: 23–25.
1977   An Inquiry into the Locations and Characteristics of Jacob Bright's Trading
        House and William Montgomery's Tavern. Arkansas Archeological Survey
        Research Series No. 11. Arkansas Archeological Survey, Fayetteville.
Martin, Patrick E., and Robert C. Mainfort
1998   Cultural Resources Survey and Evaluation within the Threemile Creek Project
        Area, Logan County, Arkansas. Arkansas Archeological Survey, Fayetteville.
Mattison, Ray H.
1957   Arkansas Post: Its Human Aspects. The Arkansas Historical Quarterly 16(2):
        117–138.
Matzko, John A.
2001   Reconstructing Fort Union. University of Nebraska Press, Lincoln.
McAlexander, William E.
1999   "A Man of Wealth and Elegance:" A Look at the Life and Style of Chester
        Ashley and His Family in Early 19th Century Little Rock, Arkansas.

Master's thesis, Department of History, University of Arkansas at Little Rock, Little Rock.

McCrocklin, Claude

1985 The Red River Coushatta Indian Villages of Northwest Louisiana, 1790–1835. *Louisiana Archaeology* 12: 129–178.

1990a *Preliminary Site Report, Tara II (3MI297): Lost Prairie, Miller County, Arkansas.* Arkansas Archeological Survey, Fayetteville.

1990b Three Historic Sites on Red River. *The Arkansas Archeologist: Bulletin of the Arkansas Archeological Society* 31: 31–41.

McGimsey, Charles R.

1972 *Public Archaeology.* Seminar Press, New York.

McGimsey, Charles R., and Hester A. Davis

1992 *History of the Arkansas Archeological Survey.* Special Publications. Arkansas Archeological Survey, Fayetteville.

Moore, Clarence B.

1908 *Certain Mounds of Arkansas and of Mississippi.* P.C. Stockhausen, Philadelphia.

Moore, Jackson W.

1962 Status of the Fort Smith Excavations. *The Arkansas Archeologist: Bulletin of the Arkansas Archeological Society* 3(10): 12.

Moore, Jackson W.

1963 *The Archaeology of Fort Smith I: Fort Smith National Historic Site.* USDI/ National Park Service, Richmond, VA.

Orser, Charles E.

1996 *A Historical Archaeology of the Modern World.* Plenum, New York, NY.

Phillips, Philip

1941 *The Menard Site on the Lower Arkansas River.* Unpublished report. National Park Service, Washington, DC.

Phillips, Philip, James Alfred Ford, and James B. Griffin

2003 *Archaeological Survey in the Lower Mississippi Alluvial Valley, 1940–1947.* Classics in Southeastern Archaeology. University of Alabama Press, Tuscaloosa.

Rose, Jerome C.

1985 *Gone to a Better Land: A Biohistory of a Rural Black Cemetery in the Post-Reconstruction South.* Research Series, no. 25. Arkansas Archeological Survey, Fayetteville.

Rotman, Deborah L., and Michael S. Nassaney

1997 Class, Gender, and the Built Environment: Deriving Social Relations from Cultural Landscapes in Southwest Michigan. *Historical Archaeology* 31(2): 42–62.

Sabo, George

1979 Preliminary Report on Test Excavations at the Walker-Stone House (3WA280) October 31–November 4, 1979. *Field Notes: Newsletter of the Arkansas Archeological Society*(170): 8–9.

Sabo, George, Ann M. Early, Jerome C. Rose, Barbara A. Burnett, Louis Vogele, and James P. Harcourt

1990 *Human Adaptation in the Ozark and Ouachita Mountains.* Arkansas Archeological Survey, Fayetteville.

Santeford, Lawrence G., and William A. Martin (editors).

1980   *The Conway Water Supply: Results of Archaeological Survey and Testing and a Historical Survey of a Proposed Reservoir Area in Conway County, Arkansas*. Arkansas Archeological Survey Research Report No. 20. Arkansas Archeological Survey, Fayetteville.

Scott, Douglas D., and Richard A. Fox

1987   *Archaeological Insights into the Custer Battle: An Assessment of the 1984 Field Season*. University of Oklahoma Press, Norman.

Scott, Douglas D., Richard A. Fox, Melissa A. Connor, and Dick Harmon

1989   *Archaeological Perspectives on the Battle of the Little Bighorn*. University of Oklahoma Press, Norman.

South, Stanley, and Kathleen Deagan

2002   Historical Archaeology in the Southeast, 1930-2000. In *Histories of Southeastern Archaeology*, edited by Shannon Tushingham, Jane Hill, and Charles H. McNutt, pp. 35-50. University of Alabama Press, Tuscaloosa.

Stewart-Abernathy, Leslie C.

1981   Historical Archaeology at Old Washington: 1981. *Field Notes: Newsletter of the Arkansas Archeological Society*(179): 4-5.

1982   *The Sawdust Hill Community: Graphic Documentation of the Historic Occupation of the Parkin Site (3CS29)*. Arkansas Archeological Survey, Fayetteville.

1985   The Block House Cellar. *Field Notes: Newsletter of the Arkansas Archeological Society* 203: 9-11.

1986a   Urban Farmsteads: Household Responsibilities in the City. *Historical Archaeology* 20(2): 5-15.

1986b   *The Moser Farmstead: Independent But Not Isolated: The Archaeology of a Late Nineteenth Century Ozark Farmstead*. Arkansas Archeological Survey Research Series No. 26. Arkansas Archeological Survey, Fayetteville.

1987   From Memories and From the Ground: Historical Archaeology at the Moser Farmstead in the Arkansas Ozarks. In *Visions and Revisions: Ethnohistoric Perspectives on Southern Cultures*, edited by George Sabo and William Schneider, pp. 98–113. Southern Anthropological Society Papers, No. 20. University of Georgia Press, Athens.

1998   Some Archeological Perspectives on the Arkansas Cherokee. *The Arkansas Archeologist: Bulletin of the Arkansas Archeological Society* 37: 39–54.

1999   From Famous Fort to Forgotten Farmsteads: Historical Archaeology in the Mid-South. In *Arkansas Archaeology: Essays in Honor of Dan and Phyllis Morse*, edited by Robert C. Mainfort and Marvin D. Jeter, pp. 225–244. University of Arkansas Press, Fayetteville.

2002   *Ghost Boats of the Mississippi: Discovering Our Working Past*. Arkansas Archeological Survey, Fayetteville.

Stewart-Abernathy, Leslie C., and Beverly Watkins

1982   Historical Archeology. In *A State Plan for the Conservation of Archeological Resources in Arkansas*, edited by Hester A. Davis, pp. HA1–97. Arkansas Archeological Survey Research Series 21. Arkansas Archeological Survey, Fayetteville.

Trubowitz, Neal L.
1984   Cedar Grove. Research Series No. 23. Arkansas Archeological Survey, Fayetteville.

Valentino, Alicia B.
2006   The Dynamics of Industry as Seen from Van Winkle's Mill, Arkansas. University of Arkansas.

Volf, William J.
2003   Geophysical Resistance Surveys at the Elkhorn Tavern and Leetown Locations within Pea Ridge National Military Park, Pea Ridge, Arkansas. USDI/NPS/Midwest Archeological Center, Lincoln, NE.

Walker, Iain C.
1967   Historic Archaeology - Methods and Principles. Historical Archaeology 1: 23–34.

Watkins, Beverly
1982   History of the Felsenthal Region. In Human Adaptation in the Grand Marais Lowland, pp. 79–98. Research Series No. 17. Arkansas Archeological Survey, Fayetteville.

West, Elliott
1998   Foreword. In Arkansas, 1800–1860. University of Arkansas Press, Fayetteville.

Westbury, William A.
1976   Archeological Assessment, Arkansas Post National Memorial. Southern Methodist University, Dallas, TX.

White, Nancy M.
1999   Hester Davis: A Legend in Public Archaeology. In Grit Tempered: Early Women Archaeologists in the Southeastern United States, pp. 206–229. University Press of Florida, Gainesville.

Wilson, Rex L.
1965   Archaeological Investigations in Pea Ridge National Military Park. USDI/ NPS Midwest Archeological Center, Lincoln, NE.
1966   Archeological Explorations at Arkansas Post, 1966. USDI/NPS/Southwest Archeological Center, Globe, AZ.

COLONEL MUSTARD AND THE DOG WITH THE CROCK IN THE BASEMENT

The Power of Things in Places in Antebellum Arkansas

Leslie C. Stewart-Abernathy

There used to be debates about what should be the proper relationship between Archaeology, however spelled, and History. Were archaeologists just hand maidens to history, servants to the true truth revealed only in documents? "Yes," said some, because service to Clio is only the proper role for folks who grub in the dirt for the bit of chamber pot or cuff link or other relic that momentarily brings said elite white male or a famous fort into a bit of humanity. "No," said others who were trained in anthropology, historians just have boring questions about the particular elite white male of the moment, and define significance of sites by their importance to perceived great themes (Little 2007a; Orser 1996; and see the debate in the early volumes of *Historical Archaeology* and the *Conference on Historic Sites* volumes).

This debate had its impact on Arkansas. For example, reticence by historians at taking significant domestic industries in a serious manner postponed progress on the extensive 19th century stoneware pottery industry in the state. Thirty years ago, a dissertation proposal to study the history of remarkable potters in Dallas County, Arkansas (Watkins 1980 and below) was rejected by a prominent department of history in Georgia, on the grounds that crocks were just the stuff of accessorizing reconstructed kitchens. Since then, graduate students in American studies programs and many history departments have contributed greatly to our knowledge of American material culture (Schlereth 1982; Buchner this volume).

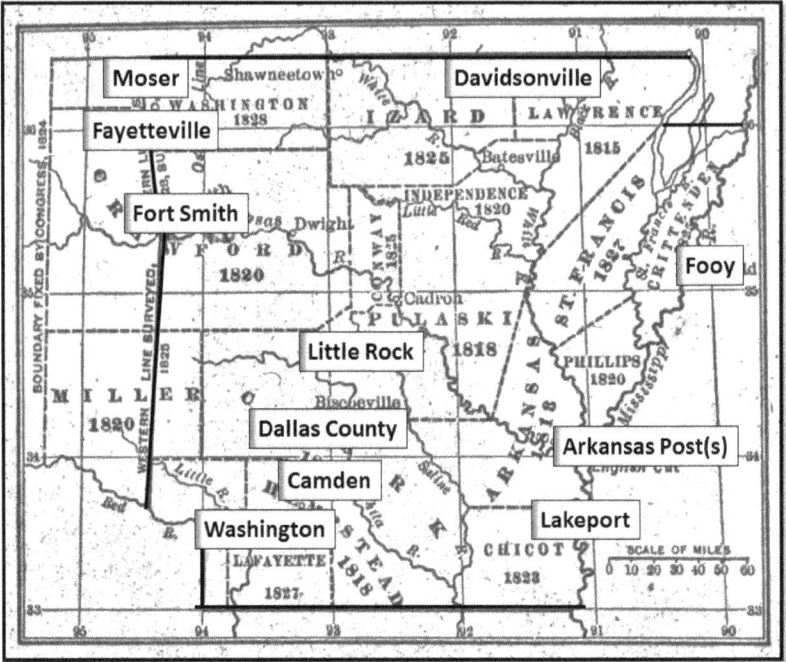

Figure 1.1. Map of Arkansas showing selected locations discussed in text.

Such debates between archaeologists are largely over, primarily because historians purloined anthropological concepts, filtered through sociology by the French Annales School, and renamed them "social history" (Little 2007b). Historians as historical archaeologists started asking more interesting questions about the role of material culture in life. Many discovered that objects and the larger domain of material culture are significant. This is often because researchers have come to recognize that individuals and social groups make daily life possible by using things of the material world in the construction of systems of meanings. Community members are taught, as children, how to read the rules that objects carry.

Even humble objects, such as dishes, provide and guide the comfortable routines and habits of daily life, because these objects can convey rules of thought, habit, and belief. Note the rules encoded at the well-dressed dinner table in the United States in the 21st century. Each person gets their own plate, a reminder about the importance of individuality in our culture. But notice also that all the plates match and so do the eating utensils and glasses, to show the diners that as individuals they belong to a group.

These codes can be changed, and negotiation, action, and reflection are intrinsic to daily life. There is continuity, provided by the shared values and behaviors of culture, and new situations are worked through using old values.

Glass canning jars, for example, are a fully modern product. Successfully using the jars depended on practical acceptance of the germ theory of disease, or one's family on consuming contaminated food from the jar could die horrible deaths from botulism. The jars were created by the millions, in factories known for the hellish heat of melting glass, and these jars had to be acquired from stores with hard-earned cash. And yet, the families who bought and used them together transformed these jars into powerful symbols and literal proof of family self-sufficiency and independence. The transformation was so successful that their origin—far away in modern mass production under harsh factory conditions—has been almost completely forgotten. Because glass jars break, the colorful fragments of blue-green canning jars found on farmstead sites in the Arkansas Ozarks, for example, thus evoke a place, a time, and the struggle against the Machine, won by co-opting the products spit out by the Machine (Stewart-Abernathy 1985; 1986a, 1987, and 1992).

Historical archaeology is a technique among many, to explore how humans construct a meaningful existence. Since most of the products used in a European or North American household in the last two or three centuries were produced outside the home and thus are identical or nearly so, the power of historical archaeology comes from finding artifacts in a particular place, for which documents and other data sources provide context.

Often the key is to be found in artifacts for which one has a reliable date of manufacture, because then one can integrate multiple sources relating to the find of an artifact in a place. For example, in Washington, Arkansas, in a trash-filled root cellar behind the house of Abraham and Fannie Block, most of a red transfer printed tea saucer was found.

On the back are a series of impressed and printed marks that show much about the manufacture, use and discard of this simple vessel. One finds the pattern name "Rose." There is also a suggested date of production, 1836, from the "3" and "6," on either side of the shank of the distinctive impressed anchor that with the printed mark "Davenport" confirms the maker as John Davenport, Stoke on Trent, Staffordshire, United Kingdom.

Also revealed are some of the commercial process that brought the saucer came to North America, in the printed importer's mark "Henderson

Importer's mark   Impressed anchor

Decorated upper surface of saucer

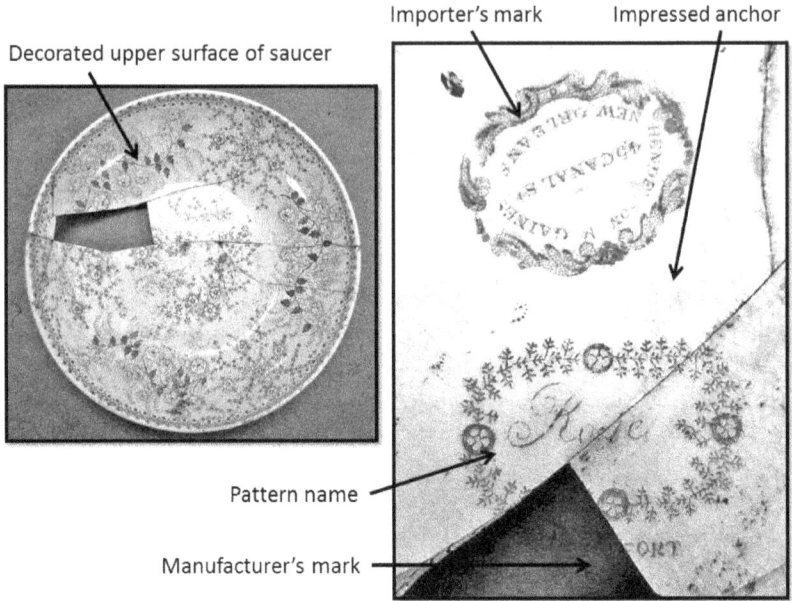

Pattern name

Manufacturer's mark

Figure 1.2. Upper and lower surfaces of a "Rose" pattern red transfer printed saucer manufactured by Davenport, excavated 1982 from the Feature 14 trash deposit in a root cellar behind the Block Family House, Washington, Arkansas. Courtesy of Arkansas Archeological Survey.

& Gaines/New Orleans/45 Canal St." However, by looking at business directories from New Orleans one also sees a conflict between the impressed date of manufacture and the printed address of the firm (Black and Brandimarte 1987; Hahn 2013). In 1836 the firm was recorded as 41 Canal Street. They are not recorded at 45 Canal Street until 1842. Davenport thus obviously produced this plate as a blank in 1836 as the impressed anchor had to be stamped on the ware before it dried out, but the company did not decorate and glaze the saucer until at least 1842. Picture the Davenport pottery facility with a warehouse full of "blanks," ready to be utilized when market forces were right. In this case, part of the delay might have been the terrible Depression that hit the U.S. in 1838 and 1839. When markets turned to normal, Davenport dug into its warehouse and started decorating that backlog of unsold blanks. One artifact, found in its place of discard thousands of miles from its place of manufacture, can then record a little bit about international economics, not to mention about the people who used these items before they were trash.

There has been a surprising amount of historical archaeology conducted in Arkansas. This dates at least back to the 1880s to Edward Palmer's description of the mid 1700s Fort San Carlos expression of the wandering Arkansas Post (Jeter 1990:240–241; Hodges and Hodges 1942). A bibliography of references to much of this work up to 1998 accompanies the essay "Famous Forts and Forgotten Farmsteads" in *Arkansas Archaeology* edited by Robert Mainfort and Marvin Jeter (Stewart-Abernathy 1982, 1999). There are useful updates as well in the articles in the Winter 2008 issue of the *Arkansas Historical Quarterly*, edited by Mary Kwas, which focuses entirely on historical archaeology (Kwas editor 2008). See also the other articles in this volume. There was also an attempt to prepare minimal guidelines for projects involving historical archaeology resources as part of environmental impact investigations (Stewart-Abernathy and Watkins 1982).

As a consequence of these developments, there has been significant historical archaeological research at antebellum sites carried out in all four corners of Arkansas, from the site and state park at Davidsonville at the northeast entry to the state on the Old Southwest Trail (Cande 2008 and this volume; Stewart-Abernathy 1980, 1983), to the cumbersome mix of site, park, and town of Washington with nearby Blackland cotton plantations, strategically located at the other end of the Southwest Trail and the gateway to Mexico and later Texas (see Kwas 2009a; Markus in this volume; Stewart-Abernathy 1986b; Stewart-Abernathy and Ruff 1989). In southeast Arkansas there has been intensive work at Lakeport Plantation mansion as part of its restoration, and site survey nearby suggests a rich array of antebellum and post bellum sites that can be explored with many questions such as the complexities of African American and European American interactions from the 1830s to the present (Kelley 1981; Guendling 2003, 2013). The three different locations of the five expressions of Arkansas Post (Arnold 1983) have been identified as well, including the probable location of the first Post des Arkansas at Wallace Bottom, occupied 1686 to 1749 (House 2002; House, Starr, and Stewart-Abernathy 1999; Martin 1978; McClurkan 1971, 1972). Finally, there has been work on a variety of sites in northwestern Arkansas, from the Ridge House in Fayetteville, Cane Hill to the west of Fayetteville, to the Van Winkle Mill Complex to the northeast (Brandon 2008; and see Brandon and Valentino this volume).

There has also further exploration at the first fort at Fort Smith (Coleman 1987, 1990; Coleman and Scott 2003) and the important Drennen-Scott Historic Site at Van Buren on the Arkansas north of Fort

Smith (Mulvihill 2007), and work eastward down the Arkansas River valley at the early town site of Cadron (Smith 1974), and at such places significant to the Cherokee Old Settlers as some of their farmstead sites (Davis 1987; Stewart-Abernathy 1998) and the trading post "fur factory" at Spadra (Westbury 1971). And one must not forget the discovery of the last bit to survive of the famous settlement of Benjamin Fooy on the Mississippi River across from Memphis, by William McAlexander of the Arkansas Highway Department. Although the locus has long been declared to have been destroyed by the Mississippi, McAlexander was examining a slight rise along the bank being considered as possible borrow for fill for a highway project. He found numerous sherds from British ceramics dating to the first decades of the 1800s, indicating that at least some of the ground at Fooy's complex survives (McAlexander 2000). This is yet another example of how often some evidence survives long after sites are dismissed as obliterated by natural or cultural events.

Why Do Historical Archaeology

The practice of historical archaeology has made great progress in understanding the complexities and dynamism of the antebellum period of Arkansas. To demonstrate some of the successes, this essay borrows a framework that traces back to the late James Deetz. There are five opportunities, or reasons, or mandates, or funding sources, or excuses, or principles, in the service of examining the evidence of the past. These all demonstrate vividly that what historical archaeologists really do work to deepen understandings of past lives.

1. To Aid in Historic Preservation

One of the first uses to which historical archaeology was put, and still a frequent initial cause for historical archaeology at a particular locus, is the ability of archaeology to provide immediate and visible assistance to restoration and reconstruction efforts at historic sites. In this search for foundations and the like, one can incorporate questions of perhaps wider interest, showing that Clyde Dollar's assertion many years ago that historical archaeology's only true orientation was in service to architects' needs was indeed a limited point of view (Dollar 1968; Drexler and Markus this volume).

Archaeologists have been conducting fieldwork in Washington, Arkansas, since 1978 as part of restoration and reconstruction efforts. Much of the work since 1984 has been carried out by the Arkansas Archeological Survey's Sponsored Research Program. As is often the case in historic preservation projects, the needs of the immediate project often did not match the anthropological problems of interest to archaeologists, but one can take advantages of opportunities (Stewart-Abernathy 2002).

One site with much interest is the Block Family house from the 1830s, as part of restoring the house and urban farmstead complex to something resembling its antebellum character. The search for the "separate" kitchen building also became an investigation of the relationships between enslaved people and their owners (see below).

A more narrow restoration question was the form of the original porch, and here as well there is a wider context. Into the 1980's, for at least two generations it had been a two story portico the width of the central hall. This portico was strongly defended by some proponents in the town, since it transformed the house from a simple two story structure, one room deep on each floor with a shed-roofed ell along the rear of the first floor, into a modest but nonetheless authentic survival of the Greek Revival classicism. This classicism has been promoted as a symbol of power and prosperity in Washington at least since the restoration of the 1836 Courthouse by the Daughters of the Confederacy in the late 1920s. Greek Revival in the antebellum South was the fashionable architectural assertion of authority and deserved privilege (Hamlin 1944:187–257). It was asserted that the Block Family home, the residence of merchants and entrepreneurs (Stewart-Abernathy and Ruff 1989; Kwas 2009a and b), must have had such a portico.

There were clues, however, that that the porch was originally much longer, for example empty mortise pockets in the plate at the top of the first floor of the front wall of the house. A small excavation undertaken as part of re-working the timber foundation discovered the original brick porch piers just below the ground surface. This allowed the reconstruction of the original porch that stretched all the way across the front of the house. This was much more in keeping with the original Federal style of the house (Guendling, Cande, Tavaszi, Stewart-Abernathy, and Ruff 2002; Stewart-Abernathy 1986). As much as some preservationists in modern Washington wanted to promote this house to the more elaborate style, a few two by two meter units demonstrated objectively that it was not.

One might also note the discovery of the sad evidence of a buried pet, an intact skeleton of a dog, on the site of the former kitchen ell and thus dating after about 1950, with a chicken bone in its larynx. Unlike a complete rooster carcass that was dumped into a hastily dug shallow

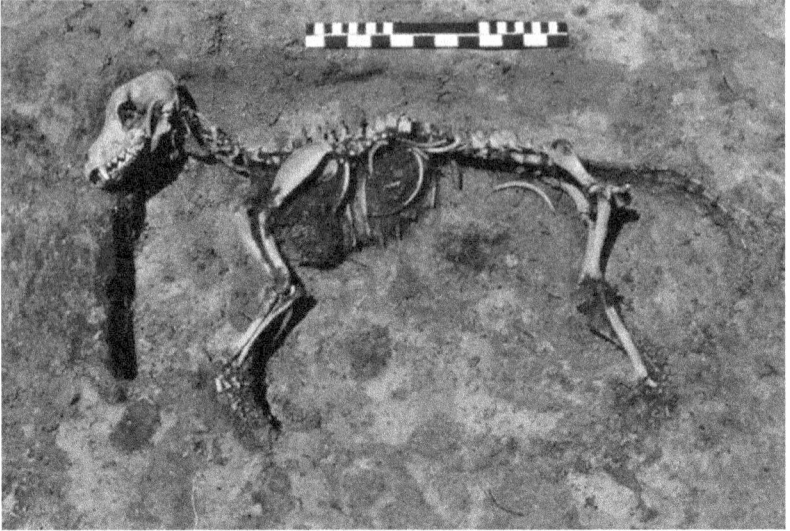

Figure 1.3. Skeleton of a dog, exposed in 1982 in the back yard of the Block Family House, Washington, Arkansas. Courtesy of Arkansas Archeological Survey.

hole outside the perimeter of the kitchen (one does not eat poultry that has died of an uncertain cause, explained informants), this dog was carefully laid down in a grave on its right side, fore and hind legs extended comfortably at right angles to the spine, its head a little higher than the rest of the body. Not incidentally, the remains were laid out with the head and back in perfect alignment with the Block House, thus ultimately with the Southwest Trail to which the town plat oriented. It was an act of the 1950s, yet deeply affected by the spatial framework of Washington established in 1824. That framework provided a perhaps comforting moment of regularity and routine a century and a quarter after the surveyor laid down his tools.

Another example of archaeology so far pretty much limited to restoration questions is the work at Lakeport, built 1859–60 for Lycurgus and Lydia Johnson. It is one of the few *Gone with the Wind* scale houses in the state. Archaeology under the direction of Randy Guendling was an integral part of the restoration over five years (Guendling 2003, 2013). It was not until 2009 that limited fieldwork in the form of controlled surface collection was carried out in the adjacent cotton fields. There it was discovered that the area of worker housing northeast of the house known as the "Quarters" was entirely post-bellum, that the housing for enslaved people owned by Lycurgus Johnson at the start of the Civil War was probably at his late father Joel Johnson's plantation headquarters within a mile southeast of Lakeport, and that there was an 1820s–1830s occupation of some sort right on the old Mississippi River bank only a hundred meters or so north of the house.

2. To Serve the Decorative Arts

The second reason for historical archaeology is to better understand the technological and economic contexts from which came the artifacts that we find. Looking at artifacts as part of the history of decorative arts encourages deeper knowledge of the techniques of production and related topics such as marketing and transport. One can better contextualize what one finds in a particular place if it is known how that object was made and where and when.

For example, Arkansas was a source of stoneware pottery from the 1820s into the 1950s. Dallas County alone had numerous potters before the Civil War. Work by Beverly Watkins (1980) has located many of the groundhog kilns commonly used there. Wasters provide an opportunity to study techniques of production and decoration, and to establish definite criteria to distinguish one maker from another. Work has also been carried out at other antebellum kiln sites in Cane Hill, near Fort Smith, and in Sharp Co. (Bennett and Worthen 1990:142–164; Blakeley 1989; Smith 1972b). Even the work at the later Howe Kiln site at Benton near Little Rock provided totally new evidence, wasters marked by a heretofore unknown potter (Buchner 2011 and this volume).

3. To Complement the Historical Record

A third reason for doing historical archaeology is to explore sites for the information they contain that enhances or complements the picture sketched by the analysis of documents, photographs, and other sources. A good example is the house built by one of the richest families in Arkansas in the 1840s. This is the Ashley Mansion. Chester Ashley was prominent in most affairs in central Arkansas from the 1820s onward. One of the founders of Little Rock, he was highly successful in business, politics, and the law. His wife Mary continued to be prominent after his death in 1848 (Rose 1911; Roy, Witsell, and Nichols 1984:30–32; Ruple 1983).

The mansion they had built for themselves in the 1840s was in the growing commercial center of Little Rock on Markham Street only two blocks from the Arkansas River. The mansion was elaborate and luxurious to the extent that it was deemed suitable for General Frederick Steele, the commander of Union forces when Little Rock fell in 1863. Thus there are official photographs, including a busy image of the front of the house taken during a party for General Steele's farewell and another taken looking west that shows the massive two story brick end wall with embedded chimney flues and an enormous U.S. flag suspended horizontally from a framework on the front porch roof (Bennett and Worthen 1991: Ph-82, p.72; Roy, Witsell, and Nichols 1984:30, 32).

Unfortunately, that part of downtown Little Rock changed character after the Civil War. By the 1880s the house was surrounded by noisome commercial property. The mansion itself was downgraded to a cheap boarding house, photographed almost hidden from the street (Roy, Witsell, and Nichols 1984:30). These transformations were documented in a master's thesis by David Earnest (1994).

Urban renewal in the 1920s converted most of the block into warehouses, and the Ashley mansion disappeared. Today the site is in a revitalized area of downtown, with a large office building at each end of the block. Half of the block is even part of the Historic Arkansas Museum's reconstruction of an antebellum pioneer farmstead.

Evidence of the Ashley mansion reappeared in 1984 when the two warehouses at each end of the block were being renovated for offices. One surprise was the discovery of the bottom of a brick-walled cistern underneath a commercial warehouse, now known as Heritage West, that had been built with two levels of basements below street level. This cistern must have been just off the back corner of the mansion and kept filled by runoff from the roof.

After the removal of the concrete slab that had been the floor of an adjacent one story warehouse along with tons of brick rubble of the house itself, and after a lot of hand excavation by many volunteers, it was realized that the east half of the bottom part of the Ashley house itself had survived. Thus the foundation of the porch and the support piers for the magnificent columns were intact. Some of the column sections were themselves still holding together in spite of having been pushed inwards through the front of the house.

These are only the third set of antebellum brick columns known in Little Rock, along with the Pike-Fletcher-Terry House and the Old State House, and all three were finished differently. The Ashley columns had a rough brick core covered thickly by mortar with a smooth finish coat. The Old State House columns have a brick core concealed by

Front porch foundation   Mansion Basement   Basement
                                                       entry

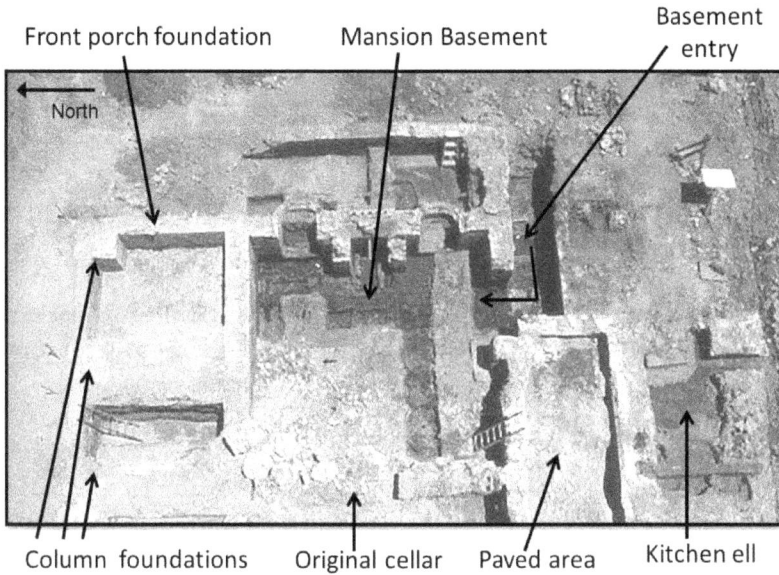

Column foundations   Original cellar   Paved area   Kitchen ell

Figure 1.4. East half of the foundations and features of the Ashley Mansion,
excavated 1984, Little Rock, Arkansas. Courtesy of Arkansas Archeological Survey.

mortar and plaster worked into vertical flutes (Kwas 2011; Guendling
and Kwas 1997). These two techniques demonstrate a common practice
with Greek Revival architecture in which the outside appearance was
the important point, not the supporting structure for that appearance
(Hamlin 1944:332). The Pike-Fletcher-Terry columns are entirely of
brick with curving bricks forming the exterior (Roy, Witsell and Nichols
1984:50, 58).

Evidence also survived of the first Ashley house built in the 1820s,
prior to which discovery had only been surmised. Remains included an
area of brick paving laid in a herringbone pattern that might have been
an outdoor work area behind or adjacent to the house, and below-grade
stone foundations that continued downwards to form the stone walls of
a cellar. Stone below-grade with brick walls above has turned out to be
common in many sites in Arkansas dating from about the first one third
of the 1800s. It can be found in Davidsonville, Fayetteville, Little Rock,
Washington, and elsewhere, though absent in stone-poor southeastern
Arkansas. Its presence is practically diagnostic of such early construction at least where building stone is available. The stonework insulates
the porous locally fired brick from rapid deterioration when the bricks
are in contact with the damp earth.

In part of the stone-walled cellar that survived were remains of some of the feasting for which the Ashleys were famous, such as a wine bottle seal "St Julien Medoc" marking a prominent French wine region. William McAlexander's master's thesis integrated documents and these and other antebellum Ashley artifacts including ceramics and even oyster shells from elsewhere on site to show just what was meant by Southern hospitality for elites (McAlexander 1999).

Also surviving was the complete east, north, and south wall of an entirely unknown brick-walled basement that was evidently dug out adjacent to the stone-walled cellar, probably when the house was transformed into the familiar mansion in the 1840s. This basement had been filled first with industrial waste from a leather-processing enterprise that stood next to the mansion in its later days, then with animal bones and broken dishes that was waste from nearby restaurants. This included stoneware jugs and crocks, and even a distinctive pitcher of Rockingham stoneware that was molded in the "Rebecca at the Well" form popular in the late 1800s. Most of the fill in the basement was the brick Ashley Mansion, pushed in on itself.

The basement was originally fitted out with amenities that made it habitable as a relatively comfortable slave quarter. These improvements included a fireplace evidenced by two brick shoulders and a horizontal wrought iron bar that supported the hearth and mantel (the flue ran inside the east brick wall of the house). There was also a window well on either side of the fireplace that provided light and ventilation. Access was down a stairway from a porch on the east side of the ell behind the house.

It was well known that the Ashley family belonged in their day to the elite of antebellum Arkansas. The grand public face of their house was not subtle in claiming and expressing this elite position. Shattered fragments of elaborate plaster eave moldings found in the rubble that filled the basement suggest the interior of the house was equally elegant, and eloquent. It is of interest perhaps that the public and private spaces known to the Ashleys have been obliterated, whereas the comfortable yet hidden spaces known to their slaves survive.

So, too, has survived a photograph of the young child Harriet Ashley, held in the arms of an enslaved African American nurse in the Ashley household who probably knew well the slave quarters in the basement of the mansion (Bennett and Worthen 1991:Ph-3 p.11). The name of the nurse is not known, but clearly the implied relationships between owned and owner are also of interest. Chester and Mary Ashley lived a highly public and well-documented life. With the discovery of the slave quarters in the basement, we now know at least a bit more about the lifeways of the urban enslaved people who made that life possible (Lack 1982).

4. To Supplement the Historical Record

A fourth reason why one does historical archaeology is that many times the documentary record holds only clues and hints, and a little digging can provide the answers. A good example is the town site of Davidsonville, on the Black River in northeast Arkansas where the Ozark Plateau drops off into the Mississippi Alluvial Plain. It was established in 1815 but largely abandoned by the 1830s. Although it was on the very western edge of Anglo North America, the plat of Davidsonville suggests the founders had more in mind than a hodgepodge of hovels strung along the Black River.

The above-ground evidence for a town is not readily apparent. Fieldwork over the last 40 years has revealed a rich variety of material culture that confirms high aspirations and connections to the wider world. Beginning with Sam Smith and Tim Klinger in the 1970s (Klinger 1976; Smith and Davidson 1975; Smith 1978;), archaeologists discovered enough data to relay the plat precisely, located the limestone foundations of the imposing brick courthouse that actually did have a brick paved floor as legend had it, and located the no less solid foundations of the house in one tiny space of which was located the first United States post office in Arkansas, in 1817 that had made the town "famous" in the common story of Arkansas history (Cande 2008; Stewart-Abernathy 1980).

Finally, Kathy Cande and her team discovered a cellar associated with a dwelling with a tavern license. In the refuse that filled the cellar was found a wonderful assemblage of ceramics (mostly from Staffordshire, Great Britain), glassware, food bones, and personal items dating before 1825. There was even a small leather bag with American and Spanish coins (Cande, Pebworth, Jenkins, and Evans 2007).

The path this bag followed into the refuse is unfathomable. What is certain is that no one can ever believe again that Arkansas was isolated during the historical period. The objects may have come in by keel boat, a train of pack mules, or heavily loaded wagons, but finding British dishes, Spanish coins, and other imported goods in situ at Davidsonville that far from the Atlantic or Gulf coasts makes such assertions as "isolation" silly at best and misguided at worst. Arkansas was connected to the wider world in the very earliest days of American settlement, and to use "isolation" as an excuse for social or economic problems at any time thereafter was and is to deny reality.

5. To Illuminate Groups and Issues Barely Mentioned

The fifth in this list of reasons to conduct historical archaeology, and the reason some find the most challenging task for historical archaeologists, deals with the least visible people in the normal historical record. One of the challenges of course in the enticement is that this allows one to look at groups within the wider context of normative culture in the region, and see how a subgroup generates and experiences variation.

In antebellum Arkansas such groups include the Old Settler Cherokee and other emigrant Native American groups. There were even left over French *habitants* and the occasional refugee Bonapartist soldier such as Antoine Barraque in Jefferson County and Jean La Caz on Petit Jean Mountain.

The greatest population of barely visible people was of course enslaved African Americans. They were in fact in 1860 a majority of the population in several counties, and almost half the population in the capitol city of Little Rock (Lack 1982). It is hard to see enslaved African Americans in historical documents unless they escape or are sold. Perhaps that is why the only attempt at a comprehensive history book on African American slavery in Arkansas is now over half a century old (Taylor 1958).

Historical archaeologists are sometimes accused of helping to construct the history of the nation as if it were actually only the history of the actions of elite white males, and their houses. Certainly much of the work in Historic Washington State Park has been usually subverted by the "Moonlight and Magnolias" view of a peaceable, harmonious Southland, visible at every turn in the town. This view has been challenged (Stewart-Abernathy 2002), so after almost four decades of effort, some of the story of African Americans is beginning to slip in. After all, they were half the population of Washington recorded in the census at the very end of Antebellum Arkansas (White 1984; Stewart-Abernathy 2004).

Ms. Mckicia Henry portrays the character of Betty Sanders at the Sanders house. The character is a composite but much is drawn from a real woman named Eliza, owned by the Sanders family. In 1847 Simon Sanders first wife Zenobia died, leaving him at age 50 with three daughters, Sarah Virginia age 13, Isabella age 10, and Zenobia age 5 (Kwas 2006; Williams 1951). They were "to be cared for in the absence of a mother's loving

Figure 1.5. Ms. McKicia Henry, interpreter at Historic Washington State Park, walking down the reconstructed rear porch of the Sanders House toward the reconstructed Sanders Kitchen, 2011, Washington, Arkansas. Courtesy of Arkansas Archeological Survey.

kindness" (Anon.:16). Fortunately, slave Eliza was present. She saved the day and probably the next seven years until Sanders remarried, for "by the aid of a faithful old colored servant he continued to keep house and keep his children together" (Anon.:16). If this is indeed the same Eliza who was reported still living in 1912 (Royston 1912:19), she herself may not have been much more than 20 at the time she found herself as defacto mother and mentor to the three girls. Eliza is thus an important element in the history of the Sanders family.

In 1853, 18 year old Sarah Virginia Sanders married Augustus Garland who would one day be Governor of Arkansas, U.S. Senator, and Attorney General of the United States (1885–1889) (Schlup 1981; Watkins 1995). At their wedding her father Simon, still a widower, gave faithful Eliza not her freedom, but as a present to Sarah (Montgomery 1980:165n.18). Such a wedding gift was not uncommon in Arkansas and elsewhere (Taylor 1958:149, 194). It helped to maintain the emotional ties, and it provided the beginning family with an important investment both in capital and experience. However, it is a stunning reminder that there was more to the ties between Eliza and Sarah than emotion—the pupil and "daughter" now owned the teacher and "mother."

Historical archaeologists found the brick underpinnings of the original kitchen that was reconstructed, in which Ms. McKicia Henry portrays the Sanders family cook. It was located primarily through excavation both by hand and by backhoe. The discovery was aided by an old photograph taken from the roof of a building three blocks away after a tornado hit the town in 1907, and oral history conducted by archaeologists (Stewart-Abernathy 2001a, 2001b, 2004). Historical archaeologists thus established the footprint of the three-dimensional space where she could perform, accompanied by the aromas of cooking food, and the sounds of annoyed chickens. That may be the best result of the power of historical archaeology in antebellum Arkansas to date.

Acknowledgments

Many people and organizations made this work possible, including the Arkansas Archeological Survey, the University of Arkansas System and many of its campuses, the Arkansas Historic Preservation Program, the Arkansas Department of Parks and Tourism, the Arkansas Highway and Transportation Department, the Little Rock, Memphis, and Vicksburg Districts of the US Army Corps of Engineers, the Pioneer Washington Preservation Foundation, Historic Arkansas Museum, the Old State House Museum, the Department of Arkansas Heritage, and others. I have been very lucky to have been a part of much of the historical archaeology carried out in Arkansas since 1977.

REFERENCES

Anonymous
n.d.   In Memoriam. Typescript biography of Simon T. Sanders. On file, Southwest Arkansas Regional Archives, Washington, Arkansas.

Arnold, Morris S.
1983   The Relocation of Arkansas Post to *Ecores Rouges* 1779. *Arkansas Historical Quarterly* 42:317–331.

Bennett, Swannee, and William B. Worthen
1990   *Arkansas Made: A Survey of the Decorative, Mechanical, and Fine Arts Produced in Arkansas, 1819–1870, Volume 1 (Furniture, Quilts, Silver, Pottery, Firearms)*. University of Arkansas Press, Fayetteville, Arkansas.
1991   *Arkansas Made: A Survey of the Decorative, Mechanical, and Fine Arts Produced in Arkansas, 1819–1870, Volume 2 (Photography, Art)*. University of Arkansas Press, Fayetteville, Arkansas.

Black, Art, and Cynthia Brandimarte

1987   *Henderson & Gaines, New Orleans Ceramic Importers.* Research Notes, Historic Sites and Materials, Texas Parks and Wildlife Department, Austin.

Blakely, Jeffery A.

1989   The nineteenth century Pottery Industry in Sebastian County, Arkansas. Paper presented at the annual meeting of the Arkansas Historical Association, Van Buren, Arkansas.

Brandon, Jamie C.

2008   Van Winkle's Mill: Recovering Lost Industrial and African-American Heritages in the Ozarks. *Arkansas Historical Quarterly* 67(No.4, Winter):429–445.

Buchner, C. Andrew

1992   *Archaeological Investigations at the Lewis Site (3LE266): A Twentieth-Century Black Owned Farmstead on the St. Francis Flood way, Lee County, Arkansas.* Garrow and Associates. Submitted to Department of the Army, Memphis District, Corps of Engineers, Memphis.

2011   *Data Recovery Excavations at the Howe Pottery (3SA340) on Military Road in Benton Saline County, Arkansas.* Panamerican Consultants, Inc., Memphis, TN, PCI No. 29228.3, Submitted to Jacobs Engineering Group, Inc., Little Rock, Arkansas.

Cande, Kathleen H.

2008   Rediscovering Davidsonville, Arkansas' First County Seat Town, 1815–1830. *Arkansas Historical Quarterly* 67(No.4, Winter):342–358.

Cande, Kathleen H., Jared S. Pebworth, Aidan Jenkins, and Michael M. Evans

2007   *"A Public House of Entertainment:" Expanding Public Interpretation at Old Davidsonville State Park, Randolph County, Arkansas.* Final Report, Project 06–1, Arkansas Archeological Survey, Fayetteville, Arkansas.

Coleman, Roger E.

1987   *The Arkansas Post Story:* Arkansas Post National Memorial. National Park Service, Southwest Cultural Resources Center Professional Papers No. 12, Santa Fe.

1990   *Archaeological Investigation for Construction of a Pedestrian Trail and Identification of Laundress Row, Fort Smith National Historic Site, Arkansas.* Southwest Cultural Resources Center Professional Paper No. 30. National Park Service, Santa Fe.

Coleman, Roger E., and Douglas D. Scott

2003   *An Archeological Overview and Assessment of Fort Smith National Historic Site.* National Park Service, Midwest Archeological Center, Technical Report No. 87, Lincoln, Nebraska.

Davis, Hester A.

1987   The Cherokee in Arkansas: An Invisible Resource. In *Visions and Revisions: Ethnohistoric Perspectives on Southern Cultures,* edited by Sabo, George III and William M. Schneider. University of Georgia Press, Athens, GA. Pp. 48–58.

Dollar, Clyde D.

1968   Some Thoughts on Theory and Method in Historical Archaeology. *The Conference on Historic Site Archaeology Papers* 2(2):1–30.

Ernest, David M.

1994   The Oakleaf Hotel: A Study of Urban Residence Dynamics in Late nineteenth and Early 20th Century Little Rock, Arkansas. Master's thesis, Department of Anthropology, University of Arkansas, Fayetteville, Arkansas.

Guendling, Randall L.

1993   *Archeological Assessment of the Sanders Block, Old Washington State Park, Hempstead County, Arkansas.* Final Report, Sponsored Research Program, Arkansas Archeological Survey, Submitted to Arkansas Department of Parks and Tourism, Little Rock.

2003   *Archeological Investigations at Lakeport Plantation, Summary Report.* Arkansas Archeological Survey Project 03–2. Submitted to Witsell, Rasco and Evans, Little Rock.

2013   *Archaeology and the Restoration of the Lakeport Plantation House, 2002–2009.* Arkansas Archeological Survey. Submitted to Dr. Ruth Hawkins, Arkansas State University, State University, Arkansas.

Guendling, Randall J., Kathleen H. Cande, Leslie C. Stewart-Abernathy, and Dawn Novak

2001   *The Archeological Investigation of the Sanders Kitchen, 1981 and 1992, Old Washington Historic State Park.* ANCRC Report, Project 01–01, AAS Project 01–1. Arkansas Archeological Survey Sponsored Research Program, Fayetteville, Arkansas.

Guendling, Randall L., Kathleen H. Cande, Maria Tavaszi, Leslie C. Stewart-Abernathy, and Barbara Ruff

2002   *The Archeological Investigation of the Block Detached Kitchen: The 1982 and 1983 Arkansas Archeological Society Digs, Old Washington Historic State Park.* Sponsored Research Program, Arkansas Archeological Survey. Grant No. 02–02, AAS Project NO. 02–1. Submitted to the Arkansas Natural and Cultural Resources Council, Little Rock.

Guendling, Randall L., and Mary L. Kwas

1997   *The Historical Archaeology of Arkansas' Old State House.* Sponsored Research Program, Arkansas Archeological Survey. Submitted to Department of Arkansas Heritage and Arkansas Commemorative Commission, Little Rock.

Hahn, Thurston

2013   The Henderson and Gaines Family of Ceramic Importers. Paper presented at the annual meeting of the Society for Historical Archaeology, Leicester, United Kingdom.

Hamlin, Talbot H.

1944   *Greek Revival Architecture in America.* Oxford University Press, reprinted 1964 Dover Publications, Inc, New York.

Hodges, T. L. and Mrs. T. L. Hodges

1942   Possibilities for the Archeologist and Historian in Eastern Arkansas. *Arkansas Historical Quarterly* 2(2):141–163.

House, John H.

2002   Wallace Bottom: a Colonial-Era Archeological Site in the Menard Locality, Eastern Arkansas. *Southeastern Archaeology* 21(2): 257–268.

House, John H., Mary Evelyn Starr, and Leslie C. Stewart-Abernathy
1999   Rediscovering Menard. *Mississippi Archaeology* 34(Winter, 2): 156–177.
Jeter, Marvin (editor)
1990   *Edward Palmer's Arkansas Mounds.* University of Arkansas Press,
         Fayetteville, Arkansas.
Kelley, David B.
1981   *A Cultural Resources Survey of Levee Enlargement and Berm Areas,
         Lakeport to Harwood, Chicot County, Arkansas.* Coastal Environments,
         Inc., Baton Rouge. Submitted to U.S. Army Corps of Engineers, Vicksburg
         District, Vicksburg.
Klinger, Timothy C.
1976   *An Assessment of Impacts on the Cultural Resources of the Historic
         Davidsonville State Park Resulting from Proposed Park Improvements.*
         Arkansas Archaeological Survey, Fayetteville. Submitted to the Arkansas
         Department of Parks and Tourism, Little Rock.
Kwas, Mary L.
2006   Simon T. Sanders and the Meredith Clan: The Case for Kinship Studies.
         Arkansas Historical Quarterly 65(3):250–273.
2008   The Growth of Historical Archaeology and its Impact on Arkansas. *Arkansas
         Historical Quarterly* 67 (4, Winter):329–341.
2009a   *Digging for History at Old Washington.* University of Arkansas Press,
         Fayetteville, Arkansas.
2009b   Two Generations of the Abraham and Fanny Block Family: Internal
         Migration, Economics, Family and the Jewish Frontier. *Southern Jewish
         History* 12:39–114.
2011   *A Pictorial History of Arkansas's Old State House; Celebrating 175 Years.*
         University of Arkansas Press, Fayetteville, Arkansas.
Kwas, Mary L. (editor)
2008   Historical Archaeology in Arkansas. Special topic issue, *Arkansas Historical
         Quarterly* 67(4, Winter)
Lack, P. D.
1982   An Urban Slave Community: Little Rock, 1831–1862. *Arkansas Historical
         Quarterly* 41(3):258–287.
Little, Barbara J.
2007a   *Historical Archaeology: Why the Past Matters.* Left Coast Press. Walnut
         Creek, California.
2007b   Topical Convergence: Historical Archaeologists and Historians on Common
         Ground. *Historical Archaeology* 41(No. 2): 10–20.
Martin, Patrick E.
1978   *An Inquiry into the Locations and Characteristics of Jacob Bright's Trading
         House and William Montgomery's Tavern.* Arkansas Archaeological Survey
         Research Series No. 11. Arkansas Archaeological Survey, Fayetteville,
         Arkansas.
McClurkan, Burney B.
1971   The Search for Fort Desha. *Arkansas Archaeological Society Field Notes*
         77:5–6.

1972   Fort Desha, the Location of Arkansas Post ca. 1735–1750. *Conference on Historic Sites Archaeology Papers* 6:32–39.

McAlexander, William E., Jr.
2000   *Cultural Resources Survey of Borrow Areas on AHTD Job Number 110235, Crittenden County.* Arkansas Highway and Transportation Department, Environmental Division, submitted to Arkansas State Historic Preservation Office, Little Rock.

McAlexander, William E., Jr.
1999   "A Man of Wealth and Elegance": A Look at the Life and Style of Chester Ashley and His Family in Early nineteenth Century Little Rock. Master's thesis, Public History Department, University of Arkansas at Little Rock, Little Rock.

Montgomery, Donald R.
1980   Simon T. Sanders, Public Servant. *Arkansas Historical Quarterly* 39(2):159–168.

Mulvihill, Tim
2007   Archeological Research at the Drennen-Scott House, Van Buren, Arkansas. *Arkansas Archeological Society Field Notes* 336:3–5.

Orser, Charles E., Jr.
1996   *A Historical Archaeology of the Modern World.* Plenum Publishing, New York.

Rose, U. M.
1911   Chester Ashley. *Publications of the Arkansas Historical Association.* Vol. 3. Arkansas Historical Association, Fayetteville, Arkansas.

Roy, F. Hampton, Charles Witsell, Jr., and Cheryl G. Nichols
1985   *How We Lived: Little Rock as an American City.* August House, Little Rock.

Royston, Charles E.
1912   *History of Hempstead County, Arkansas during the War Between the States.* Typescript on file, Southwest Arkansas Regional Archives, Washington, Arkansas.

Ruple, Susan Hamner
1983   The Life and Times of Chester Ashley, 1791–1848. Master's thesis, Department of History, University of Arkansas, Fayetteville Arkansas.

Schlup, Leonard
1981   Augustus Hill Garland: Gilded Age Democrat. *Arkansas Historical Quarterly* 40(4, Winter):338–346.

Schereth, Thomas J.
1982   *Material Culture Studies in America, an Anthology.* Rowan Altamira, Lanham, Maryland.

Smith, Samuel D.
1972a   Prospectus for Historic Site Archaeology in Northeast Arkansas. *Craighead County Historical Quarterly.* 11(2):7–17
1972b   Arkansas Kiln Sites. *Arkansas Archaeological Society Field Notes.* 95:7–10.
1974   *A Survey and Assessment of the Archaeological Resources of Cadron Settlement.* Arkansas Archaeological Survey Research Report No. 1, Arkansas Archaeological Survey, Fayetteville, Arkansas.
1978   Davidsonville Bricks. *The Arkansas Archeologist* 19:31–35.

Smith, Samuel D. and William V. Davidson
1975   County Seat Towns as Archaeological Sites: Some Arkansas Examples. *The
          Conference on Historic Site Archaeology Papers* 8:33–51.
Stewart-Abernathy, Leslie C.
1980   *"The seat of Justice, 1815–1830": an Archaeological Reconnaissance of
          Davidsonville, 1979,* Arkansas Archaeological Survey Research Report
          No. 21, Fayetteville, Arkansas.
1982   The Other Four and a Half Centuries: Historical Archaeology and the
          Arkansas Archaeological Survey, in Neal L. Trubowitz and Marvin D. Jeter,
          editors, *Arkansas Archaeology in Review,* Arkansas Archaeological Survey
          Research Series No. 15, Pp. 301– 309, Fayetteville, Arkansas.
1983   Old Davidsonville on the Arkansas Frontier: Reconnaissance at a Townsite
          for the Parks and the Past, for the Public and the Present, in *Forgotten Places
          and Things: Select Papers from the 1980 Society for Historical Archaeology
          meetings,* Albert E. Ward, editor, Center for Anthropological Studies,
          Albuquerque, NM. Pp. 141–147.
1985   The Moser Farmstead: Ethnoarchaeology in Pre-World War Ozarkia. *Pioneer
          America Society Transactions* 8:27–36.
1986a   *The Moser Farmstead, Independent but not Isolated: the Archaeology of a
          Late Nineteenth Century Ozark Farmstead.* Arkansas Archaeological Survey
          Research Series No. 26, Fayetteville, AR.
1986b   Urban Farmsteads: Household Responsibilities in the City. *Historical
          Archaeology* 20(2):5–15.
1986c   *The Block House Piers: A Contribution to the Archaeological Underpinning
          of Historic Preservation in Washington, Arkansas.* Submitted to the Arkansas
          Department of Parks and Tourism, Little Rock.
1987   From Memories and From the Ground: Historical Archaeology at the
          Moser Farmstead in the Arkansas Ozarks. in George Sabo III and William M.
          Schneider, editors, *Visions and Revisions, Ethnohistoric Perspectives on
          Southern Cultures.* University of Georgia Press, Athens, Georgia. Pp.98–113.
1992   Industrial Goods in the Service of Tradition: Consumption and Cognition
          on an Ozark Farmstead Before the Great War. In *The Art and Mystery of
          Historical Archaeology: Essays in Honor of James Deetz,* edited by Anne
          Elizabeth Yentsch and Mary C. Beaudry, CRC Press, Boca Raton, Florida.
          Pp. 101–126.
1998   Some Archeological Perspectives on the Arkansas Cherokee. *Arkansas
          Archeologist 1996.* 37(1996):39–54.
1999   From Famous Forts to Forgotten Farmsteads: Historical Archaeology in the
          Mid-South. as Chapter 11 in *On Beyond Zebree, Papers in Honor of Dan
          and Phyllis Morse,* Robert Mainfort, Editor, University of Arkansas Press,
          Fayetteville, Arkansas. Pp.225–244.
2001a   Kitchens and slavery, as Chapter 6, in Guendling et al 2001, below,
          Pp.89–97.
2001b   Research Plan for the 1981 Society Training Program at the Sanders Block at
          Old Washington (3HE236). as Appendix 1 in Guendling
          et al 2001, below, Pp. 107–119.

2002   Just Putting It Back the Way It Was: Archaeology and the Constructions of
        an Antebellum Townscape in Washington, Arkansas. Published on the web
        page of the South Central Historical Archaeology Conference, at
        http://www.uark.edu/campus-resources/archinfo /SCHACstewabernathy.pdf.
2004   Separate Kitchens and Intimate Archaeology: Constructing Urban Slavery on
        the Antebellum Cotton Frontier in Washington, Arkansas. for editors Kerri
        Barile and Jamie Brandon, *Household Chores: Historical and Archaeological
        Perspectives on Households*, University of Alabama Press, Tuscaloosa,
        Alabama. Pp.51–74.

Stewart-Abernathy, Leslie C., and Barbara L. Ruff
1989   A Good Man In Israel: Zooarchaeology And Assimilation In Antebellum
        Washington, Arkansas. *Historical Archaeology* 23(2):96–112.

Stewart-Abernathy, Leslie C., and Beverly S. Watkins
1982   Historical Archaeology, in *A State Plan for the Conservation of
        Archaeological Resources in Arkansas*, Hester A. Davis, editor, Arkansas
        Archaeological Survey Research Series No. 21, HA1–HA53, Fayetteville,
        Arkansas.

Taylor, Orville W.
1958   *Negro Slavery in Arkansas*. Duke University Press, Durham, North Carolina.

Watkins, Beverly S.
1980   The Bird and Welch Potteries: Small Industry in Nineteenth Century
        Arkansas. Paper presented at the annual meeting of the Society for Historical
        Archaeology, Albuquerque.
1995   Eleventh Governor: Augustus Hill Garland, 1875–1877. in Donovan,
        Timothy, Willard B. Gatewood Jr., and Jeannie M. Whayne, editors. *The
        Governors of Arkansas: Essays in Political Biography*. 2nd ed. University of
        Arkansas Press Fayetteville, Arkansas. Pp.64–68.

Westbury, William A.
1971   *1969 Excavations at Spadra Bluff 3JO33*. Arkansas Archaeological Survey,
        Fayetteville. Submitted to the National Park Service, Southeast Region, Atlanta.

White, Dena D.
1984   Slavery in Hempstead County, Arkansas. Honors Thesis, Ouachita Baptist
        University, Arkadelphia, Arkansas. Copy on file Southwest Arkansas
        Regional Archives, Washington, Arkansas.

Williams, Charlotte M.
1951   *The Old Town Speaks: Washington, Hempstead County*. Anson Jones Press,
        Houston.

2

ARCHAEOLOGY OF KINSHIP
AT TREAT, ARKANSAS
Intersections of Past Lives, Memory, and Identity on the Landscape

Mary Z. Brennan

The *landscape* that is the Ozark National Forest in northwest Arkansas includes remnants of 19th and early 20th century kin-based communities and several thousands of farmsteads, house places, schools, cemeteries, gristmills, timber mills, stills, and other places recorded as archaeological sites. Few have been excavated and, for most, only a cursory review of archival records has been conducted. While archival research indicates that the chronological histories of many of these communities may be similar, diversities in social behaviors that resulted in the formation of these communities and archaeological sites provide context and opportunities for interpretation of the archaeological landscape that remains.

Reconstructing accurate settlement and behavioral histories for these communities can be problematic. These were kin-based settlements, and populations were generally small. Representation in the archival record is often sketchy, as the mix of family groups changed over time and families intermarried and moved in and out of the region. Working with descendant communities provides opportunities to gather information about past landscape history and also to understand how archaeological sites and other places in the landscape are used by people today in the intergenerational transference of individual, family, and community identities. Integrating data from archaeological investigations, archival research, and collections of orally

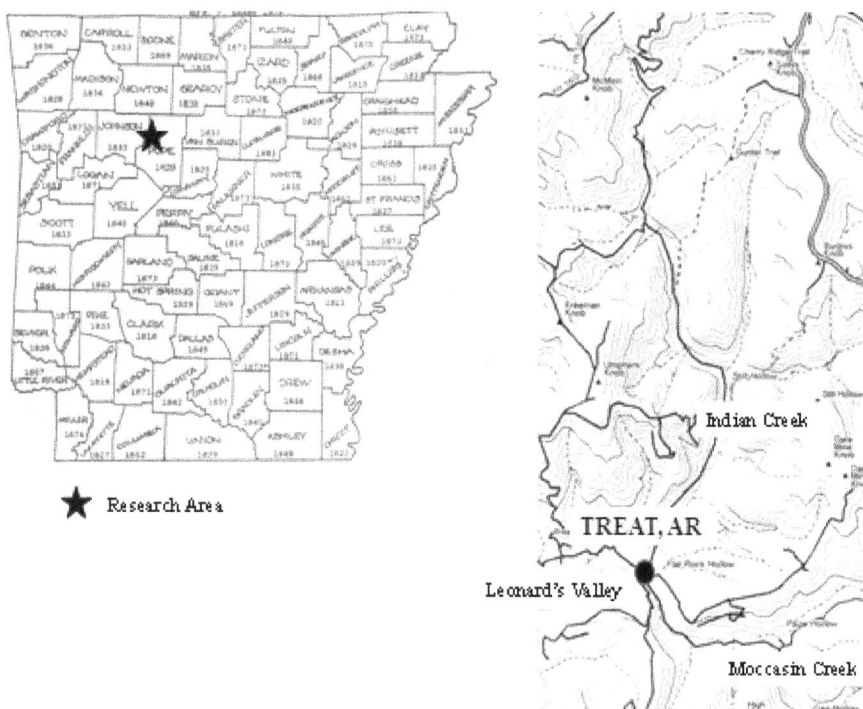

Figure 2.1. Treat, Arkansas.

communicated memories enables reconstruction and understanding of historic landscapes and memoryscapes.

One such memoryscape is Treat, Arkansas.

Treat, Arkansas

"Treat" appears as a dot on a map in the Arkansas Ozarks, on the southern slopes of the Boston Mountains in Pope County at the confluence of Moccasin, Indian, and Big Piney creeks (Figure 2.1). Today most of this area is government-owned and managed as part of the Ozark National Forest. A small percentage of land is privately held, with only a handful of full-time residents. The area is a popular recreational destination, used seasonally by the public for hunting, hiking, canoeing, and camping. The appearance of a community on a map with defined boundaries is misleading. Descendants of families who settled here say that "Treat" was the name of the post office, not how they identified themselves. In the 19th century, families used descriptors like "Leonard's Valley" and "Ross Community." "Treat" and "Big Lick" became more commonly used in the early 20th century to describe and differentiate areas of settlement. In practice, the community was dispersed across the landscape in house places, farmsteads, and agricultural fields cultivated by family groups. At one time, the community's span of control neared 10,000 acres in the drainages and watersheds of Moccasin and Indian Creeks.

The population here was never very large (Table 2.1). The earliest evidence of historic period settlement is provided by General Land Office surveyors who, in 1845, noted a "road" or trail connecting the Indian Creek bottoms with a well-traveled turnpike to the northeast (State of Arkansas Land Office 1846). Certainly by the 1850s, occupants in this area were represented in the archival record. The population count in 1860 for Allen Township, which includes this area, was 144 people in 27 households. In 1870 it numbered 224 in 41 households. Population stayed fairly constant until the 1920s (U.S. Census 1850, 1860, 1870, 1880, 1900, 1910, 1920). Archival evidence indicates that the area was settled primarily by four family groups and their extended families—the Page family who lived along Moccasin Creek, the Freeman family along Indian Creek, and the Ross and Meadows families who lived along Indian Creek and in Leonard's Valley. The location and mix of families on the landscape was fairly fluid. Whereas earlier settlement had been in distinct kin groups, over time boundaries between family settlements blurred as groups intermarried and redefined their operational boundaries and spans of control over the landscape and its natural resources.

A total of 77 archaeological sites associated with 19th and early 20th century occupation have been recorded here (Brennan 2009). A

Table 2.1. Population Returns for Allen Township

YEAR	POPULATION	HEADS OF HOUSEHOLD
1860	144	27
1870	224	47
1880	211	41
1890	not available	not available
1900	150	26
1910	201	34
1920	192	38
1930	156	31

Table 2.2. Archeological Sites

FUNCTION	KIN GROUP AFFILIATION			
	FREEMAN	ROSS	HULL/MEADOWS	PAGE
Houseplaces (56)	21	6	4	14
Mills (4)	1	1		2
Stave Mill (1)				1
Stills (3)		1		2
Schools (4)				
Cemeteries (5)				
Dipping Vats (2)				
Rock Culverts (1)				
Field Clearing Piles (1)				
Rock Fences (1)				

summary of sites by site type, function, and family affiliation is provided as Table 2.2. Family descendants occupy four houses, located on private land, at least seasonally. Two of the five cemeteries are active, and the other three continue to be decorated and maintained by descendants. Forest Service roads and trails generally follow the templates of roads used by earlier settlers. Other pioneer roads have been abandoned, but traces are still visible on the landscape.

Research of the historic community combined more traditional methods of research with genealogical methods and archaeological investigations. Families who settled in this area were not necessarily well represented or accurately represented in the documentary record. For some families who settled in this area during the mid-to-late 19th century, the need for "ownership" appears to have been satisfied with the physical making of farmsteads—clearing fields, building rock fences and structures. In some cases, they lived on the land for 10 to 20 years before applying for and receiving legal land title. Other families never legally owned land on which they settled, choosing instead to relocate elsewhere and leaving behind only archaeological evidence of their occupation. Other tracts of lands may have been patented by an individual head-of-household and later subdivided and occupied by adult children, each shaping the landscape and constructing separate farmsteads in the tract without transfers of legal title.

Combining data from documentary sources, genealogical research, oral histories, and archaeology provided a more complete record of how families operated on the landscape, using socially constructed related-ness to more effectively utilize natural resources. Data collected enabled the construction of a kinship network defined by behavior rather than biology, and this network was used as an explanatory mechanism for analyzing settlement and subsistence practices of individuals and groups in the research area. The data provided spatially relevant information and enabled the association of specific archaeological sites and other places in the cultural landscape with individuals or kin groups in the network. By compiling a record of actual kin relations that specified kinship mecha-nisms connecting known archaeological sites, the study "ground-truthed" the spatial expression of kinship structure on the landscape.

Kin-based settlement was an integral component of family and com-munity survival strategies. Families relied on subsistence agriculture and free-range grazing and annual herding of livestock to market, subsidized later by harvesting timber and producing corn liquor. The distribution of family across the landscape was integral to their survival. It provided a span of control over the available natural resources and ensured access to the labor required for harvesting these resources. Over time, group boundaries changed as families intermarried and merged—social actions that served to maintain and reinforce the span of control over resources. As the population increased, family subsistence strategies became more diversified and changing social structures were replicated in the spatial positioning of family mills, stills, blacksmiths, stores, and other places that provided community services.

The area was selected for a study of kin behavior in part because of a wealth of oral histories collected by Tate Page and Lynwood Montell, professors at Western Kentucky University (WKU). Page was raised by his grandparents on Moccasin Creek near Treat, Arkansas, living here from approximately 1912 until the mid-1920s. While dean of education at WKU, Page compiled a collection of stories he recalled from his child-hood as teaching materials and a material culture inventory of selected landscape features and structures at Treat for Montell's material cultural class. In 1972, Page's manuscript was published in book form. Following his retirement to Arkansas, Page collected more than 300 oral histories from local residents as source materials for a weekly newspaper column and daily local radio program on life in the Ozarks. In 1981 and 1982, Montell recorded 30 hours of interviews with Dr. Page, in preparation for a second book. Unfortunately, the book never materialized, and the Page and Montell materials were subsequently donated to the Manuscript and Folklife Archives of Western Kentucky University.

Oral history recordings were made in the 1990s by family historian John Page and Skip Stewart-Abernathy of the Arkansas Archeological Survey, and by the author in 2003 and 2005 during archaeological field investigations. Much information was gathered from unpublished family histories and memories compiled by family historians Anna Page Fields and Steve Page.

Field Investigations

In 1971, students from Western Kentucky University conducted a material culture survey at Treat, studying "the lifestyle of the Moccasin Creek people by viewing the cultural manifestations on the landscape" (Folk Art and Technology Students 1971:ii). Students were charged with exploring the "many old buildings standing", and each student was assigned a subject area including house types, cemeteries, food storage, building materials, type and nature of outbuildings, relationship of building sites to topography, and road conditions. The group project resulted in an unpublished manuscript, "Folk Culture along Moccasin Creek," with approximately 50 photographs and descriptions of houses, barns, outbuildings, fences, gates, latches, and other elements (Folk Art and Technology Students 1971).

In the 1990s, Phase I surveys were conducted for proposed Forest Service timber projects by forest archaeologists. Beginning in 2002 and continuing through 2008, field investigations continued as part of a graduate research project (Brennan 2003, 2009) and with assistance from Skip Stewart-Abernathy and Larry Porter, Arkansas Archeological Survey, as well as Page family descendants and other volunteers. Of the total 77 historic sites that have been recorded, included are 56 farmsteads, four schools, five cemeteries, two dipping vats, four mill sets, three stills, a check dam, miles of rock fences, and numerous rock clearing piles in formerly cleared agricultural fields (Brennan 2009).

In 2005, subsurface investigations were conducted at 3PP318, the Nehemiah Scott Page farmstead. Investigations concentrated on two areas of the farmstead (the house and the farmyard). Six units (2m x 2m) were excavated within and adjacent to the footprint of the Nehemiah Scott Page house. Another 2 units (2m x 1m) were excavated within Feature 2, thought to be a collapsed cellar or trash pit. The six units were excavated to depths of 20 cm, and most of the artifacts recovered from these units were found at depths 0–10 cm. Feature 2 was excavated to a depth of 30 cm. Archaeologists surveyed an area north of the houseplace, believed to have been the location of the barn, blacksmith shop, other outbuildings, and corrals, with metal detectors and then selective shovel testing. Using 1936 aerial photographs as a guide, a 10m x 10m grid was established over this area. Twenty-two units were surveyed with metal detectors, resulting in a total of 380 "hits." Units with the most concentrations of hits were selectively shovel tested, and a representative sample of artifacts was collected (Brennan 2009).

Above ground investigations of three community cemeteries (Shannon, Treat, and McGowan) were conducted in 2006 and 2007 to gather demographic data and information about kin group mortuary behaviors. McGowan Cemetery is the smallest of the three as measured by number of burials (36 burials), and the majority of burials here (30 burials) have fieldstones with no inscriptions. Treat Cemetery includes 89 burials—49 burials have fieldstones with no inscriptions, and 40 have inscribed stones. Shannon Cemetery, the largest of the three, has 123 burials marked with stones. Seventy-six have inscribed stones, and 47 have fieldstones with no inscriptions.

GIS Modeling and Thematic Mapping

The role of kinship in the settlement of the Arkansas Ozarks has been documented in other regional studies (Hackbarth 1980, Joyce 1980), but these were primarily described on the basis of documentary evidence. By directly associating individual archaeological sites with specific individuals and/or family groups, the expression of kin behavior on the landscape could be spatially modeled. In this study, ESRI ArcGIS was used to thematically describe and analyze past and present cultural landscapes, as well as spatially organize data and materials. The GIS model constructed for this study contained three georeferenced datasets—archaeological, current landscape, and historical landscape—and a fourth dataset for materials that could not be adequately georeferenced.

The archaeological dataset included layers that represent archaeological sites recorded in the research area, excavation and survey grids from investigations at 3PP318 (the N.S. Page farmstead), and cemetery data. The current landscape dataset included layers that represent modern roads and trails, vegetation, private ownership, and the most recent USGS quadrangles and aerial photographs. The historic landscape dataset generally replicated the landscape as it appeared in the 1930s, a point-in-time used because it represents the earliest available spatially comparable data. Layers included in this dataset included the 1932 quadrangle, 1936–37 aerial photographs, and a layers depicting issued land patents 1840–1920.

Data points and polygons contained in these layers were filtered or sorted via kinship coding, making possible the direct association of place in the physical environment with place in the social structure. This association enabled the production of thematic maps depicting landscapes specific to separate kin groups, providing data towards a better understanding of how settlement and survival strategies were defined, constructed, and negotiated within and between kin groups, how these strategies changed over time, and how they are reflected in the extant cultural landscape.

The Cultural Landscape

Archaeological Sites

Thematic mapping enabled the production of maps showing the spatial distribution of archaeological sites and land usage across the landscape differentiated by kin group association and, where known, name of the specific owner or occupant. While subsistence agriculture was the predominate use of land resources in this area, the survival strategies used by these families included diversified sources of barter, or later, cash. Family groups operated grist and lumber mills, blacksmith shops, stores, and they made moonshine. Accordingly, thematic mapping by site function and type illustrated the diversity of function across the landscape.

House places and farmsteads were generally located along creek bottoms and on terraces with good soil and water access. Almost all the recorded farmsteads included a dug or drilled well and/or were located near a spring or other water supply. Those that did not have access to water, or had water only seasonally, may have been occupied for only a short time. Site features that remain on the landscape today generally include a rock foundation line indicating the locations of the house, a hearth or chimney fall, the afore-mentioned well and/or improved spring, and sometimes a depression that might indicate a dug cellar. Most farmsteads included various outbuildings (i.e., barns, smokehouses, blacksmiths), visible on 1936 aerial photographs; however, generally these structures were ephemeral and very few surface features remain that indicate their locations. At the Nehemiah Scott Page farmstead (3PP318), for example, the location of outbuildings and the stockyard was indicated only by a stand of cedar that had grown up in their places, corroborated by scaling the aerial photograph and using a metal detector to locate subsurface remains. Claimant testimonies contained in some land case entry files provided information about farmsteads and land use at the time of application. For example, in his 1890 application for a land patent, Martin C. Ross characterizes his land as "[m]ost valuable for agricultural . . . . All was covered with the various oaks, some pine and hickory, all standing yet except on about ten acres in cultivation, and that used for fuel and improvements on the land" (U.S. National Archives 1891). He describes his house as a hewed log dwelling, 16 x 18 feet, one-story high with a side room on the north side and porch on the south side and with plank floors, a board roof, and a stone chimney. Ross identifies other improvements as a crib and stable, smokehouse, garden, and orchard. Farm implements include plows, hoes, axes, rakes, harrows, and a spade. Livestock include two mules, 12 cattle, 12 hogs, four sheep, and domestic fowls. Household furnishings include beds, bedsteads, chairs, tables, and cooking utensils. Similar information was documented on questionnaires in land case entry files for William R. Freeman, Mahala Havner, Alice Hull, Shaderick Jones, and Samuel Pain (U.S. National Archives 1890, 1891, 1896, 1896a, 1900, 1901).

No structures remain at the settlement, which is now government land, although some vestiges of collapsed outbuildings are still visible at a few sites. The lack of structural remains may result from destruction or dismantling of structures after the farms were sold to the government. Generally, the government viewed structures as potential liabilities and impediments to the management of the forest, and typically, the Forest Service gave former owners a year to remove whatever materials they wanted from the property. Jewell Page Mathis, a granddaughter of Nehemiah Scott Page, remembers that the family removed much of her grandparents' house (3PP318) as materials to build a house for her Uncle Jeff, and it was her job to pull nails. Her sister, Cledyth Page Latham, recalls that the family removed materials from their parents' house (3PP346) when they relocated to Crow Mountain (personal communication 2005, 2006). Any remaining structures were likely dozed or burned by the government. Melted glass recovered from shovel testing at several sites may indicate the disposition of the structure. The Nehemiah Scott Page house place (3PP318) includes no foundation stones and only a few chimney stones. These may have been removed and used during construction and relocation of Page Hollow road in the late 1930s or 1940s. Some structures were destroyed by recreational use of the forest. The Ross School (3PP290), for example, was still standing as recently as 1993, but due to its continued use by the public as a deer camp, it has been demolished.

Several structures remain on private property. Some were visited and recorded as archaeological sites during fieldwork. These include Louis and Norma Ross Gunter's house, a cabin still owned by descendants of the Meadows family, an early log cabin thought to have been built either by Thomas G. Page or David Hull, the Dave Waterman house, and a building that was once used as a post office by Mart and Mattie Page.

Although not all recorded as archaeological sites, there are miles of rock fences still visible on the landscape that delineate yardscapes and the once-cleared fields in creek bottoms and on terraces. Some are stacked rock fences, but many, particularly the ones that edge old cleared fields, are piled rocks likely removed from the fields they surround. In a 1982 interview, Tate C. Page describes the construction of rock fences as follows:

Montell: What kinds of fences?

T. C. Page: Now the rock fence was very common ... because there were so doggone many rocks. And a second thing that was in favor of the rock fence, they didn't burn. [E]verybody burned woods in the spring. ... Now the rocks came off the fields. We hauled rock many, many winters and built fences with them. ... [W]e built pyramid type, no that's not, conical is the term. It looked like a wigwam. We arranged those right out in the field and stacked them. And some fields ... would have, I bet you, 25 or 30 of those things in a five acre field.

Montell: You wouldn't take them over to the edge?

T. C. Page: Oh, no. You just build them. ... We just called them rock piles is all I remember right now at the moment. Then we put rocks in gullies and/or made fences. But you see, each of those meant you hauled the rock. The other you took the rock right where it was. The dogs and rabbits would run in those conical shaped rock piles. And the dogs then would start clawing around and eventually they would get a paw underneath and make a hole. A rock would fall out and the first thing you know the whole dad-gum thing would be down. And you'd have to haul them off or do it over. It was an endless battle of some sort. (Page 1982b)

In general, fences were constructed to keep livestock out, rather than in, but occasionally they were constructed as part of boundary disputes or disagreements with neighbors, as described by John Page.

Aunt Allie built her a fence, but she didn't want my father to tie on. So they both built a fence down through there, you see, just wide enough to walk down through there. It wasn't a road at all. You couldn't even get through there with a wagon and team. But each built a fence. I remember helping my father build a rail fence down through there and how mad he was because they was both contrary enough that they wouldn't let each other tie on. So it's known as the "grudge fence." (Page and Freeman 1976)

Settlement and Use of the Landscape

Thematic mapping enabled the depiction of settlement in three chronological periods (1840–1870, 1871–1900, and 1901–1920), with land tracts delineated by family affiliation. The assignment of lands to chronological periods is based on the issue date of land patents.

A review of land patent records and case entry files for these family groups indicates behavior consistent with regional trends noted by Walz (1958). For example, Nehemiah Scott Page, who is thought to have begun clearing land for his farm on Moccasin Creek by 1870, applied for a land patent in 1890. It was granted in 1895, 25 years after he occupied the land and began shaping the landscape. Others who relocated from elsewhere in Arkansas (i.e. Lazarus and Levi Freeman) did not patent lands in this area, but patents granted to their descendants may include areas these earlier settlers occupied. Tate C. Page describes legal land ownership: "This was the time when you didn't homestead, but patented your land. You squatted on it and after a certain time the land became yours if you had built a barn and a house. And then . . . at some point in time you applied for a patent and you got it" (Page 1982b).

The earliest lands patented were located in Leonard's Valley where the terrain is more suitable for cultivation (i.e. bottom lands with ready access to water). These were followed by bottom lands up Indian and Moccasin Creeks, with water supplies that are more seasonal. The last parcels patented were located on slopes and ridges above creek bottoms. The terrain and later patent dates indicate that these tracts likely were selected for their timber or potentially minerals rather than suitability for cultivation. Page describes the selection of a place for a farmstead "Water . . . probably was the number one consideration. Near a spring was the most desirable location. . . . [I]f you could find an everlasting spring . . . that was an ideal location. . . . So you couldn't just go out and locate a cabin by any spring. It had to be reasonably close to a gardening spot . . . truck patches" (Page 1982b).

In many cases, the earlier generation of the kin group settled and patented a large block of land (i.e., 160 acres). However, only a portion was cleared and improved by the first generation. The rest of the landscape was used as forage for their free-range livestock and their hunting and gathering. Page states,

> They didn't clear any more land than they absolutely had to. And then they wore that out. . . . They grew crops on it until it wouldn't grow anything. . . . The simplest thing to do was to just leave that as a pasture and move over somewhere and clear you some more land. You know, on your own, still on the same area. And you'd eventually end up with several fields. . . . Some of them wouldn't grow anything and would be used maybe for the calf pasture or your milk cows or something. (Page 1982b)

As the next generation grew to maturity and married, it was not unusual for them to settle on land owned by their parents. A block of land might contain four or five farmsteads that represented the infilling by family members.

Montell: Were there cases also of the newlyweds moving back into one of their parents' home?

T. C. Page: Was not unusual at all. . . . Usually the parents of whichever or both parents, frequently both parents, got together to help. One family might give the girl quilts and all the things that you needed to set up at least one bed and a place to cook. . . . The other parents might give them mules and wagon, some plows, and this kind of thing. The tools necessary to start in farming. If you were any good, you could usually rent land. If you couldn't rent it from anybody else, either of the parents had land. You could rent from them a year or two, but they stayed at home a lot.

Montell: How would they go about acquiring their own land?

T. C. Page: It was a long process. You inherited it just as you do today when the older people died; they divided it up among their kids. (Page 1982d)

It also was not unusual for families to move within the community, sometimes moving into cabins that been built and vacated by earlier occupants. Shaderick Jones and Samuel H. Pain both indicated on their application questionnaires that they moved into vacant houses that pre-dated their occupation (U.S. National Archives 1890, 1896a). Page confirms this practice: "When your wife died. . . . she wore out and your farm was worn out, too. You just . . . moved somewhere else and got you another woman and another farm, cleared you up some more land, and just moved on west as a rule. Now, not necessarily, you might have moved somewhere else in the community" (Page 1982b).

People also relocated in hope of avoiding disease. Robert Page initially lived in Leonard's Valley near Shannon Cemetery. Shortly after the turn of the century, he moved his family up Indian Creek near the McGowan cemetery to land that had been patented by William Riley Freeman, hoping to avoid mosquitoes and typhoid (Page 1982). John Page states,

> Uncle Bob and Gooder and Ellen were all down with typhoid fever—real bad. The nearest doctor was 25 miles to Dover, so they sent after the doctors. And usually the doctors would go in twos, so the doctors were on their way. But before they got there, Ellen died, and Aunt Nellie, who was very much wrapped up in her daughter, said, "Now, there's no use for the doctor to come on. Ellen's dead." And my father—it made him mad because he felt like Uncle Bob and Gooder needed the doctors. Anyway, Aunt Nellie didn't think about them. . . . So my father demanded that the doctors come right on and take care of them. So Uncle Bob and Gooder lived, but for a long time they were very poorly. . . . And then they found out the typhoid fever was coming [again]. . . . So Uncle Bob sold his place and moved up on Indian Creek. (Page and Freeman 1976)

Subsistence farming, hunting, and gathering required a family-based society. Clearing woodland required healthy, strong, and young people, and an abundance of labor was needed. Early marriages and the bearing of many children were encouraged, and decision-making was vested in the individual head of the family group (Jordan and Kaups 1989). Page states, "When I was a youngster, my grandfather was unquestionably in charge of the whole family and that's all his kids and the kinfolks and everybody else. . . . [T]hey came and asked him about everything: when to plant, when to do this, when to trade. He was just the authority . . . " (Page 1982c).

Family size and the division of labor that it provided were important factors in farm management. Plenty of children meant plenty of farmhands and free labor. Responsibilities were assigned based on sex, age, and skill. Men and boys worked in fields, planting and cultivating crops, caring for livestock, maintaining fences and buildings, harvesting crops, and hunting. Women and girls worked both inside the house and in the gardens and fields (Blevins 2002). Page reiterates this trend:

> A man with several kids could farm a lot of acreage if he wanted to and had it. . . . Each child knew that he was a useful member of the family by the time he was six or seven years old. . . . [H]e was carrying in the wood, he was helping in the feeding, he was going to the field and carrying. If couldn't do anything else he was carrying water and pulling weeds and . . . running the errands around the field and by the time he was seven and certainly by eight and that meant girls and boys both. (Page 1982d)

Figure 2.2 illustrates the correlation between spatial and social positioning of farmsteads along Moccasin Creek. Simply put, the farmsteads that are closest to Nehemiah Scott Page are those of his children. Farmsteads that are the farthest away are in-laws.

Montell: They had a spirit of community, didn't they?
Page: Let's put that in its proper context. Each person was taught to be self-sufficient. [Y]our number one responsibility was your own family, your own blood kin. You helped first your family and then you helped your kin folks. And that's blood kin, now, we're not talking necessarily married in kin. They'd come next in the hierarchy of things. And then, outside of those, would be your other neighbors. (Page 1982b)

These relationships also appear in land usage along Moccasin Creek, illustrated by the cleared fields shown on the 1936 landscape. Farmsteads generally were located on terraces above creek bottoms and near water sources to maximize the availability of bottomlands for cultivation. Farmstead layouts included areas cleared for yardscapes, barns and outbuildings, gardens and orchards. While these areas are visually identifiable with individual houseplaces, cleared fields in the bottomlands appear to be visually related to groups of farmsteads, not necessarily individuals. In other words, cleared fields on the eastern end of Moccasin

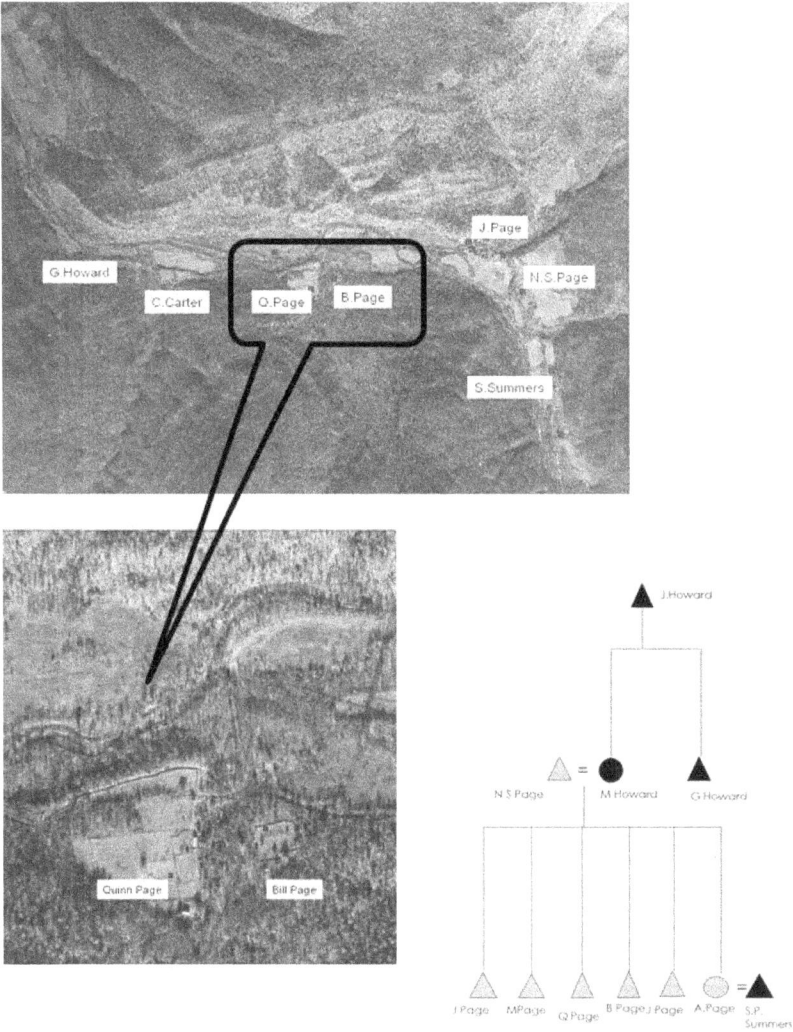

Figure 2.2. Page Family Farmsteads along Moccasin Creek.

Creek appear to be associated with the Page family, and cleared fields on the other end of Moccasin Creek appear to be associated with the Howard or possibly Ross families.

One exception might be the location of the farmstead associated with Claude Carter. Claude Carter was Nehemiah Scott Page's son-in-law, married to daughter Nora Page. Yet, their farmstead is located along

Shop Bluff Branch just across from George Howard, several miles from Nehemiah Scott Page. However, Nora Page was Claude Carter's first wife. His second wife was Clara Howard Phillips, daughter of George Howard, and archival research suggests that he may not have moved to Moccasin Creek until after this second marriage. This could explain the proximity of his farm to that of George Howard (Phillips 1981).

Cleared fields located near the S. P. "Pet" Summers farmstead are spatially separated from fields used by Nehemiah Scott Page and his sons. Topographically, the Summers' farmstead is located along the south fork of Moccasin Creek, while the other Pages are located either along the north fork or along Moccasin Creek before it forks, and this topographical distinction may account this difference. This could also replicate the genealogical connection of Pet Summers as a son-in-law, rather than as a son.

Another possible anomaly might appear to be the spatial relationship between the Bill Page and Quinn Page farmsteads, located almost directly across Standridge Branch from one another. In comparison to the Quinn Page farm, Bill Page has significantly less land cleared for gardens and few outbuildings. In fact, Bill Page's wife died at a young age, leaving him with two small children who spent most of their childhood living with their grandparents and other relatives. According to Quinn's wife Lottie Page, Bill Page was a good hunter and trapper and brought them the meat to cook since he did little cooking on his own (L. Page 1976). Both farms shared an improved spring located in the drainage that separated the two farms. The reciprocal relationship between Bill Page and his brother Quinn may be replicated in the 1936 landscape.

As family groups intermarried and population density increased, dependencies within family groups are evident in diversification of survival strategies and the specialization of jobs. Page states,

Now as time went on, and the mountain world became a little more complex. In the beginning, every man did his own everything. He had to. His neighbors didn't have time to fool with him. And then as we became more of a social group, in other words, more people came in, you had more neighbors, then some degree of specialty came in. Somebody might be a pretty good chairmaker. And so they'd get him to make chairs. . . . And you did have people who became somewhat specialized. For instance, if you wanted a still made, you had to get hold of a man who was pretty good with a soldering iron and cutting out copper and putting it together. And there were usually these specialists. (Page 1982b)

The Memoryscape

Research focused primarily on the community from 1850–1930, the period of initial settlement, population peak, and beginning of depopulation of the area. This should not be interpreted to represent that the area depopulated completely during that time. Many families did leave during the Depression years, selling their land to timber speculators or to the government, but some third and fourth generation families remained in the area as late as the 1940s and 1950s.

Beginning in the 1920s, the reciprocal relationships that allowed residents to be subsistence farmers in earlier decades did not sustain the community into the 20th century. The economic needs of the community changed; this, coupled with changes to accessibility of resources provided by family and the natural environment, meant the old survival strategies were unsustainable. The changing dynamics are reflected in the memories of Tate Page as follows:

Montell: Something happened up there that caused people ... people started moving out ... and finally everybody was gone. So name me three, four, or five things that actually caused it all to peter out.

E. Page: I think kind of the main thing was it come to the place that you've got to have to have money to get by, you know. Back when we was younger you raised what you eat and eat what you raise, and everybody done that, more or less. But it come to the place that ... that you couldn't even make enough on them little old farms to buy your sugar and salt and stuff, and you started to have to have a job, and there just wasn't no jobs there, and people had to move out to where they could get work.

B. Page: People begin to go to California. . . . They begin to have work out there, and people heared about it and they begin to go ... and then probably consolidating the schools and things of that nature helped, you know.

J. Page: [T]hat's about what I'd say: school and schooling, jobs, money. (T. Page, E. Page, B. Page, J. Page 1982)

The reconstruction of the cultural landscape discussed provides a context for exploring the sense of place which resides in the descendant community today. Field investigations included many trips to Moccasin and Indian Creeks and countless hours of discussion with the descendant community. During an initial trip in early 2003, a Page family descendant expressed the following sentiment. "This landscape is *sacred* to my family," she said (personal communication, A. Fields 2003). Over the next few years, I began to observe patterning in the mix and timing of family stories in context of driving routes. Certainly different stories were associated with different places; but in addition entire dialogues, or sets of stories, were associated with different parts of the landscape. Just as there were spatial correlates between the places on the landscape and the social context within which they were created, there are spatial correlates between how and what family dialogues are remembered and re-told. The cultural landscape and the places within it continue to function as an active part of the intergenerational transference of family histories and identities. The landscape is annotated with family geneal-ogy and social relationships, and correspondingly, spatial relationships are embedded in the identities and collective memories communicated from generation to generation.

For many descendants and the public at large, the published recol-lections of Page have become their memories of "Treat, Arkansas." In January 2007, the author accompanied a Page descendant on a hike to Shop Bluff on Moccasin Creek. When we arrived at the bluff shelter, we found a family group on off-road vehicles at the shelter, and as we approached, heard one of the adults telling the story of the William Henry Page family traveling to Arkansas and spending their first winter camped at the shelter. We asked them how they had heard the story, and were they relatives of the Page family? The man who had told the story said he was not a relative, but he was a fan of Tate Page's book. He said like the Page family, his grandparents had moved to Arkansas in the late 1800's and settled in the mountains. He didn't know where they had lived and had little information about them, but he imagined their experiences must have been similar to the stories in Page's book. Having no specific place that he could connect with his own family, he reconstructed a connection to a representative place and transferred identity to his descendants using Page family stories.

This use of family stories is consistent with Page's own view of his work, illustrated by the following excerpt from a 1972 interview with Lynwood Montell.

Montell: Okay, in your mind, [what] are you and I doing a history of? Are we doing it of Moccasin, or are we doing it of the Ozarks? . . . . Of the whole Ozark culture.
Page: [T]he whole pattern; it is representative of the pattern.
Montell: Now this makes sense. I mean to use that as the labora-tory or as the case study to illustrate all the rest of the Ozarks.

Page: I have repeatedly said . . . that my book is not a story of the Pages. It's a story of a people at a time and in a place in the Ozarks. And was an example that is typical of what you would've found anywhere else in the Ozarks. And I think it's true. (Page 1982e)

The landscape continues to be used by descendants and the public to whom these places have meaning. Although no longer bound by a physical place, a community exists today that shares a sense of place transmitted to them through family stories and shared experiences that are part of their individual and group identities. It is this "sense of place" that calls them to participate in ongoing family rituals (i.e. family reunions and cemetery decoration days).

Montell: [I]n this day and time . . . folklorists, geographers, and other people are talking about people's sense of place.
Page: What does that mean?
Montell: It simply means that people identify very strongly with a particular place. . . . If people ever moved out, would they always feel (as you feel) that sense of loyalty to what used to be?
Page: All you have to do . . . is go back to these reunions they have every spring. . . . They come from California and all over the nation to some of these reunions. And now the descendants are coming. . . . Children that are grown that didn't grow up there. And they're attached, too, and they go back and have these. . . . They go to the graveyards. They have a sort of decoration day sometimes. They started out as decorations and they have become a community reunion. (Page 1982e)

This research provides an opportunity to understand landscapes and the places they contain as spatial expressions of past and present social networks. Archaeological sites continue to be used by the descendant community to construct and reconstruct individual, family, and community identities. They provide families with places at which they can gather, remember, and re-member.

REFERENCES

Blevins, Brooks
2002   *Hill Folks: A History of Arkansas Ozarks and Their Image.* Chapel Hill: University of North Carolina Press.

Brennan, Mary Z.

2003   "Mapping the Genealogical Landscape: Kinship and Settlement along Moccasin and Indian Creeks, Pope County, Arkansas." Master's thesis, University of Arkansas.

2004   "A Tale of Three Cemeteries: Above-Ground Investigations and Construction of Meaning at McGowan, Treat, and Shannon Cemeteries, Pope County Arkansas." Paper prepared for coursework, University of Arkansas.

2008   "Reconstructing the Genealogical Landscape: Kinship and Settlement along Moccasin and Indian Creeks, Pope County, Arkansas." *Arkansas Historical Quarterly* Vol. 67 No. 4:386–397.

2009   "Sense of Place: Reconstructing Community through Archeology, Oral History, and GIS." Doctoral disseration, University of Arkansas.

Folk Art and Technology Students

1971   "Folk Culture along Moccasin Creek". Paper prepared for coursework. Lynwood Montell Collection, Manuscripts and Folklife Archives. Western Kentucky University.

Hackbarth, Mark Robert

1980   "The Effect of Kinship on Land Choice in Washington County, Arkansas 1830–1850." Master's thesis, University of Arkansas.

Jordan, Terry G., and Matti Kaups

1989   The American Backwoods Frontier. Baltimore: The Johns Hopkins University Press.

Joyce, Jane Sally

1980   "A Settlement Pattern Study of the War Eagle Creek Region, Madison County, Arkansas, During the Pioneer Period." Master's thesis, University of Arkansas.

Page, John, and Wash Freeman

1976   Interview by Tate C. Page, May 1 and May 3. Audio tape, Tate C. Page Collection, Manuscripts and Folklife Archives. Western Kentucky University.

Page, Lottie Underhill

1976   Interview by Tate C. Page, June 6. Manuscript and audio tape, Tate C. Page Collection, Manuscripts and Folklife Archives. Western Kentucky University.

Page, Tate C.

1972   *The Voices of Moccasin Creek.* Point Lookout: The School of the Ozarks Press.

1982   Stories from the Ozarks, A compilation of newspaper articles published in the Courier Democrat, Russellville, AR.

1982a   Interview by Lynwood Montell, February 10. Manuscript and audio tape, Lynwood Montell Collection, Manuscripts and Folklife Archives. Western Kentucky University.

1982b   Interview by Lynwood Montell, February 24. Manuscript and audio tape, Lynwood Montell Collection, Manuscripts and Folklife Archives. Western Kentucky University.

1982c   Interview by Lynwood Montell, March 17. Manuscript and audio tape, Lynwood Montell Collection, Manuscripts and Folklife Archives. Western Kentucky University.

1982d   Interview by Lynwood Montell, March 23. Manuscript and audio tape, Lynwood Montell Collection, Manuscripts and Folklife Archives. Western Kentucky University.

1982e   Interview by Lynwood Montell, n.d. Manuscript and audio tape, Lynwood Montell Collection, Manuscripts and Folklife Archives. Western Kentucky University.

Page, Tate C., Earl Page, Bill Page, and Jewell Page Mathis
1982   Interview by Lynwood Montell, June 30. Manuscript and audio tape, Lynwood Montell Collection, Manuscripts and Folklife Archives. Western Kentucky University.

Page, Tate C., and John Page
1982   Interview by Lynwood Montell, June 28. Manuscript and audio tape, Lynwood Montell Collection, Manuscripts and Folklife Archives. Western Kentucky University.

Phillips, Bud
1981   *The New Ozark Cousins*. Jasper: Newton County Historical Society.

State of Arkansas Land Office
1846   GLO surveyor's notes and plat, Township 12N Range 20W.

U.S. Bureau of the Census
1850   Population Schedule, Arkansas, Pope County. Microfilm, Fayetteville Public Library, Fayetteville.

1860   Population Schedule, Arkansas, Pope County. Microfilm, Fayetteville Public Library, Fayetteville.

1870   Population Schedule, Arkansas, Pope County. Microfilm, Fayetteville Public Library, Fayetteville.

1880   Population Schedule, Arkansas, Pope County. Microfilm, Fayetteville Public Library, Fayetteville.

1900   Population Schedule, Arkansas, Pope County. Microfilm, Fayetteville Public Library, Fayetteville.

1910   Population Schedule, Arkansas, Pope County. Microfilm, Fayetteville Public Library, Fayetteville.

1920   Population Schedule, Arkansas, Pope County. Microfilm, Fayetteville Public Library, Fayetteville.

1930   Population Schedule, Arkansas, Pope County. Microfilm, Fayetteville Public Library, Fayetteville.

U.S. National Archives
1890   Land case entry file, patent no. 5592, application no. 18695, Shaderick S. Jones. National Archives, Washington, DC.

1891   Land case entry file, patent no. 5592, application no. 18695, Shaderick S. Jones. National Archives, Washington, DC.

1896   Land case entry file, patent no. 5592, application no. 18695, Shaderick S. Jones. National Archives, Washington, DC.

1896a   Land case entry file, patent no. 5592, application no. 18695, Shaderick S. Jones. National Archives, Washington, DC.

1900   Land case entry file, patent no. 5592, application no. 18695, Shaderick S. Jones. National Archives, Washington, DC.

1901   Land case entry file, patent no. 5592, application no. 18695, Shaderick S. Jones. National Archives, Washington, DC.

Walz, Robert Bradshaw
1958   "Migration into Arkansas, 1834–1880: Incentives and Means of Travel." *Arkansas Historical Quarterly* 17:4.

3

A SYMBOLIC AND SACRED LANDSCAPE
The Confederate Cemetery in Fayetteville, Arkansas

Duncan P. McKinnon

The Confederate Cemetery in Fayetteville, Arkansas is tucked away in a secluded and seemingly rural location on the western slope of the heavily wooded Mt. Sequoia overlooking the hustle and bustle of downtown Fayetteville. The cemetery is on the National Register of Historic Places and has been owned and cared for by the Southern Memorial Association since its formation in 1872 and the cemetery construction and dedication in 1873. The cemetery and the monuments that define this symbolic and sacred landscape represent a "concrete and palpable connection to past generations" and a tangible repository of cultural history to all those who visit (Schantz 2008:71). More so, the Confederate Cemetery is an example of the concerted commemoration of tradition by southern women as expressed in a monumental and memorialized cultural landscape (Janney 2008:119).

Curious visitors who seek out this quiet and peaceful landscape of commemoration are greeted by a large ornate iron gate flanked by two massive cut-stone pillars. Mounted to one of the pillars is a bold sign warning that trespassers will be punished to the extent of the law, although such regulation is not enforced today (Figure 3.1). Beyond the gate are four large raised burial plots, neatly organized and oriented at cardinal directions. Within each burial plot are the remains of Confederate soldiers from Arkansas, Louisiana, Missouri, and Texas. In the center is a grand cornerstone monument, atop which stands the statue of a Confederate soldier guarding his fallen comrades.

Figure 3.1. Iron gate and stone pillars at the entrance to the Confederate Cemetery. Photo by Jamie Brandon, April 2015.

Historical documents describe how Confederate soldiers were removed from hastily dug graves at battlefields in northwest Arkansas. The majority of soldiers were removed from Prairie Grove and Pea Ridge where thousands of Confederate soldiers lost their lives and were quickly and unceremoniously buried where they fell (Shea 2004; Shea and Hess 1992). Those individuals, along with soldiers from scattered graves throughout the countryside where "every foot of soil in this part of Arkansas was marked by contest and red with the blood of valor" were gathered and reburied at the Confederate Cemetery (Confederated Southern Memorial Association [CSMA] 1904:67). The cemetery represents a constructed and deliberately laid out cultural landscape consisting of monuments, stone markers, and the Confederate dead who represent a physiognomy of symbolism, remembrance, and memorial.

This project initially began as a curiosity to explore the events that led to the construction of the 140-year old cemetery and how it came to be in its remote and solitary location. As the investigation began and the cemetery landscape was examined in more detail, the arrangement of marble stone markers within each raised burial plot was analyzed and a thesis developed: Do the marble stone markers represent each Confederate soldier, individually reburied and corresponding to each stone, or were the solders instead reburied in mass graves with the stones intended to indicate the number of individuals interred at the cemetery? Investigating this inquiry first began by reviewing historical documents to better appreciate the sequence of events associated with the construction of the cemetery, the groups involved, and the community contributions undertaken. The background research was followed by fieldwork and the use of archaeological remote sensing methods to define the spatial relationship between subsurface features (organization of burial shafts) and visible surface features (extant marble markers).

A Call to the Ladies

Discussions related to the creation of a Confederate Cemetery in Fayetteville first began in June 1872, ten years after the battles at Prairie Grove and Pea Ridge. In the June 8, 1872 edition of the *Fayetteville Weekly Democrat*, a "Call to the Ladies" was posted, respectfully requesting a meeting of southern women to come together and remedy the "culpable neglect of our brethren who lie around and about us in weed-covered and unknown graves" (*Fayetteville Weekly Democrat* 1872).

This first meeting, attended by about forty women, established the Washington County (Fayetteville is the Washington County seat) division of the Southern Memorial Association—a group of women dedicated to "see that those who gave their lives for the greatest cause the world has ever known, must live forever in the hearts of the Southern people" (O'Connell 2006). Their mission was to locate a plot of land through community contribution where Confederate soldiers who perished in northwest Arkansas could be given a final resting place. The Southern Memorial Association was one of the many groups formed by women throughout the south that were organized despite years of hardship and challenges in the struggle to commemorate the Confederate dead (Blair 2004; Janney 2008; Neff 2005).

On March 1, 1873, in anticipation of the purchase of land, the ladies of the Washington County Southern Memorial Association hosted a benefit to raise funds for the building of a wooden fence. The event, comprising of individuals contributing tableaux, charades, and musicianship, was well received in the community. The women "succeeded pecuniarily beyond their most sanguine expectations, realizing nearly two hundred dollars" (*Fayetteville Weekly Democrat* 1873a). Converted for inflation, the Southern Memorial Association raised roughly the modern-day equivalent of about three thousand five hundred dollars—a significant amount by even today's standards.

On April 11, a plot of "three acres more or less" was purchased above the city of Fayetteville and a wooden fence around the property was constructed a year later. In 1876, sandstone markers were erected within each of the burial plots. Between 1885 and 1890, the wooden fence was replaced by a stone wall about 4-feet tall and constructed of local rough hewn stone. In 1903, the four burial plots were raised with earth and bordered with horizontally placed marble slabs. Unmarked marble stone markers were also erected in each burial plot to replace the newly buried sandstone markers. In 1926, the massive stone arch, decorated with iron gates and bronze tablets, was built to formally mark the entrance of the cemetery. Both the stone wall and stone arch still stand today, although the stone wall is in need of repair in some places owing to the toppling of various iced trees over the many years. Today, the unmarked marble stones are the primary markers within each of the burial plots.

Confederate Remains

Throughout April and May 1873, the remains of Confederate soldiers were removed from Pea Ridge and Prairie Grove by Mr. J. D. Henry and were reburied within the newly established Confederate Cemetery (*Fayetteville Weekly Democrat* 1873b). Mr. Henry was paid $1.40 ($24.78 when converted to the monetary value today) for each exhumed individual from Pea Ridge and $2.50 ($44.24 when converted to the monetary value today) for each exhumed individual from Prairie Grove. Over the years that followed, additional remains were collected in adjoining counties until "every wayside grave had given up its treasure" (CSMA 1904:67). Various sources estimate that between 600 and 900 individuals were removed from the battlefields and countryside locations and are now resting at the Confederate Cemetery. If one counts the marble stones visible today, there are 622 including a few that have inscriptions and date to the 1930s, 40s, and 50s.[1]

On May 31, 1873 the Southern Memorial Association expressed thanks to the citizens in northwest Arkansas for allowing Mr. Henry and party in taking up the Confederate dead and returning them to the

Confederate Cemetery. On the same date, the Southern Memorial Association announced that the cemetery was to be dedicated on June 10.

Cemetery Dedication

On the 14th of June 1873, the *Fayetteville Weekly Democrat* reported that over three thousand persons participated in the ceremony that, with a procession one and a half miles long filled with musicians, ex-Confederate soldiers, citizens on foot, on horseback, in carriages, and in wagons, marched from the town center to the location of the Confederate Cemetery. The *Weekly Democrat* continued, "The falling rain that day did not deter little girls, maidens, young ladies, old ladies, youths, young men, and silver-haired men from moving on to pay tribute to the memory of our beloved Southern dead" (*Fayetteville Weekly Democrat* 1873c).

Upon the procession reaching the cemetery, Rev. F. R. Earle, of Cane Hill College[2], greeted the crowd and who "then delivered the dedication address, full of pathos and earnestness." The crowd then silently filed off throughout the cemetery to honor each and every grave with "flowers, evergreens, and tears... Widows and orphans were there strewing the graves of husbands and fathers who had rendered up their lives in defence [sic] of what they conceived to be right" (*Fayetteville Weekly Democrat* 1873c).

Cemetery Organization

As reported by the *Fayetteville Weekly Democrat* (1873c) and evidenced on the landscape today, the cemetery is octagonal in shape (Figure 3.2). The majority of the marble stones are unmarked. Only a few have inscriptions. Each burial plot is oriented toward one of the four primary states from which the soldiers hailed. For example, the northern burial plot contains soldiers from Missouri (located *north* of Arkansas) and the southern burial plot contains soldiers from Louisiana (located *south* of Arkansas). The western burial plot contains soldiers from Texas (located more or less *west* of Arkansas; Oklahoma was Indian Territory at that time) and the eastern burial plot contains soldiers from Arkansas (considering that the majority of the state of Arkansas is *east* of the Confederate Cemetery location).

At the time of dedication, a temporary monument filled with evergreen wreaths was erected in the center of the cemetery. In 1897, twenty-four years after the initial dedication of the ceremony, a large

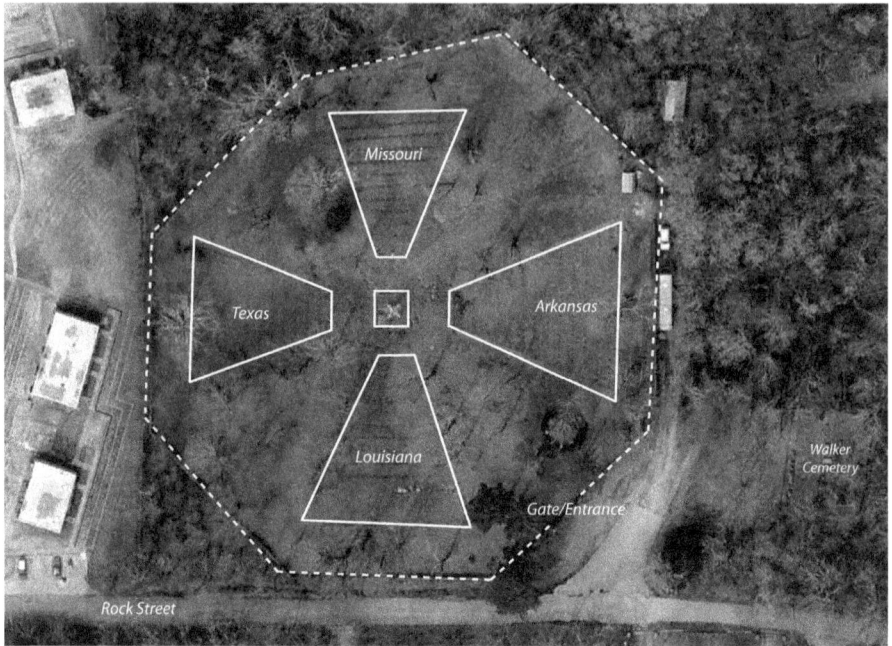

Figure 3.2. The octagonal shape of the Confederate Cemetery with the burial plots of each state labeled. Satellite image taken March 10, 2008.

cornerstone monument with the statue of a confederate solider stand-ing atop and guarding his buried comrades was erected for a sum of $3,000.00. Today, that amount is equal to roughly $76,000. In 2001, frozen limbs from an ice storm damaged the statue and portions of the granite monument and it was restored at a cost of $9,600. Etched into the monument that faces the Arkansas burial plot, which also faces the gated entrance, are the words "These were men whom power could not corrupt, whom death could not terrify, whom defeat could not dishonor." At the base of each side of the monument, the state names are etched as they correspond and face each of the burial plots. The state names on the monument are the only visible indication of the cemetery landscape layout and burial plot designations. There are no indications within the burial plots, apart from an occasional stone with an inscription stating the military appointment of the buried individual or a small state flag placed by recent a visitor - a temporary marker lasting as long as the wind will let it. Additionally, each corner of the monument base contains an artillery cannon carved from marble, each of which is oriented such that the barrel is aimed at the space between each burial plot, rather than at the burial plots.

In 1903 the cemetery was upgraded to the marble stone markers visible today. As part of the upgrade, fill was brought in to essentially raise and fully delineate the burial plots. The large unmarked marble stone markers were set within this new raised earth layer. The tops of a few of the original sandstone markers can still be seen buried within the raised surface. It is not known why the sandstone markers were not removed during this upgrade, or if some were removed and others were not. The buried sandstone markers are positioned at about a 45-degree angle to the base of the burial plot, whereas the marble markers are positioned perpendicular to the base of the burial plot. The sandstone and marble stones do not spatially correlate. Where the tops of the sandstone markers are visible, there is seemingly less than the later added marble markers. The upgraded marble stones are fairly irregular and of various sizes and might have been donated by a local business from surplus.

It is likely that the raising each of the burial plots with earth was to remedy a potential beautification issue caused by slumping of earth over time in preparation for the 30-year anniversary of the cemetery. A series of individual graves within the back section of the Louisiana plot recently showed severe evidence of slumping earth (Figure 3.3).[3] All of the stone markers associated with these graves are inscribed and date after 1903. Thus, it seems plausible, given the incidence of slumping associated with these later burials, that in the 30 years since the burial of soldiers that the cemetery landscape might have looked similar, which prompted the Southern Memorial Association to raise each of the burial plots with earth to cover the unsightly slumping throughout the site.

Geophysical Survey

While historical documentation illustrates a chronology of the events that led to the construction of the cemetery and how it came to be in its location, examined documentation does not explicitly mention if the Confederate soldiers were reburied individually or in mass graves within each burial plot. In other words, do the stones convey a mistaken impression of individual burials or are the remains en masse with the arranged stones intended to indicate the number of individuals interred at the site?

In order to address this question, a ground-penetrating radar survey (GPR) using a 400MHz antenna was undertaken. The survey was conducted as part of field instruction in archaeological remote sensing

Figure 3.3. Evidence of the "slumping" of recent burials in the Louisiana burial plot. Photo taken by author.

in the course, 'Approaches to Archaeology'—an introductory course in archaeology at the University of Arkansas. Data were collected along transects that were set up parallel to the headstones with transect spacing at approximately 50cm in order to bisect possible grave shafts. When a single transect was blocked by a row of headstones, the GPR antenna was pulled as close to the line of stones as possible. The survey areas were confined to the raised portion of the cemetery within each burial plot. To date, the cemetery has been surveyed in the Missouri, Arkansas, and Louisiana burial plots with equal results.

A GPR radargram of a single transect from the Missouri plot reveals a series of hyperbolic reflections (Figure 3.4). The apex of each reflection represents the location of a material that is different in compositional structure than the material above it. The strength of the hyperbolas represents the intensity of the radio wave reflected at a certain point. Thus, the apex of each one of these arcs might represent casket compo-

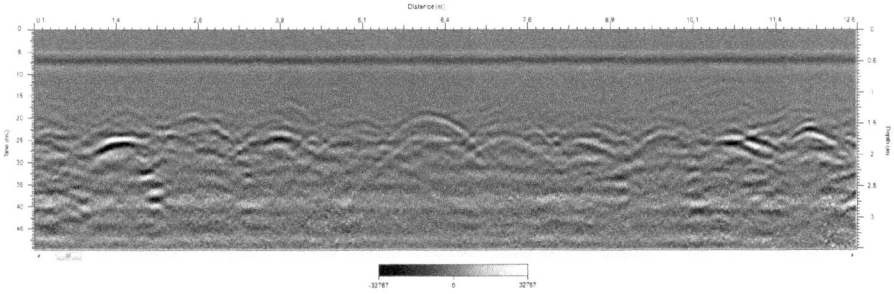

Figure 3.4. Profile of ground-penetrating radar data showing hyperbolic arcs that represent components of the bottom of individual burial shafts at approximately 4.5–5.7 feet.

nents, or at minimal they might merely represent differential moisture within certain graves that enhance radar reflections. Most importantly, they represent individual reflections related to individual burial shafts.

The hyperbolic arcs are useful to isolate areas of interest and their geometry can be used to estimate the speed at which the radio waves travel through the ground allowing for a calculation of the actual sub-surface depth of anomalies (Conyers 2004). In several of the profiles, the depth of each hyperbole apex is roughly 20–25 nanoseconds, or approximately 1.40–1.75 meters (4.5–5.7 feet) below the surface and represents components of the individual grave shafts (see Figure 3.4).

Using several combined profiles to create a "time slice" reveals that the majority of Confederate soldiers were reburied individually (Figure 3.5). With time slice processing, data are interpolated between adjacent survey profiles to create a plan map that allows for a visual representation of anomalies at various depths. A single time slice within the Missouri plot at approximately 20 ns (1.40 meters) shows several regularly spaced anomalies each measuring approximately 1.5 meters (5 ft) by 0.75 meters (2.5 ft) and organized in rows throughout the burial plot. Concentrations or groups of anomalies may represent areas where multiple burials are closely spaced as a result of obstacles, such as large boulders hidden in the rocky Ozark subsurface geology. Possibly, they might represent larger burial shafts containing more than one individual. Many of the regularly spaced anomalies more or less correspond with the stones situated along the surface. Further mapping is necessary to

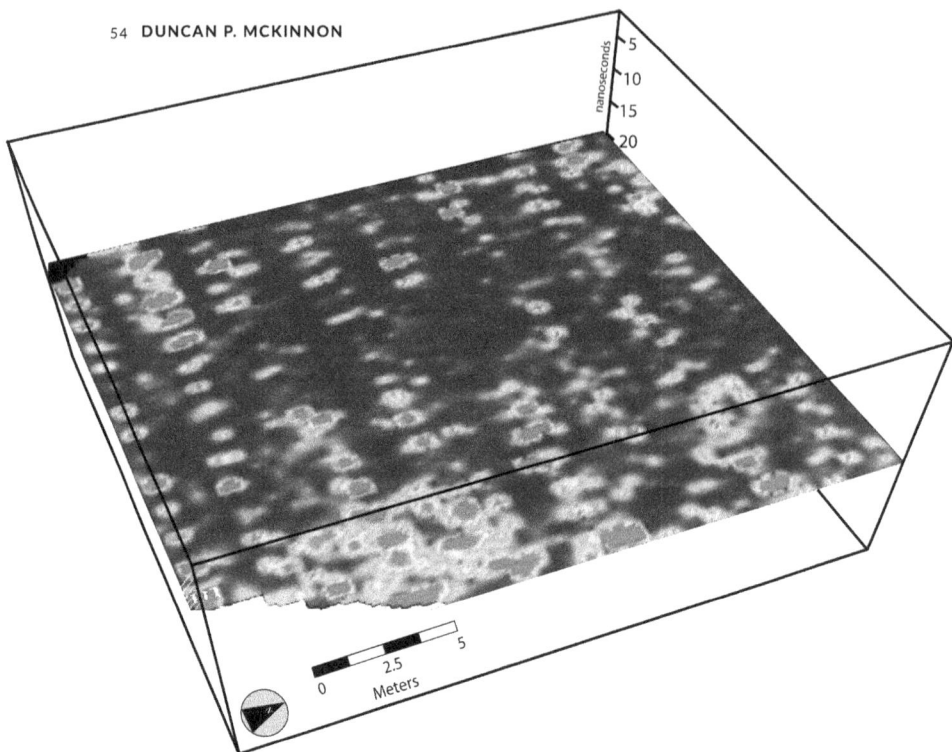

Figure 3.5. Plan view (time-slice) showing individual burial shafts at the Confederate Cemetery. Time slice is at about 20 nanoseconds in depth, roughly the bottom of the shafts. Time slice created by Jason Herrmann.

properly correlate the relationship of buried sandstone markers, marble markers on the surface, and the location of individual radar anomalies.

Conclusion

The integration of historical and remote sensing data has illuminated the symbolic and sacred cemetery landscape in Fayetteville, Arkansas. Historical documents reveal that the construction of the cemetery focused on an urgency to honor Confederate soldiers hastily buried throughout northwest Arkansas and to provide them a proper final place of rest attended with the requisite ceremonies and rituals associated with the "promise of eternal life" (Faust 2008:62). Spearheading this urgency were the members of the Southern Memorial Association, formed by local women as "custodians of the Lost Cause at a time when that role was inexpedient for southern women" (Neff 2005:147). Remote sensing data reveal that soldiers were reburied at the Confederate Cemetery primarily in individual graves that were organized in an orderly, sacred, and symbolic manner rather than buried en masse. The Confederate Cemetery, as defined by the women of the Southern Memorial Association, represents "a tangible reminder of the brave men who died for a way of life they held dear and the proud women who loved and honored them." Even today, every June 10th on the anniversary of the dedication of the cemetery in 1873, the Southern Memorial Association hosts Southern Memorial Days, where community members flock to the cemetery grounds and continue to honor and pay respect to those buried within a symbolic and sacred landscape.

Acknowledgments

Versions of this paper were originally presented at the 67th Southeastern Archaeological Conference in Lexington, Kentucky and the 71st Arkansas Historical Association Conference in Fayetteville, Arkansas. Thanks go to students in the University of Arkansas "Approaches to Archeology" course with assistance in data collecting. Many thanks to Dr. Jason Herrmann who helped with the collecting and processing of data and provided comments and contributions to earlier versions of this paper. Thanks to Jerry Hilliard of the Arkansas Archeological Survey for assistance with mapping. Thanks to Donna Schwieder, President of the Southern Memorial Association, and to the board of the Southern Memorial Association for the opportunity to investigate this interesting and important historical site.

NOTES

1. In preparation for the June 2012 Southern Memorial Day festivities, additional unmarked stones have been added based on a dowsing survey.
2. From 1834–1891, Cane Hill College was one of the earliest educational institutions in the state of Arkansas, finally closing its doors in 1891 (Basham 1969).
3. During the initial investigations outlined in this paper, evidence of slumping was apparent as shown in Figure 3.3. In preparation for the June 2012 Southern Memorial Day festivities earth was deposited to cover the former slumps of earth and once again addressing a beautification issue.

REFERENCES

Basham, Robert H.
1969   A History of Cane Hill College in Arkansas. Doctoral dissertation, University of Arkansas.

Confederated Southern Memorial Association
1904   *History of the Confederated Memorial Associations of the South.*
        Confederated Southern Memorial Association.
Conyers, Lawrence B.
2004   Ground Penetrating Radar for Archaeology. Altamira Press, Walnut Hill, CA.
Faust, Drew Gilpin
2008   *This Republic of Suffering.* Random House, NY
Fayetteville Weekly Democrat
1872   Call to the Ladies. *Fayetteville Weekly Democrat,* June 8.
1873a   Announcement of Results from Funding Event. *Fayetteville Weekly
        Democrat,* March 1.
1873b   The Re-interment of Confederate Soldiers. *Fayetteville Weekly Democrat,*
        May 31.
1873c   Dedication Ceremony. *Fayetteville Weekly Democrat,* June 14.
Janney, Caroline E.
2008   *Burying the Dead but Not the Past: Ladies' Memorial Associations and the
        Lost Cause.* The University of North Carolina Press, Chapel Hill.
Neff, John R.
2005   *Honoring the Civil War Dead: Commemoration and the Problem of
        Reconciliation.* University Press of Kansas, Lawrence, KS.
O'Connell, David
2006   *Furl That Banner: The Life of Abram J. Ryan, Poet-Priest of the South.*
        Mercer University Press, Macon, GA.
Schantz, Mark S.
2008   *Awaiting the Heavenly Country: The Civil War and America's Culture of
        Death.* Cornell University Press. Ithaca, NY.
Shea, William L.
2009   *Fields of Blood: The Prairie Grove Campaign.* The University of North
        Carolina Press, Chapel Hill.
Shea, William L. and Earl J. Hess
1992   *Pea Ridge: Civil War Campaign in the West.* The University of North
        Carolina Press, Chapel Hill.

4

THE HOWE POTTERY (3SA340)
A Traditional Stoneware Manufacturing Site
on Military Road in Benton, Arkansas

C. Andrew Buchner

The Howe Pottery (3SA340) is a small, shallow site located in an unde-veloped wooded area along Military Road (HY 5) on the outskirts of Benton, Arkansas. It is significant for being the only remaining intact archaeological site associated with the traditional stoneware potteries that formed the backbone of Benton's economy during the late 19th century. Archival research suggests that the Howe Pottery was oper-ated from before 1886 until ca. 1899, and its various potters primarily focused on the production of simple, unadorned utilitarian vessels. Fol-lowing a brief attempt to produce brick at the site, the kiln closed, the site reforested, and its existence was largely forgotten—although it was but a few steps from a busy highway.

Plans to widen Military Road resulted in the discovery of the Howe Pottery, as well as its subsequent excavation for Section 106 compliance purposes. Arkansas Highway and Transportation (AHTD) archaeolo-gists initially identified the site during a 2008 reconnaissance survey and found its archaeological signature quite curious: it contained abundance stoneware sherds, odd shaped pieces of kiln furniture, and few other artifacts. Subsequent research and informant interviews lead Hughes (2008) to recognize that the Howe Pottery, and two related nearby scat-ters (3SA339 and 3SA341), were the remains of stoneware potteries in various states of preservation. The identification of these pottery sites was a pleasant surprise, because it was widely believed that the urban

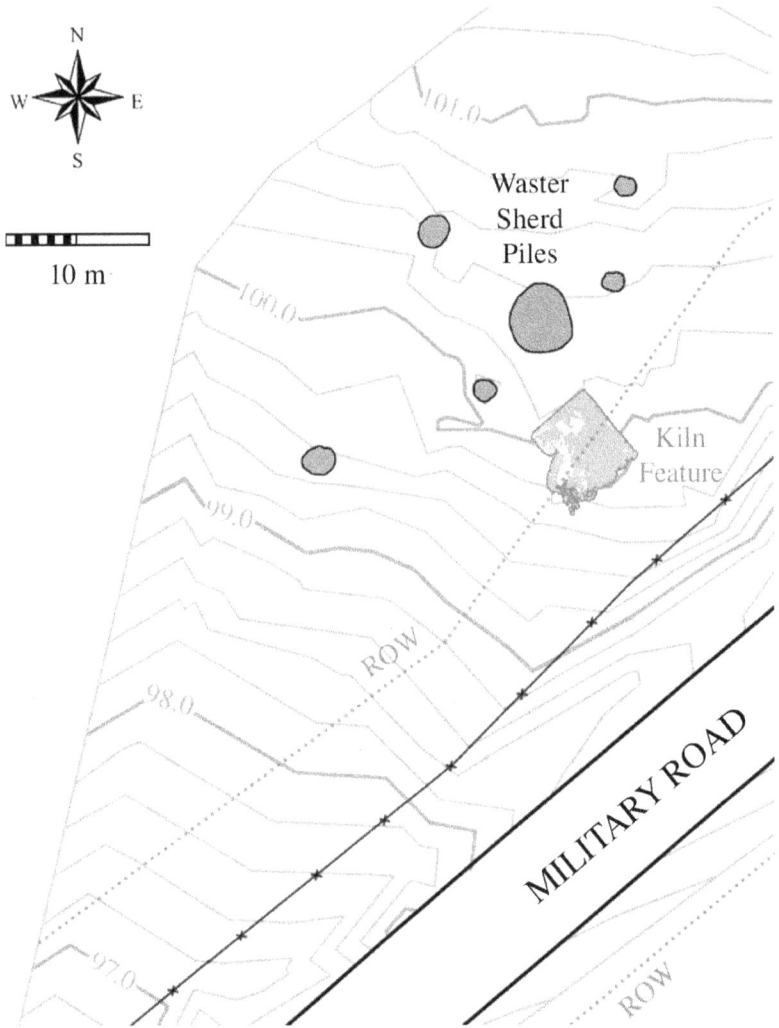

Figure 4.1. Site plan view map.

expansion of Benton had destroyed most, if not all, of the late 19th century potteries in Benton (Trubitt 2004a, 2004b).

The engineering firm responsible for the Benton Military Road widening project (AHTD Job 061257) contracted a cultural resources firm, Panamerican Consultants, Inc. (Panamerican), to conduct a Phase I survey of the proposed widening corridor, and the three pottery sites identified by AHTD were revisited (Buchner 2009). Subsequently, Panamerican conducted Phase II test excavations at the Howe Pottery and a nearby site, the Original Hyten Kiln/Eagle Pottery (3SA341) (Buchner 2010). Importantly, the Howe Pottery was found to be eligible for NRHP nomination under Criterion D, because a well-preserved brick kiln feature and waster sherd piles were identified there. There was no way the project could avoid the area, so the firm developed a data recovery plan in consultation with the SHPO, AHTD, and the Federal Highway Administration to mitigate the adverse effects of the widening of Military Road on the Howe Pottery. During the Phase III data recovery excavations a brick kiln feature was completely exposed, a pair of superimposed kilns was identified, and a large artifact sample was recovered (Buchner 2011).

Because of Panamerican's compliance studies, the Howe Pottery is now one of the best known archaeological pottery manufacturing sites in Arkansas. Previously, the archaeology of stoneware pottery sites in Benton, and more generally in Arkansas, were poorly understood because so few were investigated. Prior to the recent Military Road studies that culminated in the Howe Pottery excavation, Blakely's (1990a, 1990b) investigation of the McConnell-Osborne or Cumbie Pottery (3SB596) represented the most intensive archaeological study of an Arkansas pottery. What is known about the Benton potteries, and Arkansas potteries in general, was largely based on historic research (Gifford 2001; Starr 2003; Trubitt 2004a; Watkins 1980, 1982) and the analysis of museum pieces (Bennett and Worthern 1990). Much of the available literature regarding Benton potteries is focused on the two that survived into the 20th century, the Eagle Pottery and the Niloak Pottery (Gifford 2001). As a result, the archaeological studies at the Howe Pottery offered a unique opportunity to shed some light on Benton's traditional late 19th century family potteries.

Benton Pottery Industry

The historical sequence of Benton potteries can be viewed in terms of four periods (I, II, III, and IV). During the initial Period I (1868–1873), potteries were established and the local tradition developed. Period II, from 1873 to 1890, was the high point of the local pottery industry. During this period the Benton potteries dominated stoneware production in Arkansas. The 1890s (Period III) is an era of decline, and by ca. 1900 only one traditional pottery survived (the Eagle Pottery). Period IV is the 20th century, and is characterized by industrial pottery production. Early in the 20th century the Eagle Pottery transformed itself into a small factory and developed a decorative (non-utilitarian) product that eventually resulted in the formation of a second company (Niloak Pottery) that prospered during the 1920s. Niloak can be viewed as part of the 'art pottery movement' (Sweezy 1994:28). The Depression caused the Eagle Pottery to close in 1938 and Niloak only survived through WWII due to government contracts for war material.

Traditional potteries are family businesses, and they characterize Periods I–III. These potteries produced utilitarian stoneware with few decorations. The Howe Pottery is representative of the industry's apex (Period II) and the subsequent decline and the death of traditional potteries (Period III).

The roots of the Benton pottery industry lie to the south in Dallas County. Dallas County was the birthplace of Arkansas' pottery industry in 1843 and prior to 1870 this area was the epicenter of the industry in the state (Bennett and Worthern 1990:146; Trubitt 2004a:4; Watkins 1980, 1982). The potteries in Dallas County were the focus of various archaeological surveys and historical research, principally during 1972–1983. Some of the better-known potters in Dallas County include John Welch and the four Bird (or Byrd) brothers. The Birds were born during the 1820s within a pottery-producing region of North Carolina and by 1843 had moved to Dallas County, Arkansas (Watkins 1980, 1982). The potteries in Dallas County were located in and near the towns of Princeton and Tulip (Starr 2003:3; Trubitt 2004a:4; Watkins 1980, 1982), which are located 40 mi. and 34 mi. south of Benton, respectively.

Bennett and Worthern (1990:150) report that there were nine potteries in Dallas County; earlier Smith (1972) had noted two of these potteries. Seven kiln sites in Dallas County have been assigned archaeological site numbers, but no archaeological data is available for three (3DA540, 3DA542, and 3DA543) because they have not been field checked. The four Dallas County pottery kiln sites that have been archaeologically surveyed are significant, and are they are individually listed on the National Register of Historic Places: Welch's Kiln #2 (3DA8); the Welch Pottery Works (3DA9); the Bird Kiln (3DA12); and the Nathaniel Culberson Pottery (3DA21).

Goodspeed (1889:242) suggests that pottery was first made in the Benton area during 1866. However, most modern scholars suggest that Lafayette Glass opened the first pottery in Benton during 1868 (Rainey 1973; Trubitt 2004a:22; Winburn 1940). Prior to this, Glass had a pottery in Fordyce in southern Dallas County (Rainey 1973), thus an experienced potter from the birthplace of Arkansas's pottery industry was responsible for the initial development of the post-bellum pottery industry in Saline County. Trubitt (2004a:22) reports that Glass learned the craft from Oliver Harris, a former African American slave that he purchased in New Orleans. Interestingly, the 1870 Census indicates that Glass and Oliver Harris shared the same household.

A key natural resource that drew potters to the Benton area was extensive beds of potter's clay, and an early geologist remarked that Benton "was well supplied with excellent clays for the manufacture of the common grades of stoneware and pottery" (Branner 1908:193). Benton lies along a geological unconformity that marks the boundary between the Ouachita Mountains and the Coastal Plain, and this boundary represents an ancient shoreline. Branner (1908:193) noted that "the great pottery clay beds" lie south and east of the "old shoreline" near Benton. He described six clay pits and several other clay sources in Township 2 South Range 15 West, and reported that the best two potter's clays were reportedly from the Rhodenbaugh and Woosley pits (Branner 1908).

Lafayette Glass's first kiln is believed to have been located northwest of the Market and South streets intersection in Benton (Rainey 1973). He operated this kiln from 1868 to 1870 when it was sold. The 1870 Saline County Census "Products of Industry" reports that Lafayette Glass manufactured stoneware, had two employees, and produced $800 annually (Trubitt 2004a:22). After selling out in 1870, Glass built another kiln "at a clay pit east of Benton on the old Military Road" (Rainey 1973). This kiln has been archaeologically identified as 3SA341 and was later the location of the Eagle Pottery.

In 1873 the Cairo & Fulton Railroad extended their tracks southwestward across Saline County (Goodspeed 1889:234). Benton was on this trunk line (later known as the Iron Mountain Railroad) and, as a result, it developed into an important commercial center. After 1873, stoneware production in Benton greatly expanded, and Benton came to dominate pottery production in Arkansas (Bennett and Worthen 1990:151; Gifford 2001:11; Goodspeed 1889:242).

The 1880s were the 'golden years' of the Benton stoneware industry, and various sources suggest that from five to seven factories operated at that time. An 1880 *Arkansas Gazette* article stated that 181,620 gal. of stoneware had been produced at the Benton potteries and that 44 railroad car loads of ware had been shipped out. This would be the equivalent of producing 60,000 vessels (12,000 each in 1, 2, 3, 4, and 5 gal. sizes). The industry was characterized by multiple, small, traditional, family-oriented workshops that were strung out along Military Road on the rural outskirts of Benton (in close proximity to the pottery clay pits), and continuing into town.

During the 1880s, the local potters organized the "Benton Stoneware Association" and a list of its members was published in 1886. Gifford (2001:11) lists five Benton potteries during the 1880s: Alfred Wilbur Pottery, the Dixie Stoneware Company, and potteries operated by Lee Davis, Samuel Henderson, and David Womack. In 1889, Goodspeed (1889:237, 242) reported that pottery manufacture was the "leading industry" in Benton. At this time there were "seven good factories, producing various grades of ware and ... large shipments are constantly being made to the outside world" (Goodspeed 1889:242). The Howe Pottery was one almost certainly of the seven "factories" mentioned by Goodspeed.

By the late 1890s the Benton pottery industry was in decline, as a result of competition with mass-produced factory products, changing transportation systems, and shifting populations centers (Trubitt 2004a; Bennett and Worthen 1990:149). This was a national trend during the 1890s that is documented in other pottery regions as well, such as Illinois (Mansberger 1995), Tennessee, and Kentucky (Peres and Connatser 2008; Smith and Rogers 1979). During this era, tinware replaced milk pans, and mass-produced glass pitchers, flasks and jars "stole" the potter's market (Bennett and Worthen 1990:149). Some traditional potteries responded to the falling market by attempting to shift to production of brick and tile. The Howe Pottery appears to be a local example of this short-lived trend. Most traditional potteries were ultimately put out of business, and by 1900, only one traditional pottery remained, the Eagle Pottery, which was located outside the Benton city limits near an established clay source.

The Eagle Pottery is closely associated with C.D. "Bullet" Hyten, who had grown up in the Benton pottery industry and learned to 'turn' from this father and stepfather. By 1897 he and his two brothers ran the Hyten Bros. Pottery at Lafayette Glass's second kiln. Ca. 1900–1901, C.D. Hyten had sole ownership of the business and changed the name to the Eagle Pottery. The Eagle Pottery produced utilitarian wares, such as salt and sugar jars, crocks, and jugs. Most examples of Eagle Pottery ware are wholly or partly Bristol-glazed. This glaze was favored by almost all industrialized potteries in the U.S. after 1884, and after 1920 it was "almost always used alone" (Greer 1981:212).

In 1904, the Eagle Pottery was touted as the "largest pottery ware business" in or near Benton and it had recently expanded (Arkansas Democrat 1904). The pottery could produce up to 6,000 gallons of ware in one firing of its new Stewart patent kiln (Gilford 2001:12). There were 20 employees and the clay source was located near the shop. In 1912, a creosote fire in the kiln chimney resulted in the destruction of this pottery (Rainey 1987:66). C.D. Hyten chose not to rebuild at this location, but instead built a new factory along the railroad on Pearl Street in Benton. The Pearl Street location is recorded as Site 3SA307, and there are two Sanborn maps and numerous historic photos of this facility. The Eagle Pottery continued to produce utilitarian ware until closing in 1938.

Importantly, C.D. Hyten developed the decorative Niloak-style pottery in collaboration with Arthur Dovey at the Eagle Pottery during 1909–1910 (Gifford 2001). Niloak was a popular art pottery that was produced in Benton from 1909 until 1946 (Gifford 2001; Rainey 1973). Niloak is best known for producing a collectable, Mission-swirl pottery that was non-utilitarian and very distinct from the utilitarian stoneware produced at the Eagle Pottery. The name Niloak is a kind of wordplay, as it is kaolin, a kind of fine-grained potter's clay, spelled backwards.

In 1912, Niloak production began at the new factory on Pearl Street in Benton. The 1920s were the most prosperous era for Niloak and in 1929 they built a "magnificent" showroom on Military Road (Gifford 2001:24). This is where the historic marker for Niloak is located today. Niloak introduced a new art line "Hywood" in 1931. Sales lagged during the Great Depression and H.L. Winburn III bought the company in 1934. Winburn began competing for government contracts and during WWII the company produced over one million clay pigeons a month for the military. In 1947 the Niloak Pottery Company was dissolved and the old works later became the Winburn Tile Company.

Four Potters and a Dealer

Review of historic tax books housed at the Saline County Courthouse Annex yielded significant information regarding who operated the Howe Pottery, when they operated it, as well as the appraised value of its 14-acre lot over time. This research indicates that four potters were associated with the site, during a period from before 1886, to when production is thought to have ceased ca. 1899. Archival records suggest connections among the various traditional potters in Benton, and this is evocative of tight knit local community. Additionally, a marked sherd suggests that a former potter turned stoneware dealer is associated with the Howe Pottery.

It is unfortunate that there is no tax book data prior to 1886, as it appears the Howe Pottery was operational before this date. In 1886, Amos L. Herrick paid the taxes and the assessed value at this time is the highest that we documented throughout the history of the tract ($500). As most other lots in this area were assessed at $2 to $5 per acre, the higher rate here ($35.71 per acre) implies that the property contained an improvement of some type, and it is speculated to be a pottery works. It is comforting to note that A. L. Herrick is listed a potter the 1880 Saline County census and another E. L. Herrick opened a pottery in Saline County in 1878 (Trubitt 2004a:23). During 1880, Amos and his wife shared a household with the Leech family (another potter family, see below) and were neighbors of the Hytens (the potter family that dominated the industry during the 20th century).

Two years later J. J. Leech paid the taxes. While the assessed value in 1888 had dropped rather dramatically (from $500 to $200), it remains much higher per acre ($14.29) than the surrounding tracts (again, typically $2 to $5 per acre). J. J. Leech is listed as a potter in the 1886 Benton Stoneware Association (Trubitt 2004a:25–26). Another potter named Samuel Leech is enumerated in the 1880 Saline County Census (Trubitt 2004a:23). During the archaeological fieldwork, two stoneware sherds embossed LEECH were recovered from the Howe Pottery, thus Leech clearly produced pottery at the site. Earlier, during 1880, the Leechs cohabitated with the Herricks (who paid the taxes in 1886).

From 1891–1896 James H. Howe paid the taxes on the Howe Pottery lot, as well as several other lots in the immediate vicinity. The assessed value remained stable at its 1888 rate ($200) throughout this period. As a result, it is assumed that that kiln operation continued, but that no other improvements were made during the Howe tenure. Another family member, J. K. Howe, leased the Herrick-Atchison pottery on Military Road from 1891–1897. The Herrick-Atchison pottery has been archaeologically identified as 3SA339 and it is located a short distance southwest of the Howe Pottery, across a drainage. Thus, the Howes operated two adjacent potteries along Military Road during the 1890s.

James H. Howe was born on September 3, 1849 in Missouri. The 1880 Saline County Census described him as a potter with three Arkansas born children. He is verifiable as a Benton potter in various other sources as well (Trubitt 2004a:Appendix). Branner (1908:183) notes that Mr. J. Howe "reopened" the Hicks clay bank in 1889. This was the first clay pit in Benton and was formerly known as the "old Leach bank" (Branner 1908:183). An Arkansas Historic Commission photo of James Howe was recovered that shows him in an apron, the photo label indicates he is either a "butcher or potter" (Buchner 2011:Figure 4–8). The 1900 and 1910 Saline County censuses describe James H. Howe as a butcher; he changed careers after the Howe Pottery closed. J.H. Howe died on May 14, 1914, and was buried at the Hicks Cemetery, which is 1.1 mi. south of the Howe Pottery.

There are two 1897 tax books, one lists James H. Howe as the tax-payer and the other has A.W. Warren as the taxpayer. In both cases, the assessed value is stable at $200; it is assumed that the kiln operation con-tinued. Trubitt (2004b:29) identified Albert W. Warren as a Benton potter, but relatively little is known about Warren. He was born in Iowa ca. 1892, and he ran a pottery with C. D. Hyten for a short time (1900–1901).

J.H. Howe paid the 1899 and 1901 taxes. At his time there is a steep (80 percent) drop in the assessed value of the property: from $200 to $40. This is interpreted as evidence that the pottery works ceased operat-ing. After 1901, J. H. Howe never again paid the taxes on the property.

Archaeological evidence for a local stoneware dealer believed to be H. T. Caldwell was recovered at the site. The evidence consists of a stenciled cobalt blue mark on a salt-glazed vessel (see Buchner 2011:Figure 6–5a). The stenciled lettering on several conjoined sherds reads ". . .DWELL/ W. . .LE DEALER/ IN/ STONEWARE/ BENTON/ ARK" and is surrounded by a tied wheat crescent or sprig motif. H. T. Caldwell is the only name among Trubitt's (2004b:Appendix) list of "Individuals Associated with the Saline County Pottery Industry" that can reasonably be inferred from the stenciled word fragment ". . .DWELL."

Prior to 1868, Henry T. Caldwell was involved in potteries in Wash-ington, Arkansas, and Louisiana. During 1868–1870, he worked at Lafayette Glass' pottery in Benton. In 1870, Caldwell purchased the Lafayette Glass pottery. After 1872 Caldwell ceased being a potter and became a merchant. The Howe Pottery "DEALER IN STONEWARE" marked sherds reveal that Caldwell was a wholesale dealer in stone-ware, so although he ceased being a stoneware manufacturer, he was still involved in the pottery business. It is suspected that during "early" pottery production period at the Howe Pottery (1886 and before) H. T. Caldwell hired A. L. Herrick to produce salt-glazed cobalt blue jugs stenciled "DEALER IN STONEWARE" for the wholesale market.

Fieldwork

The Howe Pottery setting is a mature oak-pine forest with dense under-growth where, among the leaf litter and undergrowth, abundant stone-ware waster sherds can be observed and occasionally felt "crunching" under your feet. The site covers a 40–x–40 m area on a gentle slope to the southwest, and the subsurface deposits range from 20–40 cm deep in the core 20–x-20 m area of the deposit. After cutting back the vegetation, several small mounds were discerned and mapped, and the unit excavations targeted these features. Six of these represent waster piles; they are heaped masses of broken vessels and kiln furniture with artifacts densities ranging from >1,000 artifacts/m³ to >14,000 artifacts/m³. The two largest of these had old oaks growing out of them and their size suggests the site was abandoned—but undisturbed—for a considerable period of time. The low mound that was nearest to the Military Road was found to be the remains of two superimposed brick kilns.

Work conducted during the Phase III data recovery included unearthing and exposing the brick kiln feature in a 6–x-6 m area and formally excavating four units (covering 5.5 m²) and one feature (F-1) within the kiln (Buchner 2011). One unit (Unit 11) and F-1 sampled a sealed "early" site context below the exposed kiln's floor. Three units (Units 9, 10, and 12) sampled waster sherd piles. The kiln feature was exposed via shovel skimming, troweling, and sweeping with straw brooms and a gas blower. Previously during the Phase II testing eight 1–x-2 m test units were excavated (covering 16 m²), including six on the kiln feature (Units 2, 3, 4, 5, 6, and 8) and two on waster sherd piles (Units 1 and 7) (Buchner 2010). The site was shovel tested at 10 m intervals during the Phase I, and 13 tests were positive (Buchner 2009).

Kiln Construction

Determining the type of kiln employed at the Howe Pottery was a major research goal. As there is no other remaining intact late 19th century kiln site in Benton, the characteristics and technology revealed at the Howe Pottery are locally and regionally significant. Previously it was speculated that the Howe Pottery was not a singleshot- or groundhog-type kiln, because of the high frequency of kiln furniture documented at site. One of the archaeological signatures of groundhog kilns is an absence of kiln furniture (Greer 1981:220). There are no documentary records that document the type of kilns used at the Howe Pottery. The best clue as to the appearance of the kilns at the Howe Pottery is offered in the 1895 photo of the Henderson Pottery in Benton (Smith and Rodgers 2011:Figure 3–84).

The excavations revealed two superimposed kilns: a rectangular kiln over an earlier round kiln. The rectangular kiln is interpreted as a brick-making scove kiln, while the round kiln is interpreted as a pottery-making kiln. There may have been an earlier pottery kiln that predated the round kiln, but this is inferential.

The rectangular kiln is 17.39–x-14.10 ft. in size, with the long axis perpendicular to Military Road. Blackened stains, slag deposits, and brick patterns are aligned along the long axis of the kiln, which are suggestive of at least three firing lanes, are similar to patterns observed at brick kilns in Tennessee and Kentucky (Peres and Connatser 2008; Smith and Cox 1977; Smith and Watrin 1986). The brick stack in the southwestern portion of the rectangular kiln is interpreted as a group of over-heated bricks or burned bricks that were unsuitable for use, and thus were left on the floor of the kiln. Because there are no significant piles of waster bricks at the Howe Pottery, it is believed that the rectangular kiln was only used a few times and that most of the bricks that were manufactured were sold or removed from the site.

The round kiln is represented by an approximately 3.5 m (11.5 ft.) long curved section of brick. The curved section is three bricks wide and one course thick, and represents between one-fourth and one-third of a complete circle. Extrapolations based on the curvature of the intact section of the round kiln suggest that it had an exterior diameter of 5.0 m (16.4 ft.) and an interior diameter of 3.76 m (12.33 ft.). The interior floor of the round kiln is thus estimated to have covered 11.1 m² (119.2 ft.2). The ends of the bricks on the interior of the round kiln were heavily glazed and suggestive of the production of salt-glazed vessels. Two "key stone" shaped gaps in the curved wall section are suggestive of firebox openings. Given the location and orientation of the two openings, we suggest that the round kiln most likely had four openings (one every 90°), but it possibly had five openings (one every 72°). The round kiln is interpreted as a "beehive" kiln that likely had a low domed roof and is thought to be similar to ones shown in archival photos of late 19th century potteries in Benton.

The F-1 excavation and a transverse cut through the round wall section reveal that the round kiln was constructed on a shallow basin that was backfilled with a compact and dense deposit of kiln furniture and waster sherds. This backfilled basin (F-1) is interpreted as the foundation of the round kiln. A foundation was needed to support the brick walls and chimney of the round kiln. Rhodes (1968:143) illustrates a similar foundation in his section on kiln construction, but suggests using gravel fill rather than kiln waste, as here at the Howe Pottery.

Because the round kiln's foundation was constructed using kiln furniture and waster sherds it implies that there was an earlier kiln at the

Figure 4.2. Photo of the exposed kiln feature; view west.

site that pre-dates the round kiln. Alternatively, the kiln furniture and waster sherds used in the F-1 foundation could have been transported to the Howe Pottery from another pre-existing local pottery, such as the Original Hyten Kiln/Eagle Pottery, which is only a quarter mile to the southwest down Military Road.

The waster sherds and kiln furniture that were used to backfill the round kiln's foundation exhibited notable differences from the general site assemblage; including a higher frequency of salt-glazed and cobalt blue decorated sherds, the abundant presence of milk pan rims (which are generally absent elsewhere), and larger and heavier pieces of kiln furniture categorized as Type D. This sealed deposit is viewed as an early site context and its assemblage contrasts with the later and more typical site assemblage that is characterized by the recovery from the rectangular kiln and the deposits around the kiln feature, including the bulk of the massive recovery from the waster sherd piles.

It is uncertain if the round kiln was updraft or downdraft, because only a portion of the kiln was preserved. However, the simplicity of the round kiln's wall and floor hints that it was an updraft kiln, possibly similar to a bottle kiln. Updraft bottle kilns were used in the South into

Figure 4.3. Plan view drawing of the exposed kiln feature at 3SA340.

the early 20th century (Sweezy 1984:77). Downdraft kilns required bag walls, slotted floors, and/or tunnel systems to re-direct the heat (Sweezy 1984:74). The limited preserved section of the round kiln does not exhibit patterns consistent with such features.

More generally, Sweezy (1984:74–75) remarks that that "the use of round kilns spread from the Midwest through Tennessee and into the South between 1875 and 1900." The round kiln at 3SA340 thus falls within Sweezy's (1984) date range for this type of kiln in the South. During the late 1800s there was a shift from updraft to downdraft round kilns as the technology radiated into the South. In 1904, the Eagle Pottery, located only ¼ mi. from the Howe Pottery, installed a new "Stewart patent kiln," which is a type of round downdraft kiln (Gilford 2001:12).

Waster Piles

Smith (1972:9) regards the most important characteristic of a well-preserved kiln site as the presence of "large waster dumps." Waster piles consist of broken stoneware sherds and pieces of kiln furniture. Within

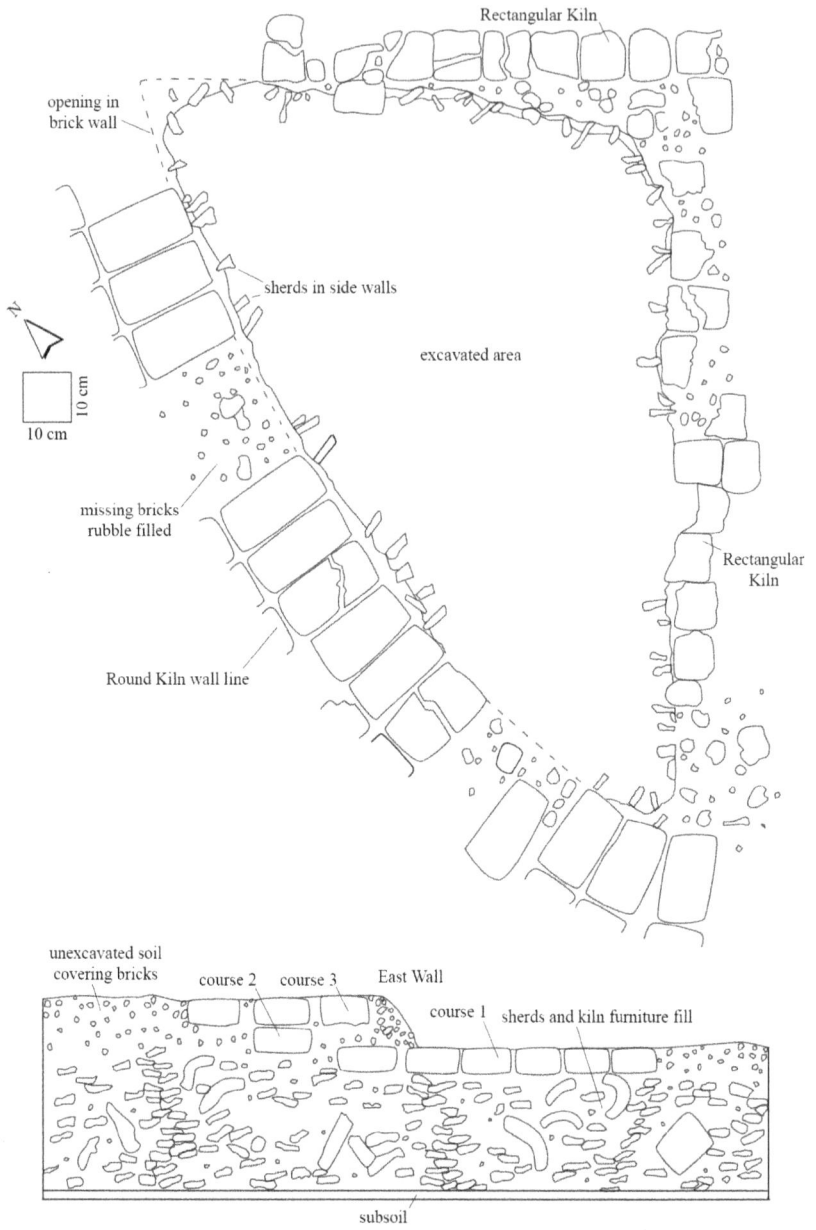

Figure 4.4. Detailed plan and profile drawing of Feature 1 showing relationship of the round kiln and the rectangular kiln.

the waster piles, sherds are typically more common than kiln furniture and at the Howe Pottery the ratio is roughly 4:1. Waster piles are variably sized, and the most prominent waster piles at the Howe Pottery are from 1.0–4.0 m in diameter and from 0.3–1.0 m tall. However, the level ground between the waster sherd piles contained a 20–30 cm thick deposit with a content similar to the piles, so in essence, the piles are just the "tip of the iceberg" of an extensive waster deposit covering a roughly 20-x-20 m oval area at the site core. The waster pile in the 1895 Henderson Pottery, also known as the Benton Jug Factory, photo (Smith and Rogers 2011:Figure 3–84) is an example of a large active waster pile.

The waster pile unit excavations at the Howe Pottery covered 9 m^2 and produced 85.8 percent (n=21,370) of the counted artifacts recovered during the Phase II and Phase III combined. These waster pile units were important for providing an abundant excavated artifact sample, and produced some of the most rare and archaeologically significant sherds. For example, the northwestern waster pile, located 14 m from the kiln feature, produced the only two examples of the LEECH marked sherds. One waster sherd pile (sampled by Unit 9) was disturbed and produced most of the 20th century artifacts that are found in the site assemblage (primarily bottle glass and metal can fragments).

Artifacts

Artifact recovery at the Howe Pottery was heavy, but redundant (Table 4.1). Stoneware sherds form 77.9 percent of the combined recovery and kiln furniture forms most of the remainder of the assemblage (19.5 percent). This is a clear indication that the Howe Pottery was a stoneware manufacturing facility throughout most of its life span.

Table 4.1. Howe Pottery Artifact Recovery Summary.

ARTIFACT CATEGORY	PHASE I	PHASE II	PHASE III	TOTAL
Stoneware	582	4,817	14,652	20,051
Kiln furniture	105	1,440	3,475	5,020
Activity Group		112	70	182
Kitchen Group		46	232	278
Architectural Group	81	29	54	164
Other items	6	3	14	23
Lithic debitage		1		1
Total counted artifacts	774	6,448	18,497	25,719
Brick mass (g)		126,149	18,499	144,648

Table 4.2. Howe Pottery Stoneware Surface Treatment Frequencies

TYPE	EXTERIOR	INTERIOR
Albany or Albany-like	77.2%	95.6%
Salt glaze	18.8%	1.1%
Unglazed	3.8%	2.8%
Bristol and other	0.2%	0.5%
Total:	100.0%	100.0%

Stoneware manufacturing technology at late 19th century kiln sites is better documented and understood in other areas of the South, such North Carolina (Sweezy 1984). At the Howe Pottery, the analysis revealed that the potters principally focused on the production of plain Albany-like brown-slipped utilitarian vessels. Over three-quarters of the Howe Pottery sherds are Albany or Albany-like brown-slipped on the exterior and over 95% are similarly slipped on the interior (Table 4.2). Less than one-fifth of the stoneware sherds exhibit salt glaze, but for those that do, salt glaze is better represented on exterior surfaces and nearly absent on interior surfaces. Sweezy (1984:24) indicates that the quality of salt-glazed pottery across the South declined after the Civil War.

The Hicks clay bank is believed to be a primary source for the Howe Pottery, because James Howe reopened the pit in 1889 (Branner 1908). This clay would not burn into solid stoneware, but could be used to manufacture "pots, churns, crocks, or milk pans, or into any article in which the liquid contents are not allowed to sand long," because it is very porous and absorbent (Branner 1908:183). Attempts to seal it with slip resulted in the discovery that only "Albany slip-black glaze can be used with it, as all attempts hereto made at salt glazing has resulted in failure owning to the inability of the ware to bare a sufficiently high heat" (Branner 1908:183). The use of the Hicks clay explains why such a large percentage of the Howe Pottery's stoneware is Albany or Albany-like brown-slipped.

Decoration is rare at the Howe Pottery, as less than 1 percent of the stoneware recovered is ornamented in any way. This implies that that throughout the use life of the Howe Pottery its various potters focused on the production of simple, unadorned, utilitarian vessels. Two types of decoration were recognized in the assemblage: trailed cobalt blue oxide designs and linear incised. The linear incising appears to have function as visual guides to allow for the symmetrical placement of handles.

All of the pottery at the Howe Pottery was hand "turned" on a potter's wheel. Some of the bases exhibit concentric marks on their

Figure 4.5. Drawings of representative Howe Pottery vessels.

exteriors that resulted from a twisted wire being pulled in a loop to cut a pot from the potter's wheel (Buchner 2011:Figures 6–9a and 6–11a). There is no evidence for the use of jiggers or molds at the Howe Pottery. During the early 20th century, Niloak began producing some smaller pieces on a jigger and about the same time (ca. 1915) replaced wood with natural gas for fuel (Gifford 2001:37). These changes reflect the increasing industrialization of the Niloak pottery.

No whole stoneware vessels were recovered; the site contains only 'waster' stoneware sherds—that is pieces of vessels that broke during production. Just over 20 percent of the stoneware assemblage consists of vessel sections or parts other than "body" sherds (i.e., handles, rims, bases, lids, shoulder, etc.). An attempt was made to categorize all of the vessel sections following Greer's (1981) terminology. In the Phase III recovery the most common type of vessel section is base (n=1,721), followed by rims (n=505), jug mouths (n=326), handle (n=288), shoulder (n=113), lids (n=18). Vessel types are discussed in the Consumer Behavior section.

Top row represents early (pre 1887) phase (top row) a-cobalt blue trailed salt-glazed jug; b-salt-glazed and Albany-like brown-slipped milk pan; c-salt-glazed semi-globular jug. Two lower rows represent late phase (1887–1899): d and h-Albany-like brown-slipped jugs; e and g-Albany-like brown-slipped churns; f-wooden dasher; and i and j-Albany-like brown-slipped jars.

Diameter measurements were estimated for bases by placing base fragments against a concentric arc chart. The measured bases ranged from a minimum of 3 in. to a maximum of 13 in., and the average diameter is 6.6 in. A histogram was prepared using 1–in. intervals, and it reveals that the most common three base diameters (6 in., 7 in., and 8 in.) form over 72 percent of the sample.

Sherds with capacity marks are rare. Combining the Phase II and III results, the most popular capacity mark at the Howe Pottery is the 3–gallon (n=5), followed by the 5–gallon (n=2) and the 2–gallon (n=2).

Kiln furniture refers to various clay forms that are employed during the loading kilns to "ensure the proper position of the pots" during firing (Greer 1981:217). This artifact category is unique to pottery production sites and must be considered part of the archaeological "signature" of kiln sites. With only a handful of possible exceptions, all of the 5,020 pieces of kiln furniture that were recovered during the various investigations are informal and disposable spacers that were made expeditiously while loading the kiln. The frequency of kiln "spacers" within the Howe Pottery assemblage reveals that green vessels were stacked inside the kilns, thus the kiln(s) at the Howe Pottery site must have been some type of upright kiln.

A diverse variety of kiln furniture shapes are present within the Howe Pottery assemblage. There were some general trends or types present among the kiln furniture, and one of the goals of the Phase III was to establish a kiln furniture typology. Ten types (A–J) were defined based on morphology. The most popular type (G) formed 20 percent of the typed kiln furniture, and functioned as jug mouth stoppers (Buchner 2011:Figure 6–33 and 6–37).

Draw trails are another unique artifact type that and should be considered part of the archaeological "signature" of kiln sites. They are stoneware sherds with circular to oval perforations that were placed into a kiln to test the temperature and the progress of the firing. Four draw trials were recovered from the Howe Pottery (Buchner 2011:Figure 6–8). Similar draw trails are reported from the Wilhelm's Kiln in Illinois (Gums 1996).

Discussion

Site Types

There are at least five site types associated with the Benton Pottery Industry: (1) traditional family potteries; (2) industrial potteries; (3) clay pits; (4) potter's residences; and (5) showroom locations.

Traditional Potteries The archaeological characteristics of traditional family potteries in Arkansas are best understood from the excavations at the Howe Pottery on Military Road and the McConnell-Osborne or Cumbie Pottery at Ft. Chaffee, as well as from the survey level investigations at nine other kilns, including the four in Dallas County that are NRHP-listed. The most outstanding trait is the presence of dense waster sherd piles in close proximity to a kiln feature. The sites are typically small, but have extremely high artifact densities and contain almost exclusively stoneware (or redware) fragments and kiln furniture. There is little evidence of domestic occupation at the kiln/waster sherd pile locations, but some sites exhibit evidence for related occupations nearby (i.e., within 200 m) that are interpreted as workshop facilities and/or potters' residences.

Industrial Potteries The two industrial potteries in Benton—Eagle Pottery and Niloak—were interrelated, shared facilities. C.D. "Bullet" Hyten owned or managed both. The original location of the Eagle or Niloak Pottery (3SA341) was archaeologically tested and a disturbed waster deposit was found that was generally similar to the Howe Pottery; the kiln here had been destroyed by land leveling years before the testing (Buchner 2010). Its archaeological profile is similar to the Howe Pottery because it was a family pottery established in 1870 that developed into a small factory around 1904 and was abandoned in 1912. One archaeological distinction between these two potteries is the frequency of Bristol-slipped sherds at the Eagle Pottery (12.8 percent) is much greater than at Howe Pottery (0.1 percent). Also the Eagle Pottery used ink stamped marks, versus cobalt blue stencil marks or impressed block letters at Howe Pottery.

The post-1912 the Eagle/Niloak Pottery location at Pearl Street, Site 3SA307, has not been subjected to intensive fieldwork. A walkover revealed that it is an empty lot with stoneware sherds scattered among modern dump piles (Trubitt 2004a:8). Structural remains should be more extensive there, as Sanborn Fire Insurance maps reveal that the layout of this commercial plant included multiple kilns and related facilities such as stock room, clay mill, crusher shed, and drying room. None of the other industrial potteries in Arkansas—such as the Ouachita Pottery in Hot Springs, Camark Pottery in Camden, and the Interstate Pottery in Texarkana—have been investigated archaeologically.

Clay Pits   The Benton potteries consumed large quantities of clay. It is estimated that 4,275 pounds (> 2 tons) of potter's clay were required every day at the Eagle Pottery when production was only 900 gallons per; this amounts to 555.75 tons of potter's clay per annum (Buchner 2011:8–9). As a result, numerous clay pits were developed to supply potters with their most basic and important raw material. These clay pits are a third type of landscape feature that can be interpreted as a site type associated with the Benton Pottery Industry.

Branner (1908) described eight historic potter's clay pits in Benton just after the death of the traditional pottery industry. Krueger (2008) provides a map showing the general distribution of over 30 "old pottery clay mines" distributed along Military Road and Congo Road in the Benton area. While modern developments in Benton have obliterated most of these, a few remain.

An old clay pit was found behind our hotel during the fieldwork. It is located between the I-30 frontage road and the Niloak Shopping Center on Military Road (behind the 1929 Niloak showroom). This former clay pit (now recorded as archaeological site 3SA359) has the appearance of a borrow pit on a hilltop. Following its abandonment as a clay pit it was graded and then used temporarily as an asphalt plant (probably during I-30 construction or resurfacing). A narrow band of white kaolin is clearly exposed in an eroded cut bank on the hillside. This pit is not one of the pits noted by Branner (1908), so it must be a 20th century feature. Niloak reportedly used the clay from here for one of the swirl colors.

Potter's Residences   AAS investigations at the Hyten House, the Niloak Pottery Company owners' residence, produced a fairly typical late 19th to 20th century domestic assemblage (Trubitt 2004b). Importantly, however, some limited evidence for pottery manufacture was recovered, including a concentration of stoneware waster sherds in a fill zone where a garage was once located. Three pieces of kiln furniture were also recovered (Trubitt 2004b:Figure 2), which indicates that the fill represents waste from a pottery. Only four of the distinctive swirled Niloak sherds were recovered, which was disappointing. Nonetheless, the Hyten House excavations demonstrated that unique archaeological deposits exist at potter's residences. This Craftsman style house was recently listed on the NRHP.

To the above, we can add that during the Military Road project a local informant reported that he had found Niloak pottery sherds and "nearly whole" Niloak vessels from a "test hole" in his front yard at 703 Pearl Street. This reported find is now recorded as 3SA360. Its location is only about two blocks from the Niloak Pottery, and much closer than the Hyten House, at Main and Smith streets, is to the pottery. Reportedly, Niloak potters tossed wasters into a street side ditch here that subsequently was buried. The presence of this material here suggests that waster disposal patterns at the Niloak Pottery had an informal element.

Showrooms There is archival evidence for two showrooms where finished vessels were sold. One was the original Niloak/Eagle showroom at 3SA341 on Military Road (Gifford 2001:36) and the other was the 1929 Niloak showroom on Military Road where the historic marker for Niloak is located today. The pre-1912 showroom was a vernacular frame structure, while the 1929 Niloak showroom was a "magnificent" structure with a Spanish façade (Gifford 2001:24). There is no archaeological data available regarding showrooms. The artifact pattern of showrooms is expected to be similar to potters' residences: a fairly typical domestic assemblage with the addition of breakage from the showroom.

Archaeological Correlates

The archaeological correlates of kilns vary depending on the type and preservation. At the Peebles Place Kiln (3SH15), the only evidence for a kiln is a burned area 9.1 m (30 ft.) in diameter surrounded by waster sherds, while at the J.D. Wilbur Pottery (3WA208) a well-preserved groundhog kiln exists as an above ground feature. Depressed features with glazed brick or stone are interpreted as collapsed groundhog kilns.

They are reported at Welch's Kiln #2 (3DA8), Welch Pottery Works (3DA9), Bird Kiln (3DA12), and at the McConnell-Osborne or Cumbie Pottery (3SB596). At the latter site, the collapsed kiln measured 6.1–x-3.0 m (20–x-10 ft.) and was built almost entirely of sandstone and mud mortar. In Benton, the remains of what was probably a ca. 1904 Stewart patent kiln were discovered during land leveling at the original Hyten Kiln/Eagle Pottery (3SA341); this kiln was destroyed/melted in a fiery accident and was fully loaded with warped vessels when found. Finally, there are the two superimposed brick kilns at the Howe Pottery, with the more recent scove kiln being well preserved and the underlying Round Kiln was only partly preserved.

The attributes of the other features and facilities associated with traditional potteries in Benton–such as clay mills, vats, woodpiles, and workshops—are not well understood.

Pottery Layout and Patterns

Because there is little information regarding this theme for late 19th century kiln sites in Benton, the Howe Pottery data is significant. The locations of the waster sherd piles offer some clues to pottery layout. They were likely located in low-traffic areas in the immediate vicinity of the kiln(s). Pottery layouts, and workshop interiors in general, tend to be compact (see Sweezy 1984 for various examples) and the reason is assumed to be associated with economy of effort as clay moves from the mill to the wheel, to the drying racks, and then to the kiln. Based on this information, archaeologists developed an interpretive drawing of the Howe Pottery layout (Buchner 2011:Figure 7–5).

The Howe Pottery deposit only extends over a 40–x-40 m area, thus it follows the tight or small site size pattern. We can only speculate how the Howe Pottery was laid out based on a few archival photos (Smith and Rodgers 2011:Figure 3–84; "A pottery scene sixty years ago" in the *Benton Courier* [1937]; and the Marshall Pottery in Texas [Sweezy 1984:147]). These photos suggest that late 19th century traditional potteries in Benton contained a fairly compact or clustered set of facilities, with round kilns standing in close proximity to a frame workshop, with woodpiles and waster piles being clustered around the kiln(s). At the Howe Pottery, the workshop was most likely a vernacular frame structure that was aligned parallel to the Military Road. Given the locations of the major waster sherd piles and the round kiln, it was inferred where the workshop was not located. The Phase I survey shovel testing results (see Buchner 2009:Figure 3–2) suggest that the workshop was likely located downhill (southwest) from the Round Kiln, because the area to the northeast produced limited evidence of use or occupation. The southwesterly location places the workshop closer to a water source, an intermittent stream a short distance down from the site.

More generally, the presence of nearby clay pits was probably one of the driving factors in the kiln site selection process, along with the presence of the Old Military Road. Branner described two Woosley clay pits (1908) within a half mile of the Howe Pottery. The Woosley clay was reportedly one of the two best local potter's clays. However, although the Woosley pits were closer, Mr. J. Howe reopened the Hicks clay bank in 1889 (Branner 1908:183), a pit that was located approximately one mile south-southeast of the Howe Pottery, near the Iron Mountain railroad.

Consumer Behavior

Consumer behavior was traced through an in-depth analysis of the quantity and types of vessels that were produced at the Howe Pottery. The vessel types and capacity frequencies documented via the analysis of the waster sherds are assumed to reflect consumer behavior. That is, the more frequent vessel types and sizes were more popular, and this reflects stoneware customers' needs. Combined, jugs, jars, and churns form over 86 percent of the known vessel type sherd assemblage at the Howe Pottery. This statistic reveals that the potters there were largely focused on the production of these common and utilitarian vessel forms. Because so few of the pieces were decorated, it is assumed that the consumers were interested in functionality above all else.

During the early 20th century there was a reaction to the banal design of mass-produced products that, in part, caused the death of the Howe Pottery and many other traditional stoneware potteries. The art pottery movement introduced artist designed and decorated non-utilitarian wares to the market. The Niloak Pottery in Benton was the local expression of the art pottery movement and the swirled, Mission-style pottery they produced until the 1940s is still collected. Today the Niloak Pottery, not a traditional pottery, is the best known pottery from Benton (Bennett and Worthen 1990:149).

Data from the Howe Pottery suggest that during the golden age of traditional potteries in Benton, the vessel type most in demand were jugs. Jug sherds represent over 49 percent of the known vessels in the sherd assemblage. Other potteries in Benton also focused heavily on jug production—the Henderson Pottery was also known as the Benton Jug

Factory. Additionally, period newspapers jokingly referred to Benton as Jugtown.

Jars and churns are the second best represented vessel form within the combined Phase II and III Howe Pottery assemblages. Jar and churn sherds form 37.4 percent of the of the known vessel type sherd assemblage. Jars and churns were combined for analysis because they can be mistaken for each (Greer 1981:93), particularly when dealing with sherds (as archaeologists often are), as opposed to whole vessels.

Bowls are less well represented (13.4 percent), and we can only infer that demand for them was much lower. Nearly all the bowls are milk pan sherds recovered from an early, sealed site context associated with the round kiln. We interpret this to mean that bowl production was a minor focus during the early period of production at the Howe Pottery, and that during the later period (post ca. 1888–1899) the production shifted almost entirely to the manufacture of jugs, jars and churns.

Several other clay products were produced at the Howe Pottery. During the early phase, domed-topped ornamental brick appears to have been produced, given the recovery of one whole and one fragmentary specimen from the round kiln foundation (Buchner 2011:Figure 6–44). The exterior surface of these bricks is rough and pitted, and given their rough appearance, they were most likely intended to be garden path or driveway borders.

A unique thick base, which is tentatively construed as a pediment for a ceramic funerary marker (Buchner 2011:Figure 6–24), was recovered in the general surface collection and is interpreted as part of the late phase production. As noted above it is highly similar to a pediment used to support a 1916 ceramic grave monument in an Upshur County, Texas, cemetery (Greer 1981:125). Benton potters produced a few ceramic grave monuments in the late 19th century; an example is on display at the Gann Museum in Benton. As only one example of this artifact category was recovered, it is believed that the potters at the Howe Pottery rarely made such items.

The rectangular scove kiln is the most visible evidence for the production of other clay products at the Howe Pottery.

Arkansas Stoneware Manufacturer's Marks

In general, there is limited data regarding 19th century Arkansas potter's marks. Bennett and Worthen (1990) illustrate the following 19th century marks on whole vessels:

Inscribed Joseph & Nathaniel Bird, 1843
Impressed/Stamped J.N. BIRD
Impressed/Stamped WB on an alkaline glazed jug (attributed to
the Bird Family)
Impressed/Stamped W (for Welch)
Impressed/Stamped J.D. WILBUR over Boonsboro, Ark.
Impressed/Stamped ROARK & WILBUR over Boonsboro, Ark.

Among the Benton potteries, the best known marks date to the 20th century and are associated with the Eagle Pottery and Niloak Pottery; Gifford (2001:47–51) illustrates many of these. Archaeological investigations at the Original Hyten Kiln/Eagle Pottery (3SA341) resulted in the recovery of two types of Eagle Pottery marks: a blue rubber-stamped eagle in circle mark (Buchner 2010:Figure 6–10a) and a blue rubber-stamped EAGLE POTTERY mark. A butter crock on display at the Gann Museum exhibits a black rubber-stamped eagle in circle mark that is identical in all aspects except color to the archaeologically recovered example. Gifford (2001:13) dates the black eagle in circle logo to ca. 1905. The eagle in circle motif appears to have been replaced by the plain block EAGLE POTTERY mark and/or "The Eagle/ POTTERY/ Benton, Ark." enclosed within a rectangle mark (Buchner 2011:Figure 7–6). This shift appears to have started ca. 1910, before the pottery relocated to Pearl Street in 1912.

Nineteenth century Benton pottery marks are not well known or well documented. However one example exists in the Historic Arkansas Museum's collection. It is a late 19th century salt-glazed vessel with two Lafayette Glass marks (Buchner 2011:Figure 7–7). It is impressed or stamped GLAƧƧ (the SS are backwards) in an arch below the rim and under that, a cobalt blue stencil reads L. GLASS./ BENTON./ ARK." This mark is highly significant because it is associated with the founder of the Benton Pottery Industry. It is tentatively dated ca. 1868–1872.

As a result of the excavations at the Howe Pottery, two types of previously unrecognized late 19th century potter's marks were identified. Three fragmentary examples of an embossed mark on the heel of Albany-like slipped vessels were recovered, and all are from the northwestern waster pile. When whole this mark is believed to have read:

MANUFACTURED BY
J. J. LEECH
BENTON, ARK.

The discovery of the impressed LEECH stoneware sherds at the Howe Pottery is significant, as we have archival evidence associating J. J. Leech with the site. These sherds provide a critical link between the archaeological record and the archival record. The LEECH marked sherds are tentatively dated ca. 1888 because that is only year J. J. Leech paid the taxes for the site property.

Archaeologists recovered two fragmentary examples of the second recognized mark. Both exhibit a stenciled, cobalt-blue mark on a cream-colored, salt-glazed vessel exterior. The larger specimen consists of several conjoining sherds from Unit 10 Level 3, and on it the stenciled lettering is surrounded by a wheat crescent or sprig motif (Buchner 2011:Figure 6–5a). When whole, this mark is believed to have read:

CALDWELL
WHOLESALE DEALER
IN
STONEWARE
BENTON
ARK.

As previously noted, Henry T. Caldwell worked at Lafayette Glass' pottery in Benton during 1868–1870 and purchased it in 1870. After 1872 Caldwell ceased being a potter and became a merchant stoneware dealer. This mark must date after 1872, and is thought to be associated with the A. L. Herrick period (1886 and before) at the Howe Pottery. More generally, Greer (1981:174) notes that after the mid-19th century, cobalt blue stencils gained popularity for labeling vessels with merchant's names.

Unfortunately no Howe marks were recovered despite the recovery of over 21,000 stoneware sherds during the various investigations at the Howe Pottery. The implication is that James Howe rarely, if ever, marked his pottery during the decade he operated the pottery.

Conclusion

The excavations at the Howe Pottery resulted in the recovery of important new information regarding the late 19th century Benton Pottery Industry. Probably the most significant archaeological findings were the discovery of the superimposed kilns and the identification of two previously unrecognized maker's marks. The Howe Pottery flourished during the peak period of traditional stoneware pottery production in

Benton, and was one of several potteries on Military Road near the clay pits. Combined, these potteries were the leading industry in Benton and they dominated stoneware production in Arkansas. The rise and fall of the Howe Pottery mirrors local and national trends in traditional stoneware pottery production. The knowledge and skill accumulated by these 19th century potters laid the foundation for the development of the art pottery, Niloak, in Benton during the early 20th century. While the Howe Pottery is interpreted as just one of many typical, late 19th century, traditional, small, family stoneware works, its archaeological record is a treasure, because all the other contemporary potteries have been destroyed or heavily impacted by modern developments.

Acknowledgments

A number of archaeologists, historians, and interested individuals assisted me during the various phases of the Howe Pottery investigations and I offer my warmest thanks to them. In particular, Milton Hughes and John Miller (Arkansas State Highway and Transportation Department) provided support throughout the project, and supplied copies of valuable research materials they had assembled. Mary Beth Trubitt and Skip Stewart-Abernathy (Arkansas Archeological Society), and Beverley Watkins also provided important research materials that improved the quality of the technical reports. George McCluskey (Arkansas Historic Preservation Program) and Randal Looney (Federal Highway Administration) offered guidance during the preparation of the data recovery plan. Swannee Bennett took the time to show me the Historic Arkansas Museum's impressive collection of whole stoneware vessels. Arline Rainey, daughter of C. D. Hyten, was also kind enough to visit the site after the kiln was exposed. My apologies to anyone inadvertently omitted.

REFERENCES

Arkansas Democrat
1904   Benton, Capital of the Saline, Prosperous and Progressive. *Arkansas Democrat*, 5 June 1904, Section II, Pages 10–11.
Bennett, Swannee, and William B. Worthen
1990   *Arkansas Made: A Survey of the Decorative, Mechanical, and Fine Arts Produced in Arkansas, 1819–1870.* Volume One. The University of Arkansas Press, Fayetteville.
Blakely, Jeffrey A.
1990a   *Archeological Testing of Three Euro-American Sites, Fort Chaffee, Arkansas.* Archeological Assessments Inc. Report No. 99 and Fort Chafee

Cultural Resources Studies No. 9. Submitted to the U.S. Army Corps of Engineers, Little Rock District. On file at the Arkansas Archeological Survey, Fayetteville as AMASDA #3308.

1990b   The Nineteenth Century Pottery Industry in Sebastian County, Arkansas. *Arkansas Historical Quarterly* 49(1):57–77.

Branner, John C.
1908   *The Clays of Arkansas.* United States Geological Survey Bulletin 351.

Buchner, C. Andrew
2009   *Phase I Cultural Resources Survey of the Benton Military Road Improvement Corridor, Saline County, Arkansas.* Panamerican Consultants, Inc. Report 29228. Final report submitted to Carter Burgess, Inc.

2010   *Phase II NRHP Testing of Two Kiln Sites on Military Road in Benton, Saline County, Arkansas.* Panamerican Consultants, Inc. Report 29228.2. Final report submitted to Jacobs Engineering Group, Inc.

2011   *Data Recovery Excavations at the Howe Pottery (3SA340) on Military Road in Benton, Saline County, Arkansas.* Panamerican Consultants, Inc. Report 29228.3. Final report submitted to Jacobs Engineering Group, Inc.

Gifford, David Edwin
2001   *Collector's Encyclopedia of Niloak: A Reference and Value Guide.* Collector Book, a division of Schroeder Publishing Co., Inc.

Goodspeed Publishing Co.
1889   *The Goodspeed Biographical and Historical Memoirs of Southern Arkansas.* Goodspeed, Chicago.

Greer, G. H.
1981   *American Stonewares, The Art and Craft of Utilitarian Potters.* Schiffer Publishing, Exton, Pennsylvania.

Gums, Bonnie L.
1996   Yellow Ware in Illinois: The Wilhelms' Kiln. *Ohio Valley Historical Archaeology* 11(1996):69–86.

Hughes, Milton
2008   3SA340 Site Survey Form. Arkansas Highway and Transportation Department. On file at the Arkansas Archeological Survey, Fayetteville.

Mansberger, Floyd
1995   "Nineteenth Century Pottery Production in Illinois." Paper presented at the Society for Historical Archaeology Conference on Historical and Underwater Archaeology, Washington, DC

Peres, Yanya M., and Jessica B. Connatser
2008   Brick Making as a Local Industry in Antebellum Kentucky and Tennessee. *Tennessee Archaeology* 3(2):105–122.

Rainey, Arlene Hyten
1973   The History of Niloak Pottery. Four part series in the *Saline County Pacesetter*, March 21 and 28, April 4 and 11.

1987   The Hytens of Saline County—111 Years. *The Saline* 2(2):64–69. The Saline County History and Heritage Society, Inc.

Rhodes, Daniel
1968   *Kilns: Design, Construction and Operation.* Second Edition. Chilton Book
        Company. Radnor, Pennsylvania.
Smith, Samuel D.
1972   Arkansas Kiln Sites. *Field Notes* 95:7–10. Arkansas Archeological Society.
Smith, Samuel D., and Stephen D. Cox
1977   Archaeological Investigations of the Hermitage Brick Kilns. In *Results of
        the 1976 Season of the Hermitage Archaeology Project,* S. D. Smith, F. W.
        Brigance, E. Breitburg, S. D. Cox, and M.Martin, Pp. 81–95. Tennessee
        Division of Archaeology. Report submitted to the Ladies Hermitage
        Association and the Tennessee American Revolution Bicentennial
        Commission.
Smith, Samuel D., and Stephen T. Rogers
1979   *A Survey of Historic Pottery Making in Tennessee.* Tennessee Department of
        Environment and Conservation, Division of Archaeology, Research Series 3.
2011   *Tennessee Potteries, Pots, and Potters—1790s to 1950, Volumes 1 and
        2.* Tennessee Department of Environment and Conservation, Division of
        Archaeology, Research Series 18.
Smith, Samuel D., and Charlotte A. Watrin
1986   Zimmerle Brick Kiln. *Tennessee Anthropologist* 11(2):132–144.
Starr, Mary Evelyn
2003   Exploring the History of the Arkansas Stoneware Industry. *The Arkansas
        Archaeologist* 42:1–14. Arkansas Archeological Society, Fayetteville.
Sweezy, Nancy
1984   *Raised in Clay: The Southern Pottery Tradition.* The University of North
        Carolina Press, Chapel Hill.
Trubitt, Mary Beth
2004a   The Archaeology and History of Charles Hyten's Niloak Pottery.
        Unpublished manuscript on file at the Arkansas Archeological Survey,
        Henderson State University, Arkadelphia.
2004b   Archeology at the Hyten House. *Field Notes* 319, July/August, 2004.
        Arkansas Archaeological Survey Newsletter.
Watkins, Beverley
1980   The Bird and Welch Potteries: Small Industry in Nineteenth Century
        Arkansas. Manuscript on file at the Arkansas Archeological Survey.
1982   The Bird, Welch, and Culberson Potteries: Local Industries in Nineteenth
        Century Dallas County, Arkansas. Arkansas Endowment for the Humanities
        Mini-grant 248–62–82M. On file at the Arkansas Archeological Survey.
Winburn, Hardy L., Jr.
1940   *Saline County Pottery Since 1868.* Niloak Pottery Company, second printing.
        Benton, Arkansas.

5

THE SPREAD OF TECHNOLOGY TO A RURAL ARKANSAS BLACKSMITH SHOP

Alicia B. Valentino

In the 1860s, Peter Van Winkle established what would become known as the "most modern and powerful mill in the west" in northwest Arkansas. Since 1997, archaeologists have studied the mill complex in Van Hollow, including its enslaved worker housing; the Van Winkle home and garden; the saw and gristmill area; and on-site ancillary facilities, including the blacksmith shop.

While archaeological investigations and the documentary record have focused on the saw- and gristmill complex, excavations at the blacksmith shop have yielded interesting data about pre- and post-Civil War operations of the shop. This article describes the excavations of the blacksmith shop, including its layout after the war, material remains, and the shop's role among the larger Van Winkle operations. Additionally, this paper touches on the workers' integration of new industrial practices in blacksmithing, based on practical details of daily operations observed in the archaeological record.

Introduction

The site of Van Winkle's mill in northwestern Arkansas remains well known within the contemporary community. Peter Van Winkle established a legend there. Unfortunately, only derivative and vaguely cited historical reports exist to tell the story of his legacy (such as Black 1960; Black 1979; Elliott 1959).

In the 1850s, Peter Van Winkle, a New York-born Arkansan of Dutch decent, left breaking land and building wagons to start a sawmill in Benton County. His operation began like others in the area, with a small, animal-powered outfit. Shortly after the establishment of this first mill, Van Winkle moved several miles from the White River into Van Hollow, rebuilding his facilities with a steam-powered engine. The success of this endeavor allowed him to develop a self-contained community with a plantation style home, housing for the twelve enslaved African American laborers who were the core of the mill's work force, and ancillary facilities including a blacksmith shop (Brandon and Davidson 2003:9).

Van Winkle had obvious Confederate sympathies, having been contracted to build Confederate barracks for soldiers stationed nearby, and having named two of his children after prominent Confederate figures: Jefferson Davis Van Winkle (b. 1861) and Robert E. Lee Van Winkle (b. 1863) (Brandon and Davidson 2003:9; Hicks 1990:175–262). During the Civil War, Peter Van Winkle, his family, and his eighteen enslaved workers fled to Texas. In their absence, Confederate forces burned the mill and other structures in the hollow to the ground to prevent them from falling into Union hands (Hicks 1990:23; Rothrock 1973:64). Upon his return, Van Winkle rebuilt his small community and constructed a steam-powered sawmill and gristmill complex. Said to be the most advanced mill in the region, it reportedly had a 150-horsepower engine with a 24-foot flywheel and three steam boilers (Hicks 1990:26; Rothrock 1973:65; United States Census Office 1880). Further expansion of these operations included three satellite mills in nearby towns (Brandon and Davidson 2003:12).

Peter Van Winkle died of a stroke on February 16, 1882, while walking with his wife, Temperance, on the streets of Fayetteville. For the next year, John Steele took over the operations of the mill until J.A.C. Blackburn, a neighbor and Peter's son-in-law, could manage the mill. He assumed Peter's title as "Lumber King" (Goodspeed Publishing Company 1884:107–108). When Blackburn moved with his second wife to nearby Rogers in 1890, he combined the operations in Van Hollow with his own at the War Eagle Mill. The machinery in Van Hollow was subsequently purchased by Tom Blackburn in 1902 and shipped to Danville, Arkansas (Benton County Pioneer 1963:13–14; Brandon and Davidson 2003).

A group called the Pathfinders purchased the Van Winkle Mill site at this time, later defaulting on payment (Brandon and Davidson 2003:14; Conable 1903; Rogers Democrat 1910). There are no indications that the mill was in operation during World War I when a group of workers dynamited the flywheel to sell as scrap metal, given the high prices at the time (Arkansas Democrat 1959; Benton County Pioneer 1962:17;

Brandon and Davidson 2003:14; Mitchell 1969). From 1944 until 1960, Vernon T. West and his wife lived in the Van Winkle house and operated a small sawmill for the Hobbs Western Tie and Timber Company. In 1960, they moved to a nearby hilltop and operations ceased (Brandon and Davidson 2003:14; Miller 1966; Mitchell 1969).

Present day Van Winkle Hollow (hereafter called Van Hollow following USGS conventions), is located in the Hobbs State Park and Conservation Area on Highway 12 near Rogers, Arkansas. Development of the area, including the addition of Highway 12 and the creation of Beaver Lake in 1960, caused adverse effects to the preservation of the Van Winkle site. However, subsequent interpretation efforts in the hollow helped to preserve the integrity of subsurface materials.

Study of the hollow began in 1997 with survey and limited testing at the Van Winkle house site. Continued investigation in 1999 consisted of excavating a single-family residence: likely that of Aaron Van Winkle or another one of the freedmen and their families who remained at the mill after emancipation (Brandon et al. 2000:55). Excavation of the mill area began in 2003 (Brandon and Davidson 2003). Unfortunately, geophysical testing at the mill proper, using electrical resistance, magnetic susceptibility, and ground penetrating radar, yielded poor results. This is likely due to site degradation and flooding from nearby Beaver Lake and Little Clifty Creek. Geophysical results from the blacksmith shop area, on the other hand, helped identify the forge and the rear wall of the shop (Brandon and Davidson 2003:36), which underwent partial excavation. The blacksmith shop was excavated almost in its entirety in 2005.

Peppering the landscape during the 18th and 19th centuries, blacksmith shops provided essential services to the public, repairing and manufacturing items for most everyone. These artisans were essential to the success of early settlement and the development of new areas (Sabo III 1990:146). Everyday tasks of the frontier blacksmith included making nails, tools, wagon parts, agricultural and domestic products, and shoeing horses, to name only a few (Lasansky 1980:24; McBride 1988:87; Reichman 1991:122). Historic records suggest that in an average day, a smith spent 40 percent of his time horseshoeing, 20 percent working on agriculture-related pieces, 14 percent on wagon repair, and the remainder associated with tinkering or making and repairing building or carriage hardware (Wylie 1990:47).

As the 19th century progressed, many people turned to mass-produced items, and as a result, economic and social patterns changed.

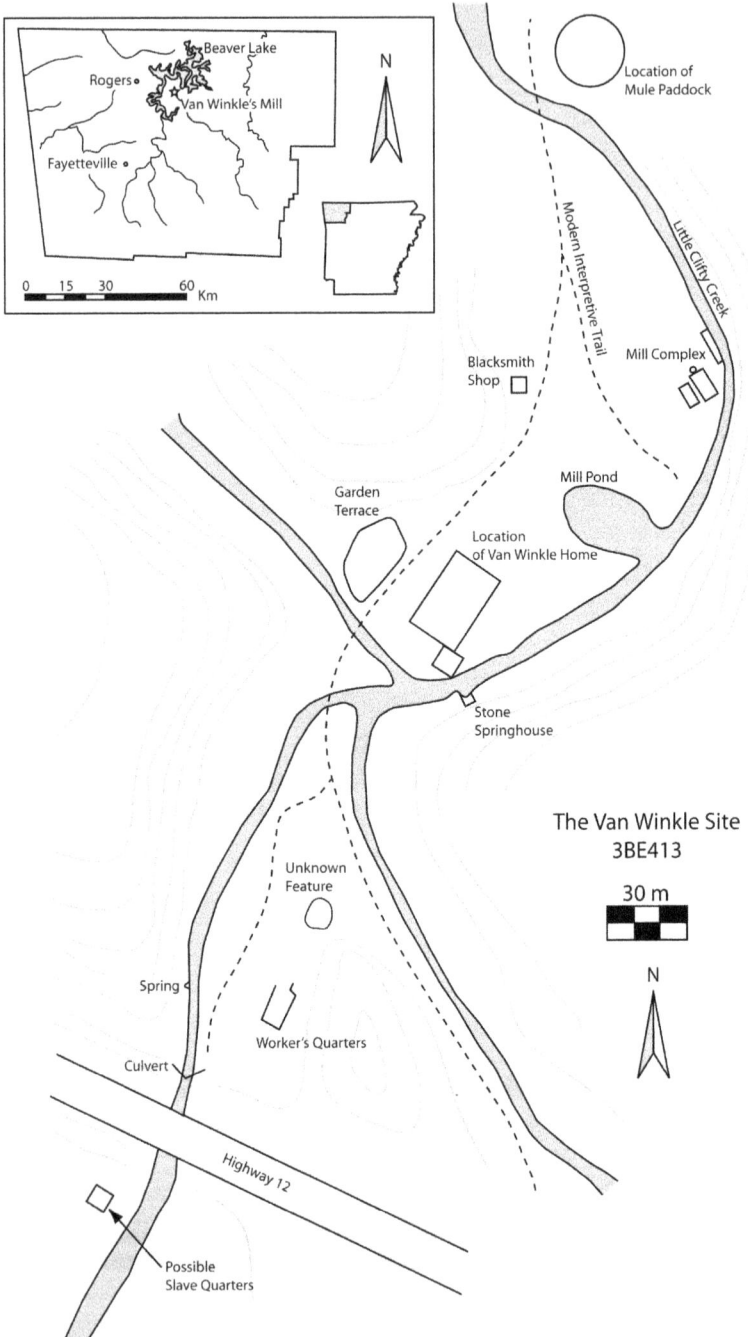

Figure 5.1. Features identified in Van Hollow, as of 2003 (after Brandon and Davidson 2003:16).

People purchased inexpensive new products rather than paying a black-smith to sharpen or restore older items (Smith 1966:44). The blacksmith, too, was not immune to changing consumer practices. Often, smiths bought factory-made tools that were as good as, if not better than, those tools they made themselves (Smith 1966:44). Eventually, blacksmithing declined almost completely.

Excavation of the Van Winkle shop offers a look at smithing practice within this rural hollow, and the results of work at the site contribute to our understanding of cultural memory in the Arkansas Ozarks (Brandon 2004). These excavations have provided interpretations of the layout of the shop both before and after the Civil War, offer an assessment of the impact and contributions of the shop to Van Winkle's operations and the local economy, and suggest how the Van Winkle blacksmith attempted to integrate new industrial practices on this backwoods frontier upon his return to the hollow following the Civil War.

Excavations at the Blacksmith Shop

Testing of the blacksmith shop began in 2000 with the identification of the shop itself during a systematic survey of the northern portion of the hollow. A single one-by-one meter test unit yielded horse tack, mule shoe fragments, nails, bolts and washers, along with handfuls of rusted, un-diagnostic metal (Brandon and Davidson 2003:31). Geophysical testing of the area between 2001 and 2002 revealed three anomalies (Lockhart and Brandon 2003). Ground-truthing of the first anomaly revealed the shop's rear wall on the western edge of the grid, comprised of a continu-ous line of stone slabs—up to two courses thick in some places—and 20–50 centimeters wide. Excavation at the second anomaly uncovered a large amount of ferrous metal, mostly stock, but no structural remains (Brandon and Davidson 2003:44).

The third anomaly was discovered to be the forge box. Excavation units here revealed large stone slabs finished with a thick layer of mor-tar to even the surface and allow for level placement of brick walls—approximately four courses as deciphered from the brick scatter. This means that the forge box would have been roughly hip-height for the smith. Sand and native sediment filled the interior of the box (Brandon and Davidson 2003:42).

Archaeologists also used magnetic fractioning to determine the work zones in the shop. When work is performed on an anvil, small sparks fly off the metal, cooling and turning to hammerscale. As more work occurs, concentrations of hammerscale collect on the shop floor. This waste, usually flat and thin, can be a telltale sign of the primary work zone. Magnetic fractioning is performed by systematically collecting soil samples, which are subsequently ground and dried. After combining a 10 gram sample in a beaker with 100 mL of acetone and a pre-weighed Teflon-coated magnetic stirring bar, the mixture is shaken. The original bar is then removed and replaced with a second pre-weighed bar. The beaker is shaken for another 30 minutes, at which time the two bars are dried and weighed. The magnetic fraction for each of the systematically collected samples uses the formula: [(weight of bars after immersion-weight of clean bars)/10g] x100 (Light 1984:41).

Use of magnetic fractioning at Fort St. Joseph in Canada (Light 1984:40–42) and the Pittsburgh and Boston Copper Harbor Mining Company in Michigan (Madson 2002:130) indicated a clear pattern across those shops, identifying the work area and anvil location. Magnetic fractioning was also successful here (Brandon et al. 2003). The results indicated that the smith might have used the area west and southwest of the forge for heavy metal working. Artifacts recovered in those areas support this, including horse and mule shoes and wagon parts (Brandon and Davidson 2003:49–50).

Data recovery excavations of the blacksmith shop in 2005 uncovered the location of the anvil base (which was indicated with the magnetic fractioning) and unearthed the entirety of the hearth. The interior of the box had a sandy soil, as first discovered during the 2001 excavations. In addition to the fallen courses of brick that originally composed the forge walls, fallen stones west of the forge likely represented the chimney.

Also identified in 2005 were two occupation zones, pre-1860 (Layer 3) and post-1865 (Layer 1), separated by a thick layer of native sediment (Layer 2). The pre-1860 zone had a boundary just beyond the western and southwestern edge of the forge box, continuing north for an unknown distance. It ended just past unit 20. Although the edge of the pre-1860 zone could not identified, it could not continue much further due to topographic constraints.

Excavation of the shop did not reach the depth of Layer 3 in all units because towards the end of excavations, the intention was to focus on locating the boundaries of the shop, necessitating the opening of more units to cover a larger area. Regardless, the data collected was sufficient for material comparison of both the pre-1860 and post-1865 occupations.

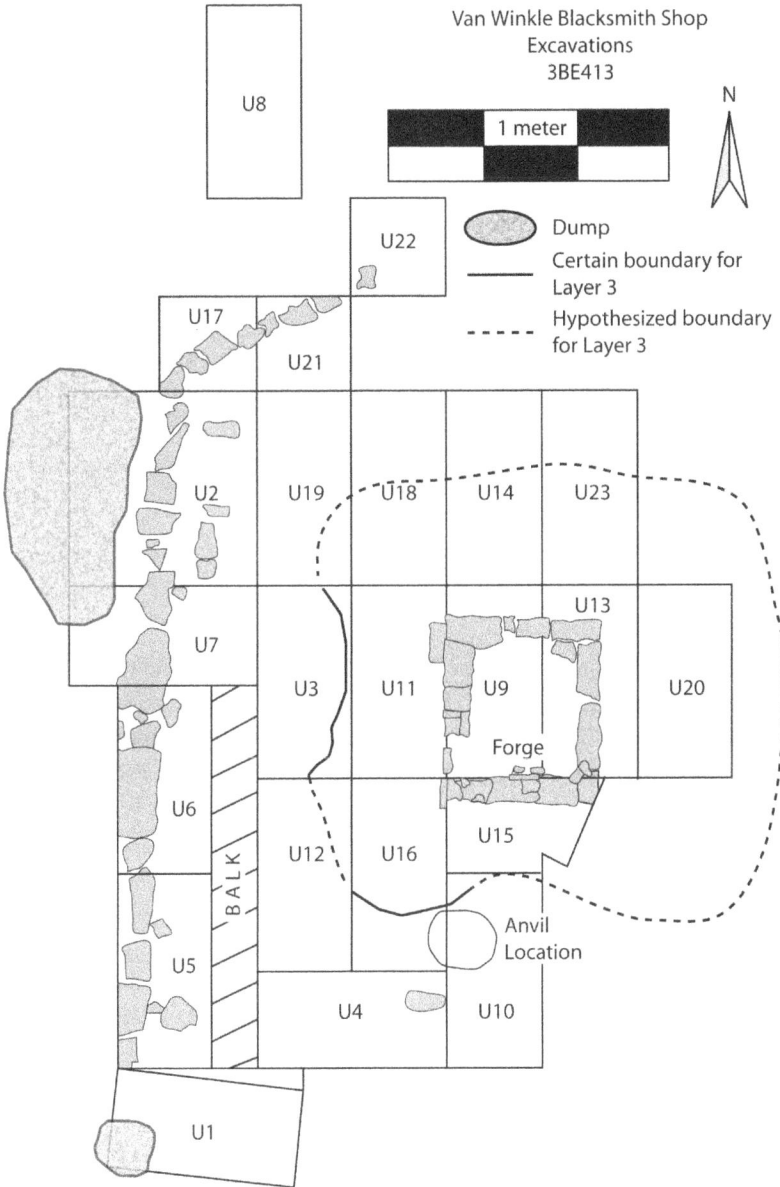

Figure 5.2. Delineation of Layer 3 and dump areas from the blacksmith shop excavations.

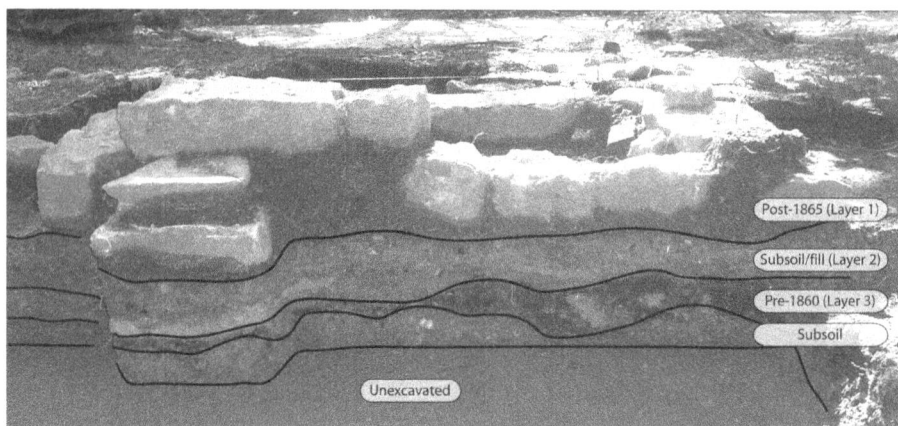

Figure 5.3. Stratigraphy underneath the forge box, looking east.

Layout

When used together, the magnetic fractioning, artifacts, and wall remains helped differentiate the post-1865 layout. The rear (west) wall generally ran north to south, taking a 45-degree turn at its northern end. This wall probably functioned as reinforcement, preventing erosion from the hillside behind the shop from entering the building, rather than as a structural foundation. This hypothesis was supported by the quantity of colluvium found in the units nearest the slope (units 1, 2, and 17). The remaining three walls not represented by archaeological features were probably timber, as evidenced by the quantity of large pennyweight nails found during excavation. Although these three walls may have been open, oftentimes blacksmiths relied on darkness to gauge metal color (Andrews 1994:10). Likewise, any drafts from having an open shop could affect the fire.

Work Area

The forge box provides a clear indication of the major work area because the feature itself is extant. Near the forge box was the anvil stump's former location as determined by its size and depth, the magnetic fractioning data, and the quantity of materials pulled from this feature. Upon removal of the stump by the smith, scrap metal lying in the area was pushed into the void.

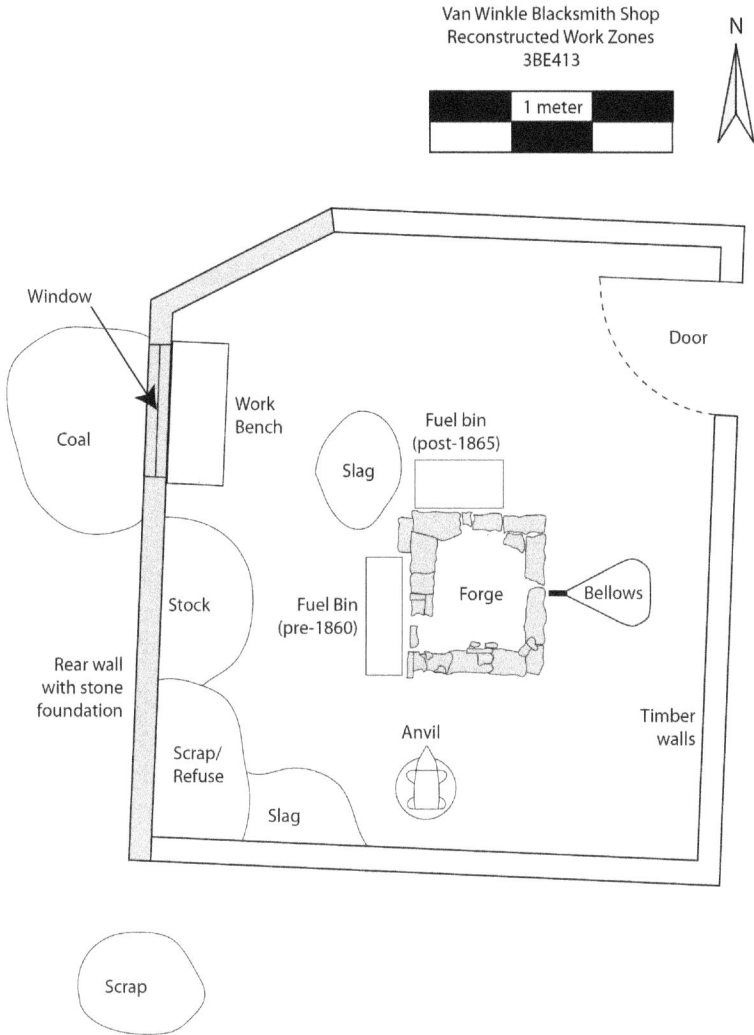

Figure 5.4. Proposed layout of the Van Winkle Blacksmith Shop.

There is no evidence of a floor-mounted bellows, which is also part of the work area. This may be because it hung from the ceiling, leaving no signature, or the signature was disturbed. Aside from the presence of a post-mold, the other way to ascertain the bellows' location is the presence of scrap or stock at its base from metalworking, much like that found in unit 20 to the east of the forge box.

The workbench, the final component, is typically located close to the anvil, within one to one-and-a-half meters, and was distinguished by magnetic fractioning data, nearby scrap, and its location near a window for proper lighting (Light 1984:58–59). Though window glass was found throughout the shop, the highest concentration was near the northern end of the west wall in unit 2. Although this area is not directly adjacent to the primary work zone, there are many high magnetic fractioning readings from this area.

General Storage Areas

General Stock Area   To differentiate the general stock area required the classification of 'stock.' The framework used here included the metal being in those forms in which stock is available: bar, strap, or sheet. The majority of the stock recovered came from along the middle interior of the west wall of the shop in both the pre-1860 and post-1865 occupations. Smaller scatters near the forge box and at the south wall of the shop are probably the result of cutting during anvil work.

General Scrap Area   The remainder of the unidentifiable metal was classified as scrap. The dispersion of this metal across the shop, corroborated by the low magnetic fractioning results, indicates that the general scrap area was in the southwest corner of the shop in both pre-1860 and post-1865 layers. The other high concentrations were found in the extensive rodent burrows encountered throughout unit 20. An external scrap area was found just south of the shop as well.

General Fuel Storage Area   The third component of the general storage area is the fuel bin. The distribution of charcoal in the pre-1860 and post-1865 occupations indicate that prior to the Civil War, the highest concentration of charcoal was just west of the forge box. Following the War this area was north of the forge box near the slag pile.

In the postbellum period, the highest coal deposits are near the pre-1860 charcoal distribution to the west of the forge box, as well as in a dump area on the exterior of the back wall in unit 2. Before the war, the highest coal concentration was in unit 20. While trade manuals do not suggest keeping the fuel as close to the forge box as demonstrated here, the blacksmith apparently had little concern for the safety hazard.

Based on recovery, coal became prominent in the post-1865 occupation layer, suggesting that it became the fuel of choice for the blacksmith here. The quantity of charcoal present is perhaps a non-issue in the post-

1865 layer since many smiths who used coal continued to use charcoal to initiate the forge fire.

The choice of coal is interesting, as the smith used anthracite, not bituminous coal. The latter was scant throughout the shop. Anthracite was not the preferred coal for blacksmithing because it did not burn freely and went to ash before forming coke, making it impractical (Lasansky 1980:14). The use of anthracite does not appear to be due to non-availability of bituminous coal, as seven western Arkansas coal fields were producing bituminous coal and only two local mines produced anthracite (Collier 1907:85).

Domestic Area

The distribution of personal artifacts, including tin cans, buttons, ceramics, and bottle glass, to name a few, were highly concentrated in the southwest corner of the shop. Otherwise, there is no clear pattern to the personal artifacts, and the shop may only have been used for blacksmithing, with most of the food consumption off-site. It is also possible that the few containers recovered were used for storage within the shop.

Refuse Area

Because of the locations of the scrap pile and domestic remains, the southwest corner of the shop was probably a refuse area. The distribution of slag across the site indicates a dumping area northwest of the forge for the post-1865 occupation. The pre-1860 occupation has the majority of the slag concentrated in unit 20. The concentration of slag in the northern part of the shop also could have resulted in the high magnetic fractioning data and presence of hammerscale in unit 11. This would have been an advantageous place for a slag pile because it was close to the forge and was out of the way of the blacksmith's work area.

Layout Interpretation

In determining the layout of the Van Winkle blacksmith shop, three points of interest arise. First, the reconstructed work areas of the Van Winkle blacksmith shop suggest that this blacksmith was not necessarily following a preferred shop layout. The most obvious difference here as compared to other blacksmith shops is that the forge is not against a wall, making it an obstacle in the center of the shop. This is not extraordinary, merely uncommon for the period. Another difference is the proximity of the fuel area to the forge box, creating a fire hazard. There is also no designated domestic area, which is uncommon. Moreover, the workbench is far from the anvil and primary working side of the forge, yet the density of window glass from this area and its proximity to the scrap pile make a decent case for its location (as well as the lack of space near the working side of the forge to place a workbench). Second, the smith appears to have switched from charcoal to coal upon his return to the shop following the Civil War, using anthracite coal, not bituminous. Third, the post-1865 forge is a charcoal designed-forge, rather than a coal forge, despite the fuel being used.

The Artifact Assemblage

During the 2000, 2001, 2002, and 2005 field seasons, archaeologists recovered over 4,300 artifacts from the blacksmith shop feature, not including counts for coal, charcoal, slag, mortar, or brick. The artifact categories below primarily relate to activity. The remaining categories include architectural parts, personal and household, and slag.

Tools

The tools recovered from the excavations of the blacksmith shop relate to everyday workings of a 19th century blacksmith. Included in this collection are several punches (including a horseshoers' pritchell and machine punch), files, and bolt headers. There is also a screw stock used to thread uniform screws, which may have been used to create the threads on the numerous bolts found throughout the excavations, as well as the tie-down rods found at the mill complex for the steam engine (Kelleher 2002:112).

Wagon Making

Evidence of wagon making is apparent from the recovery of wagon axle boxes, a bolster plate, a wagon seat spring, and wagon staples. These could also have been part of a carriage.

Farriery

Excavation recovered 31 shoeing nails. Other identifiable farriery-related items recovered include mule shoes, ox shoes, a harness ring, and a tie ring. This seems reasonable, as Van Winkle used mule and oxen extensively for transporting his lumber, maintained a mule paddock, and owned 32 mules at the time of his death (as listed in the probate record). The lack of horseshoes, however, suggests that the blacksmith did not shoe horses for the public. Since two horses are listed in the probate, this may be an example of skewed representation in the archaeological record, that shoeing took place somewhere else, or that horseshoeing was very limited.

Barstock

Over 25 kg of barstock was recovered from the excavations. Classified as round, square, and flat stock (based on form), most of the pieces exhibited some form of cutting using a hot set. Any stock exhibiting modification other than cutting was categorized as scrap. Precise measurements, including diameters, were not taken due to the variety of sizes found and range of sizes available from stock suppliers.

Samples of barstock from the pre-1860 and post-1865 occupations were examined with a spark test (as described by Andrews 1994:222–223), to determine if they were iron or steel. All of the Van Winkle samples were iron, perhaps due to availability, preference, or lack of knowledge. The probate inventory, however, lists 111 lbs. of 'to[ol] steel' and 44 lbs. of 'steel' as being held in the storehouse on-site. Why the smith did not use steel for everyday repairs at the blacksmith shop is unknown.

Blacksmithing Slag

Over 45 kg of blacksmithing slag was found throughout during excavation. A general cataloging of the slags took place following a typology created by Timothy Mancl and influenced by Hans-Gert Bachmann (Bachmann 1982; Mancl 2003:32–52). The creation of Mancl's typology was to serve studies of the iron bloomery process, not blacksmithing, though many of the techniques are similar. As detailed by T. Egleston, there are three major slag-like materials resulting from metalworking in a hearth: cinder, coal-crust, and emery. Cinder, the material of interest here, is the product that can be found with secondary ironworking, such as blacksmithing (Egleston 1879:531–536). It is the liquefied gangue (waste) material in the ore. Throughout this paper, all metalworking waste, including cinder, is referred to by the general term 'slag.'

The first slag type exhibited in this collection is a tap slag. These are dense and heavy pieces with a flowing appearance, dark brown, or black in color. Also found were sponge, cinder, and combination slags. Sponge and cinder slags are lightweight and porous with a rough surface, while combination slags are an amalgam of tap and sponge slag (Mancl 2003:40–41). Another commonly found type was a slaggy conglomerate, a mass that contains various slag types fused together with rocks and other scrap that made contact with the slag pile (Mancl 2003:42).

Perhaps one of the most interesting pieces came from the post-1865 occupation and resembled what researchers commonly refer to as a plano-convex bottom (PCB). In general, larger PCBs are the result of refining, with secondary smithing such as blacksmithing resulting in smaller PCBs. The sample from the Van Winkle blacksmith shop is substantial, considering the size of the hearth (2,029 g, 14x14x8 cm). It is flat or slightly concave on one side (caused by the air from the tuyere) and convex on the other side (formed by the shape of the firebed). Although this is somewhat large for secondary smithing, size is often influenced by the quantity of iron forged, the amount of impurities in the iron, how frequently the smith used fluxes, and the cleanliness of the hearth (Crew 1996:1).

There is also evidence of the forge having a side-tuyere as seen from samples of slag that were possibly shaped by the tuyere pipe. This slag collected around the tip of the tuyere and left a circular impression. Judging from the curve on these pieces, the tuyere pipe measured about one centimeter in diameter. Light notes that the diameter of the tuyeres is often less than a couple of inches and the fire itself is usually no larger than six inches in diameter (Light 1984:59). It may be possible that such a small tuyere as indicated here could have serviced the forge, and support for this are the numerous pieces that have this circular impression.

Another slag type found was a sample of hammerscale, the result of anvil work. Only unit 11 (in the post-1865 layer) had hammerscale. Its distance from the anvil is somewhat surprising, and there is no evidence of a second anvil near the scale. Hammerscale's absence from other units may be due in part to its size and fitting through the 1/4-inch mesh used for screening, as well as the difficulty of identifying it among the ubiquitous rocks. Hammerscale was primarily identified in this area during the magnetic fractioning tests completed earlier.

Architectural

Archaeologists collected over 24 kg of brick and 29 kg of mortar (only a sample), from the chimney fall at the forge box and at the back wall of the shop. Some of the bricks, as expected, showed vitrification from having been near very high heat. The density and spatial distribution of the bricks suggests that these were once part of the forge box, not used for any structural means in the architecture of the building. Window glass shards, however, provide evidence for glass pane windows, not simply window openings. Although the thickness of window glass may help with dating a structure (as glass thickness increases though time), there was not a large enough sample in this collection for that analysis (Moir 1983:12).

In all, archaeologists collected over 84 kg of nails and nail fragments—including 863 intact nails. Of these, 821 were cut nails, 41 were wire nails, and one was handmade. Cut nails dominated the industry from the 1800s until the late 19th century when the wire nail became popular. The abundance of cut nails over wire nails at the blacksmith shop indicates that the structure was built during the 19th century (Loveday Jr. 1983). The majority of the nails were of the pennyweights 10d, 8d, and 4d. Typically, 10d and 8d nails are used for framing walls, while 4d nails are for roofing and flooring. Although some blacksmith shops had wooden floors, this is not common practice due to the fire hazard. Stratigraphy indicates no evidence of a wooden floor ever existing here.

The quantity of pulled nails also indicates that there may have been salvage taking place at the site (839 pulled/unmodified out of 865). The distribution of large pennyweight nails across the site may show the locations of the timber walls, as mentioned above. There is an even distribution of the 4d nails throughout the site, which may have been from a roof, except for a large concentration in unit 1 in what appears to be a dump just outside the building.

Household and Personal

The few ceramics recovered during excavations are undiagnostic, except to say they are the result of 19th century use. The collection consists of undecorated whiteware and earthenware plates and bowls. One item is an Albany glaze stoneware jug.

Also recovered were 309 pieces of bottle glass. Identifiable glass includes three fragments of a cathedral-type or gothic-style pepper sauce bottle. These began to appear around 1850, but were also popular in the late 19th century (McKearin and Wilson 1978:92). There were also fragments of a hand manufactured medicine bottle.

Other personal items recovered include several metal buckles, a bullet, a 4-hole prosser button, a metal jack, half a clay marble, a metal latch for a box or bag, a metal table knife, several bullet cartridges, a fastener, grommets, a porcelain collar or cuff stud fragment, a black glass button, suspender or overall gallus hooks, a shield nickel, and tin can fragments. Some of the tin can fragments had soldered closures (dating at the earliest to the mid-1870s), and key-opening non-reclosure cans dating to 1866. These may be the remains of food consumption or were personal knick-knacks.

Artifact Interpretation

Artifacts recovered from the Van Winkle blacksmith shop demonstrate the operations of a typical, late 19th century mill smithy. As part of the support network in Van Hollow, the blacksmith here provided integral services to mill operations. Some industry-related items found include numerous chain links and chain link fragments, hooks, loops, and threaded bars and rods identical to those used to tie down the machinery at the mill complex. There are many nuts and bolts, and previously useful or in-repair items now unrecognizable and categorized as scrap. There is no evidence that the smith took on work for people outside of the mill community or if there were visitors to the mill, so it is important to examine the role of the shop within the community. Any horseshoeing that may have been done was probably for Van Winkle's own horses.

Role of the Blacksmith Shop in the Community

One of the most interesting aspects of the blacksmith shop operations learned from excavations is the shop's overall use in the community. In the larger document discussing the archaeology of the Van Winkle site's industrial sector (Valentino 2006), a considerable section was devoted to understanding the role of the mill in the local community based on material evidence and economic geography. The mill was centrally located to five major, growing northwest Arkansas towns (Fayetteville, Rogers, Eureka Springs, Huntsville, and Springdale), near thick hardwood and pine forest stands, and sited on a major thoroughfare. Van Winkle considered topography, demand, capital investment, and availability of raw materials to determine if this site would be suitable for his complex. Using these factors, calculations of least cost paths to and from local cities and access to local and regional railroad networks, were performed to see exactly how well Van Winkle situated his mill. The results suggest that local residents may have come directly to the mill, but people living in the cities would not have traveled over the distances and terrain required to make it to the mill to purchase lumber or grain direct from the miller, or have their equipment repaired at the blacksmith shop.

While it was possible for locals to support the mill, the sheer quantity of production, establishment of satellite mills and lumberyards, difficult transportation networks, and archaeology of the blacksmith shop, suggests that Van Winkle intended to supply the non-local area. Van Winkle produced far too much lumber (and grist for that matter), to supply only local residents. His establishment of satellite mills and lumberyards took the main processing away from the home mill in Van Hollow and put it at the largest markets. The home mill then focused on specialized finishing processes, working with cherry, oak, ash, walnut, and pine wood (as noted in the probate record) while the satellite mills may have performed the raw processing and distribution to the lumberyards.

The transportation networks further indicate that Van Winkle wanted to get products out—primarily suggested by the late-development of his White River ferry. If Van Winkle wanted more people to come to the mill, he likely would have established this ferry sooner, not 25 years after the mill's initial operation. Finally, the archaeology of the blacksmith shop does not indicate service for the public (such as horseshoeing). Rather, the majority of the work performed there was probably for repairs and maintenance of the mill facility.

More support for this idea is that the gristmill did not operate year-round. The 1870 census states that the gristmill only operated for three months of the year, and in 1880, the mill is only listed as a sawmill (United States 1872a, 1883). If the Hollow were bringing in people for all of their shopping needs, the gristmill would operate more frequently, like the census records indicate for other mills of the period.

The data recovered from the blacksmith shop is perhaps the most telling and most concrete. As Van Winkle maintained horses, it would also make sense to have horseshoeing done on-site. Since there is so little evidence of horseshoeing (only a horseshoers' pritchell was recovered), it may be possible that the smith restrained his shoeing activities to the maintenance of Van Winkle's team, ignoring the public. Sampling and perhaps not excavating more of the exterior scrap piles may have influenced the recovery of horseshoes and horseshoe nails. The evidence suggests that Van Winkle maintained this blacksmith shop purely for the support of his mill and not for the outside community.

Interpretation

Van Winkle performed his own logging, as determined by the census data and the probate record (Bureau of the Census of the United States 1880). Those loggers and teamsters who ran the mule teams to transport the logs would have needed quick manufacture and repair of items. Van Winkle had 32 mules at the time of his death, two horses, a colt, wagons (including parts, tires, and lumber), log chains, mule road wagons, log wagons, and other items for the transportation of lumber and raw materials in Van Hollow. Therefore, the industrial operations in the hollow, as evidenced from the archaeology, appear to have occupied the majority of the blacksmith's time. One of the primary advantages of this site was its access to the large, developing cities in northwest Arkansas, as well as having a local demand for product. Environment seemed secondary, as the pine stands for which Van Winkle became famous could be accessed from any number of other locations.

If Van Winkle intended to serve local settlers; however, his location does not imply ease of shopping. The slope of the area illustrates that the mill is in some of the most difficult terrain in the study area. The White River and bluffs surround his mill for almost 300 degrees. Van Winkle seemed more interested in purchasing land near his timber stands than near the local population, which is typical because of the material-oriented nature of the industry. Also, the only interest Van Winkle indicated in serving the local demand was his operation of a ferry on the White River which he started in 1882 (Hicks 1990:38). Although the ferry operation may have been as much for Van Winkle's benefit as it was for the public. Unfortunately, there is no information on whether Van Winkle's gristmill was a custom mill (for the processing of wood or grain for the local area), or a merchant mill (for exporting products to other markets). That information could have helped in determining Van Winkle's intent.

The material-oriented nature of this sawmill found Van Winkle between five large markets and enabled him to take advantage of events at the time to sell his lumber and develop an industrial powerhouse in southeast Benton County. His lumber went towards building roads, structures, and cities such as Eureka Springs and Fayetteville. Van Winkle seemed deliberate in his efforts to select a beneficial location, maintain a steady workforce, and adopt the newest technologies, as elaborated upon in the next section.

Technology and the Community

One fortunate result of the blacksmith shop excavations is that inferences can be made about the level of technological advancement of the Van Winkle shop. Three major changes occurred in blacksmithing during the second half of the 19th century: the transition from charcoal to coal, the incorporation of new forge designs, and the increased use of steel over iron. Based on material remains, it appears that the Van Winkle blacksmith shop operators attempted to implement these changes upon their return to the hollow following the Civil War. Archaeology of the rural Van Hollow blacksmith shop provides an intriguing example of how the technological changes were implemented with only mixed success.

Charcoal vs. Coal

The transition from charcoal to coal as the principle forge fuel is the first major industry change. Both charcoal and coal were recovered in the pre-1860 and post-1865 depositions. The highest charcoal concentration in the post-1865 layer came from unit 14, just north of the forge box. Charcoal collected from the pre-1860 layer came from this same unit in a smaller quantity.

The coal distribution was somewhat different, having been primarily found in the western half of the shop for the post-1865 layers. Most of this came from a deposit just outside of the back wall of the shop in unit 2; there were high quantities of coal in each of the units between the back wall and the forge box (just over 25 kg). Some of the coal from the pre-1860 layer was west of the forge box, while the majority came from unit 20 in the eastern part of the shop.

Without considering the spatial distribution of the charcoal and coal, there is a clear distinction between the use of the two fuels in the Van Winkle blacksmith shop when considering pre-1860 and post-1865 operation. Based on the volume recovered, coal became prominent in the post-1865 occupation layer, indicating that it became the fuel of choice for the blacksmith here. The quantity of charcoal present is perhaps a nonissue in the post-1865 layer since many smiths who used coal continued to use charcoal to initiate the forge fire. Regarding the coal, however, as explained earlier in this chapter, the smith used inferior anthracite coal rather than bituminous.

Forge Type

The second technological change is the use of a coal forge instead of a charcoal forge. Although construction techniques vary, a basic charcoal forge, constructed of stone or brick, had a rubble interior with a sand firebed and a side tuyere (Wylie 1990:89). The firebed was typically no larger than six inches in diameter. Coal forges differed in that they had a brick or metal firebed (often laid on sand) with a bottom tuyere (Light 1987:600).

The forge in the Van Winkle blacksmith shop is an excellent example of a charcoal forge, including a stone foundation and brick walls, sand firebed, possible side tuyere, and stone chimney. The inconsistency here is that the forge design does not match the primary fuel used. This may be due to a lack of knowledge about coal forges. The excavated forge, built following the Civil War, does not match the new fuel type used.

Iron vs. Steel

The third technological change is the adoption of steel over iron. Samples of barstock from the pre-1860 and post-1865 occupations were tested with a spark test, to determine if they were iron or steel. Each of the Van Winkle samples were iron, perhaps due to availability, preference, or lack of knowledge. The probate inventory, however, lists 111 lbs. of 'to[ol] steel' and 44 lbs. of 'steel' as being held in the storehouse on-site. Why the smith did not use steel for everyday repairs at the blacksmith shop is unknown.

Conclusion—A Mixed Success

Excavations of the blacksmith shop in Van Hollow have provided researchers information on the layout and daily operations of a pre- and post-Civil War blacksmith shop. Two interesting aspects of this shop are the architecture and the shop's overall use in the community. Regarding the architecture, the forge in the center of the shop creates an obstacle in the work zone, and the workbench and fuel stores are not in typical locations. These are not unheard of placements, just not recommended.

For the shop's overall use in the local community, the siting of the shop gave the potential for the smith to provide services for the public—those who came into Van Hollow for lumber and grain. As Van Winkle maintained horses, it would also make sense to have horseshoeing done on-site. Since there is so little evidence of horseshoeing (only the horseshoers' pritchell), it may be possible that the smith restrained his shoeing activities to Van Winkle's needs, ignoring the public. The evidence suggests that Van Winkle maintained this blacksmith shop purely for the support of his mill and not for the outside community.

Van Winkle performed his own logging, as determined by the census data and the probate record (Bureau of the Census of the United States 1880). Those loggers and teamsters would have needed quick manufacture and repair of items. Therefore, the industrial operations in the hollow, as evidenced from the archaeology, appear to have occupied the majority of the blacksmith's time.

In terms of technological advancement, the material remains provide a cursory look at attempted integration of new blacksmithing technologies. In comparing the pre-1860 and post-1865 occupations, it is apparent that the smith successfully switched from using charcoal to coal following the

Civil War. This is typical of most blacksmith shops in the United States; however, the smith used anthracite, not bituminous coal. Another aspect of the shop that is somewhat out of the ordinary is the forge construction. As seen from the stratigraphy underneath the forge, the hearth was rebuilt after the Civil War. Nevertheless, the design of the new forge is not for coal; it is a charcoal-fueled forge. The use of coal in a charcoal forge may be an example of limited knowledge of blacksmithing, as is the continued use of iron over steel. This smith apparently had heard of the new methods, yet lacked the ability to implement them. In addition, the transition from iron to steel is not apparent here, failing to follow the industry trend.

The Van Winkle blacksmith shop exhibited many differences from what was common practice in the 19th century. Regarding the technology in use, the Van Winkle blacksmith was able to implement at least one of the three changes in blacksmithing method: the switch from charcoal to coal to fuel the forge.

REFERENCES

Andrews, Jack
1994   *New Edge of the Anvil: A Resource Book for the Blacksmith.* Drexel Hill, Pennsylvania: SkipJack Press, Inc.
Arkansas Democrat
1959   No title. *Arkansas Democrat,* August 2. Little Rock, Arkansas.
Bachmann, Hans-Gert
1982   *The Identification of Slags from Archaeological Sites, Occasional Paper No. 6.* London: Institute of Archaeology.
Benton County Pioneer
1962   No title. *Benton County Pioneer,* July. Bentonville, Arkansas.
1963   No title. *Benton County Pioneer,* January. Bentonville, Arkansas.
Black, J. Dickson
1960   Van Winkle Mill Provided Lumber For Towns Throughout This Area. *Northwest Arkansas Times.*
1979   Van Winkle Mill Helped Build NW Arkansas. *Northwest Arkansas Times,* 52:1.
Brandon, Jamie C.
2004   *Van Winkle's Mill: Mountain Modernity, Cultural Memory and Historical Archaeology in the Arkansas Ozarks.* Unpublished PhD dissertation, Department of Anthropology. University of Texas at Austin.
Brandon, Jamie C., James Davidson, and Jerry Hilliard
2000   *Preliminary Archeological Investigations at Van Winkle's Mill (3BE413), Beaver Lake State Park, Benton County, Arkansas: 1997–1999, Final Report, AAS Project 99–05.* Fayetteville: Arkansas Archeological Survey.
Brandon, Jamie C., James M. Davidson, and Edward W. Tennant
2003   Archeological Testing of Van Winkle's Mill Features 30, 31, and 32. In *Archeological Investigation and Testing of Cultural Resources at Van Winkle's Mill (3BE413) and Little Clifty Creek Shelter (3BE412), Beaver Lake, Benton*

County, Arkansas. Final Report, AAS Project 03–04, ed. Jamie C. Brandon and James M. Davidson, 40–53. Arkansas Archeological Survey, Fayetteville.

Brandon, Jamie C., and James M. Davidson

2003　Archeological Investigation and Testing of Cultural Resources at Van Winkle's Mill (3BE413) and Little Clifty Creek Shelter (3BE412), Beaver Lake, Benton County, Arkansas, Final Report, AAS Project 03–04. Fayetteville: Arkansas Archeological Survey.

Bureau of the Census of the United States

1880　United States Manuscript Census: 1880. Washington, DC.

Collier, Arthur J.

1907　The Arkansas Coal Field. Washington, DC.: Government Printing Office.

Conable, E. W.

1903　The Old Van Winkle Home. In The Path-Finder. Roswell, Colorado: Pathfinder.

Crew, Peter

1996　Bloom refining and smithing slags and other residues. Historical Metallurgical Society Archaeological Datasheet No. 6 (hist-met.org): 1–2.

Egleston, T.

1879　The American Bloomery Process for Making Iron Direct from the Ore. Transactions of the Institute of Mining Engineering 8: 515–550.

Elliott, Blanche H.

1959　Story of a Sawmill King. Arkansas Democrat, August 2, Sunday Supplement edition:5–6.

Goodspeed Publishing Company

1884　Benton County Section of Goodspeed's Benton, Washington, Carroll, Madison, Crawford, Franklin and Sebastian Counties Arkansas. Bentonville, Arkansas: Benton County Historical Society.

Hicks, Marilyn Larner

1990　The Van Winkle Family. Wolfe City, Texas: Henington Publishing Company.

Kelleher, Tom. 2002 Nuts and Bolts. The Chronicle of Early American Industries Association Sept.

Lasansky, Jeannette

1980　To Draw, Upset, and Weld: The Work of the Pennsylvania Rural Blacksmith 1742–1935. Lewisburg, Pennsylvania: Oral Traditions Project.

Light, John D.

1984　Tinker, Trader, Soldier, Smith: A Frontier Fur Trade Blacksmith Shop, Fort St. Joseph, Ontario, 1796–1812. Ottawa: Parks Canada.

1987　Blacksmithing Technology and Forge Construction. Technology and Culture 28(3): 658–665.

Lockhart, Jami J., and Jamie C. Brandon

2003　Archaeo-Geophysical Prospecting and Mapping at Van Winkle's Mill (3BE413). In Archeological Investigation and Testing of Cultural Resources at Van Winkle's Mill (3BE413) and Little Clifty Creek Shelter (3BE412), Beaver Lake, Benton County, Arkansas. Final Report, AAS Project 30–04, ed. Jamie C. Brandon and James M. Davidson, 34–39. Arkansas Archeological Survey, Fayetteville.

Loveday, Amos J., Jr.

1983   *The Rise and Decline of the American Cut Nail Industry: A Study of the Interrelationships of Technology, Business Organization, and Management Techniques.* Westport, Connecticut: Greenwood Press.

Madson, Michael

2002   *History and Archaeology of the Pittsburgh and Boston Copper Harbor Mining Company and Blacksmith Shop.* Master's thesis. Houghton: Michigan Technological University.

Mancl, Timothy J.

2003   *Archaeometallurgy of the Carp River Forge*, chapter 3: "Slag types and chemistry. Master's thesis. Houghton: Michigan Technological University.

McBride, W. Stephen

1988   A Village Blacksmith in the Antebellum South: Archaeological Investigations at the Griswold Shop, Barton, Mississippi. *Southeastern Archaeology* 6(2): 79–92.

McKearin, Helen, and Kenneth M. Wilson

1978   *American Bottles & Flasks and Their Ancestry.* New York: Crown Publishers.

Miller, Dorothy

1966   For Vernon T. West, Log Business in His Blood. *Oklahoma Ranch and Farm World* March 13.

1969   The Van Winkle Heritage at War Eagle. *Ozark Mountaineer* October.

Moir, Randall

1983   Windows to our past: a chronological scheme for the thickness of pane fragments. Presented at the Society for Historical Archaeology, Denver, Colorado, January 7.

Reichman, Charles

1991   The Daily Transactions of a 19th Century Rural Blacksmith. *Chronicle of the Early American Industries Association* 44(4): 122–123.

Rogers Democrat

1910   No title. *Rogers Democrat*, May 5.

Rothrock, Thomas

1973   Peter Manelis [*sic*] Van Winkle. *Arkansas Historical Quarterly* 32: 61–70.

Sabo, George, III

1990   Historic Europeans and Americans. In *Human Adaptation in the Ozark and Ouachita Mountains*, ed. George Sabo III, Ann M. Early, and Jerome C. Rose, 135–170. Research Series 31. Arkansas Archeological Survey, Fayetteville.

Smith, H. R. Bradley

1966   *Blacksmiths' and Farriers' Tools at Shelburne Museum—A History of their Development from Forge to Factory.* Museum Pamphlet Series No. 7. Shelburne, Vermont: The Shelburne Museum, Inc.

United States, Bureau of the Census

1872   *Compendium of the Ninth Census, Vol 4.* Washington, DC.: Government Printing Office.

1883   *Compendium of the Tenth Census, Part 1.* Washington, DC.: Government Printing Office.

United States Census Office

1880   *Tenth census of the United States, 1880, Arkansas, manufactures.*

Valentino, Alicia B.

2006   *The Dynamics of Industry as Seen from Van Winkle's Mill, Arkansas.*
        Doctoral dissertation, Department of Anthropology. University of Arkansas,
        Fayetteville.

Wylie, William N. T.

1990   *The Blacksmith in Upper Canada, 1784–1850.* Gananoque, Ontario:
        Langdale Press.

6
ZACHARY TAYLOR AND THE SISTERS OF MERCY
An Archaeology of Memory, Landscape, Gender, and Faith on Arkansas's Western Frontier

Jamie C. Brandon and Jerry E. Hilliard

In Fort Smith, Arkansas, behind the Immaculate Conception Church at 13th Street and Garrison, stands a lonely looking chimney (Figure 6.1). This stone feature has long stood at this location—first as the chimney belonging to a building that was associated with old Camp Belknap and then, finally, as a part of a decorative "grotto" on the grounds of St. Anne's Academy and the convent of the Sisters of Mercy.

The text of the plaque reads as follows:

General Taylor's Home.
Site of the home of General Zachary
Taylor whose headquarters were at Camp
Belknap, Fort Smith, 1844–45. It was from
Here he departed to win imperishable
Glory in the Mexican War and afterward
To become President of the United States.
Erected as a public service by
The Noon Civics Club.
1936

Early in the summer of 2004, Deacon Ray Brust of the Immaculate Conception Church of Fort Smith contacted the Arkansas Archeological Survey. He was inquiring about conducting excavations at the chimney prior to a landscaping project. Deacon Brust and several

Figure 6.1. Chimney standing behind the Immaculate Conception Church, Fort Smith.

other community members had made it known that they were keenly interested in recovering proof that this had been, in fact, the home of Zachary Taylor while he was in command at Fort Smith. Before we go further into the archaeology of this site small, compact site, however, allow us to take a detour to explain a bit about the site's history and how Zachary Taylor and the Sisters of Mercy came to be associated with this site.

Historical Context: Fort Smith, a Future President, and Irish Nuns

As early as 1814, Major William L. Lovely, Indian Agent to the Western Cherokee, recommended that a military post be established on the Arkansas River in western Arkansas to help keep peace in the region (Faulk and Jones 1983:14). It was not until 1817, however, that Majors Bradford and Long were sent to locate the most suitable position for a post and erect a stockade (Patton 1992:55). Located on a high bluff at the confluence of the Arkansas and Poteau Rivers, this military outpost was known as Fort Smith (after General Thomas A. Smith) by the following year, 1818 (Mapes 1965: 6–7; Patton 1992:56–57).

Naturalist and explorer Thomas Nuttall visited Fort Smith in 1819. He gives us a brief picture of Fort Smith in its earliest incarnation.

> The garrison, consisting of two block-houses, and lines of cabins or barracks for the accommodations of 70 men whom it contains, is agreeably situated at the junction of the Pottoe [*sic*], on a rising ground of about 50 feet elevation, and surrounded by alluvial and uplands of unusual fertility. The view is more commanding and picturesque, than any other spot of equal elevation on the banks of the Arkansa [*sic*]. (Nuttall 1999:157).

The post seems to have served the dual duties of keeping peace between relocated and indigenous Native American groups and keeping white settlers from encroaching on Indian Territory (Faulk and Jones 1983:20–22; Patton 1992:60). The civilian population of Fort Smith grew rapidly as the post became an important service-center and market for the emerging frontier and Native American groups (Faulk and Jones 1983:22).

Zachary Taylor and Old Fort Smith

Born in Virginia in 1784, Zachary Taylor was raised in Kentucky on a plantation. He was a career soldier in the Army and was also a cotton planter with holdings in Mississippi and Louisiana (Bauer 1985:2; Dyer 1946:5; Fry 1848:14; Hamilton 1941:21).

He was first commissioned in 1808 as a first lieutenant in the Seventh Infantry Regiment and was one of the prominent figures in the war of 1812—successfully defending Fort Harrison from a Shawnee attack (Bauer 1985:13–28; Dyer 1946:24–26; Fry 1848:19–29; Hamilton 1941:40–44). After a brief break from the military following the War of 1812, Taylor rejoined the army as a major and was stationed at a variety of locations along the frontier (Bauer 1985:29; Fry 1848:30).

In 1841, Taylor became the commander of the Second Department, Western Division at Fort Smith, Arkansas (Bauer 1985:97; Dyer 1946:132–148; Fry 1848:68; Hamilton 1941:142–155). By 1844, however, he had moved on and had become the commander at Fort Jessup in Louisiana (Bauer 1985:103; Dyer 1946:147–148).

During his three-year tenure at Fort Smith, local oral history and several of the few published histories of the city claim that Taylor made his home in the "weather-boarded log house" that was once attached to our chimney; this was then adjacent to Camp Belknap, a temporary cantonment area established to house the troops while construction continued on Fort Smith (Faulk and Jones 1983:28–29; Mapes 1965:13–15; Patton 1992:72, 74, 219).

Of course, Fort Smith was but a brief stop on his trek. From here, Zachary Taylor went on to become a hero of the war with Mexico and is credited with major victories at Monterey and Buena Vista (Bauer 1985:166–214; Dyer 1946:184–206, 226–254; Fry 1848:215–321). In total he spent almost a quarter of a century as a soldier on the frontiers of the ever-expanding United States.

The Mexican-American War transformed Taylor from a minor military figure into a presidential contender and eventually took him, although briefly, to the White House. Taylor served a president only from March 5, 1849 until July 9, 1850 (Bauer 1985:314–327; Dyer 1946:397–410). After about sixteen months in office—and shortly after participating in the groundbreaking ceremonies at the Washington Monument on July 4, 1850—Taylor fell ill. Within five days he was dead. The cause of death was listed as gastroenteritis (inflammation of the stomach and intestines).

Taylor's story can be seen as a metaphor for 19th century America. His climb through the military ranks during a series of expansionist wars meant to fulfill our manifest destiny and his subsequent election to the highest office in the land tell a story of a very active, turbulent, expanding America with the militarism and sectional tension that eventually would lead to the Civil War.

Back in Fort Smith, however, Taylor's story is intersected by another 19th century story—the story of the Sisters of Mercy.

The Sisters of Mercy on the Arkansas Frontier

The State of Arkansas and the Indian Territory were formed in 1843 into the Catholic Diocese of Little Rock—while Zachary Taylor was still in command in Fort Smith (Church of the Immaculate Conception 1999:2; Sisters of Mercy 1989:7).

Andrew Byrne, born in Ireland, was chosen the first Bishop of this diocese—"a vast wilderness with no real city, only a few emerging towns, no reliable means of transportation over the long distances that separated towns and a very small Catholic population" (Sisters of Mercy 1989:8). The Catholic population of the diocese was not more than 1000, and perhaps as few as 400, when Byrne was appointed (Sisters of Mercy 1989:13).

At some point during his first years of service in the Little Rock Diocese, Byrne decided to develop a colony of Irish Catholics in Fort Smith. He acquired the land and buildings to start this colony when he bought 640 acres (at a price of $5,250) from the Fort Smith School Commissioners—this was the land and buildings that had comprised Camp Belknap (Sisters of Mercy 1989:14).

Bishop Byrne traveled back to Ireland with the intent of bringing back Irish immigrants and clergy in order to establish an Irish colony in his new diocese (Church of the Immaculate Conception 1999:6–7; Sisters of Mercy 1989:47–57). The few historians who have tackled the specifics of this endeavor are not sure as to how many Irish souls Father Byrne actually managed to recruit, but it seems that between 1200 and 300 would-be colonists left Naas, Ireland with between 8 and 5 Sisters of Mercy (Church of the Immaculate Conception 1999:3; Sisters of Mercy 1989: 55, 59) to start a new life on the what was then the western edge of the Western world in the wilds of Arkansas.

On January 19, 1853, the Sisters and Bishop Byrne boarded a steamboat in Little Rock and traveled up the Arkansas River to Fort Smith. The party arrived, and

... the first night in their new home the Sisters slept in one of the small two room buildings on the Camp Belknap property. The next morning they toured the Camp Belknap buildings and began to move into General Taylor's old residence, which was large enough to serve as their first convent, which they named St. Anne's. (Church of the Immaculate Conception 1999:18–19)

It was only a short time before the Sisters had organized two schools (one for girls and one for young boys), as well as catechism classes and instruction for adults. They, as their order demanded, committed their lives and resources to act in solidarity with persons who were sick or economically poor, especially women and children.

The faith of all the Sisters at St. Anne's was sorely tried on December 8, 1875. The Sisters had gone to the Parish church near the convent and were waiting for 10 a.m. Mass to begin when a cry went up that the convent was on fire! By the time the Sisters and congregation reached the scene, *the main building of Gen. Zachary Taylor's residence*, which was used by the Sisters as their convent, had been completely destroyed. A defective flue was blamed for the fire (Sisters of Mercy 1989:129, emphasis added).

Early in 1876 a new two-story frame building was built on the site of the Taylor residence and the Sisters lived in this structure until the construction of the third, brick convent in 1905 (Church of the Immaculate Conception 1999:26–27; Sisters of Mercy 1989:129). The Sisters eventually grew their compound to include not only St. Anne's Academy and their convent, but also (in the early 20th century) St. Edward's Infirmary and the Church of the Immaculate Conception.

Following the completion of the new convent, the Sisters tore down the two-room cabin that had served as the kitchen and dining room for the Zachary Taylor family, but left the solitary chimney—transforming it into a three-sided native stone grotto (Figure 6.2) which held statues of Our Lady of the Immaculate Conception, St. Joseph and St. Aloysius (Sisters of Mercy 1989:145). This grotto became a landmark itself to the Fort Smith community. The grotto appears in many local photographs—not only appearing in pictures of the Sisters, but also of photographs of school classes, weddings, and other events.

The grotto is mentioned in every Fort Smith history. It is even strangely present in some works when St. Anne's Academy and the Sisters of Mercy are *only* mentioned in connection with the grotto (e.g., Mapes 1965:15).

The Sisters operations in Fort Smith struggled through the 1960s and 1970s due to lack of teachers and funds. Eventually (in 1972) the Sisters were forced to leave the 1905 convent, as the structure was in need of repair and no funds were available for that purpose (Sisters of Mercy 1989:191). The Sisters eventually abandoned their Fort Smith presence and the Church of the Immaculate Conception purchased the grounds and buildings, and renovated them to their current state (Sisters of Mercy 1989:192).

Reconstructing the Historical Landscape

The historical record can provide us with important information when it comes to understanding the historical landscape around our chimney (state site number 3SB1088). In particular, the Sanborn Fire Insurance Maps for the city of Fort Smith help us understand the evolution of the

The "Grotto," Convent Grounds, Fort Smith, Ark.

16629-N

Figure 6.2. Postcard showing the chimney as converted into a grotto.

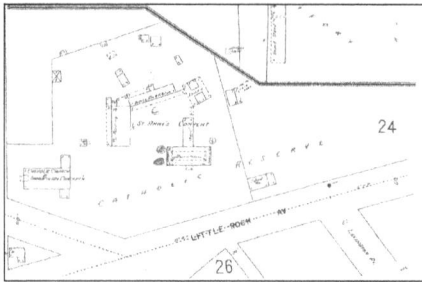

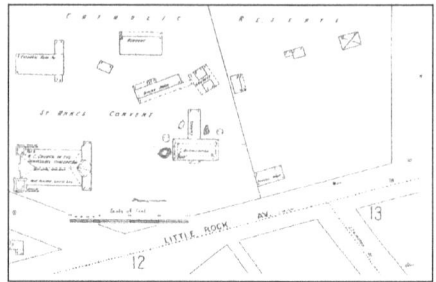

(a)   (b)

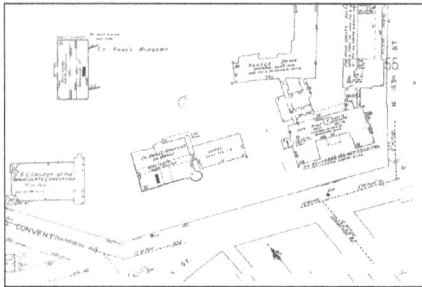

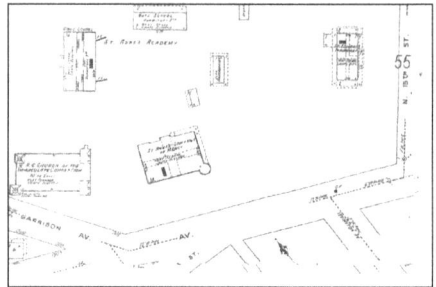

(c)   (d)

Figures 6.3a-d. Sanborn Maps Showing the Sisters of Mercy Complex.

Sisters of Mercy's compound. Figure 3a is the first available Sanborn map for our project area—1897. Thus we do not have a depiction of the original configuration of the "Zachary Taylor" cabin, but we can easily see the T-shaped second convent that incorporated a part of what remained of the 1840s structure. Given the second convent's configuration, we believe that the northern ell of the convent is the kitchen area belonging to the earlier structure and our chimney is still attached to its northern face. In the 1897 map you can also see the building housing St. Anne's Academy and the Church of the Immaculate Conception (in the bottom left). This building would have been the "white frame church" that served the community from 1867 until it was damaged during the cyclone of 1898 (Church of the Immaculate Conception 1999:34).

Figure 3b is the 1901 map over the 1897 map. By 1901 we can see some growth in the Catholic Reserve—various ancillary structures and outbuildings have been added. Also notice that the Church of the Immaculate Conception is now housed in the larger brick structure that still stands overlooking the Avenue. The "white frame" church is still present, however. It was repaired and moved north, but continued to serve the community as a Catholic Hall. It was later moved again north of Midland Boulevard where it served as the African American mission of St. John the Baptist (Church of the Immaculate Conception 1999:35).

In Figure 6.3c you see our map with the addition of the 1908 Sanborn map. We can see that the second convent has been razed and the third convent built partially over the footprint of the 1870s building. Our chimney now stands alone and had been transformed into "the grotto." Note also the addition of St. Edwards Infirmary, the addition of new St. Anne's Academy building, and the disappearance of the "white frame" church. Additionally, the busy, late 19th century landscape has been cleaned up and many of the ancillary buildings are gone.

Finally we have added the 1940 Sanborn map (Figure 6.3d). By 1940, the old St. Edwards Infirmary building and Boys School are gone. A large complex on the right-hand site of the map is St. Edwards Mercy Hospital. Also, a chapel has been added to the third convent structure.

Compiling maps such as these helps to make sense out of the current landscape as well as understanding how historical photographs are related to the current landscape. It seems to make clear that our chimney was, in all likelihood, never attached to the main residence of Zachary Taylor at Camp Belkap. Instead, it seems to be the chimney serving a detached kitchen behind the main structure. This structure survives the 1870s fires (unlike Taylors main residence), and by 1897 is used by the Sisters of Mercy as a laundry (as it is labeled in the Figure 3a Sanborn Map). However, this building is gone by 1908 and our still-standing chimney has been transformed into the ever-present grotto.

Archaeological Investigations at 3SB1088

In 2004 representatives of the Immaculate Conception Church contacted the Arkansas Archeological Survey (AAS). By then, the grotto had been dismantled amid concerns that it was no longer structurally sound. The representatives indicated that artifacts had been found in the past near the chimney and that the architects working for the church with plans for landscaping the site had recommended that the church contact the AAS before disturbing the deposits.

In late June of 2004, AAS-Sponsored Research Program personnel along with one of the authors (Hilliard) met with Deacon Burst about the site. As a result of that meeting, parties agreed to conduct a brief, three-day excavation in October 2004 to assess if there were any intact archaeological deposits around the chimney. These test excavations found intact deposits dating from the mid- to late-19th century.

In March 2005 (14–18 and the 21–23), the Arkansas Archeological Survey's University of Arkansas at Fayetteville Research Station (AAS-UAF) held a week-long Archeology Month dig at the site to expand excavations and learn more about who lived here. We ultimately completed six two-meter-by-two-meter excavation units, and recovered thousands of artifacts.

The stratigraphy of the site was certainly the product of urban construction, but it was quite helpful in understanding the chronology of the site and site formation processes (Figure 6.4). A thick, orange clay zone proved to be construction fill from the building of the current St. Anne's Academy in 1905. It is largely sterile clay with a few bricks and other construction debris present. This construction fill also alerts us to the fact that the landform was extensively leveled during the 1905 construction.

Removing the clay fill revealed the contours of the pre-1905 landform and a very compact, burned lenses of ash, charcoal, and wall plaster packed full of artifacts dating to latter half of the 19th century. This stratum seems consistent with historical accounts of the 1875 fire that destroyed what had been Zachary Taylor's residence and the Sisters of Mercy's first convent (Sisters of Mercy 1989:129).

Almost 14,000 individual artifacts (weighing almost 93,000g) were recovered from the six excavation units around the chimney. All materials from project excavations were washed and processed following standard AAS laboratory procedures, organized by provenience and analyzed using the XENA cataloging system developed by the Arkansas Archeological Survey specifically for artifacts from historical period sites. This system, although still in the development stages, fills the need for a standardized cataloging system equivalent to the DELOS system long used to catalog prehistoric artifacts in the state of Arkansas (Cande 1992).

Like South's (1977:95) seminal classification system, the XENA system divides artifacts into activity groups (i.e., foodways, household, structural, personal items, tools and equipment, clothing, etc.) as opposed to using a material-based schema. These activity groups are in turn classified by sub activity, function, and material type (ceramic, metal, glass, etc.). This system allows for quantitative data to be extracted by individual excavation context. This chapter goes on to explore the data to understand the character of the assemblage—charting information about architecture, activities conducted in the area, and chronological indicators.

Figure 6.4. Unit 2, west profile.

Finally, extensive notes are taken on all artifacts deemed chronologically or functionally diagnostic, which provides qualitative data on the artifact assemblage.

Artifacts: Faith, Service, Healing and Nuns with Guns

Unfortunately, for those who were looking for evidence of Zachary Taylor, none of the artifacts recovered from our excavations could be absolutely dated to before 1850. Some of the recovered artifacts have manufacturing ranges, which could place them as part of Zachary Taylor's household of the early 1840s, but none of these artifacts were diagnostic of solely an 1840s occupation. Likewise, none of the archaeological contexts excavated seemed to be made up of solely 1840s material. This made the association of particular artifacts with the Zachary Taylor occupation difficult at best. However, the vast majority of these artifacts can be attributed to the Sisters of Mercy occupation of the site from 1853 to around 1910. Moreover, these artifacts do tell a story of hidden diversity in Fort Smith. They tell the other 19th century story of the relocated Irish women of faith on the frontier—and they tell it in detail.

It will not come as a surprise to discover that there are many artifacts recovered from 3SB1088 that reflect the religious nature of the Sisters of Mercy—including a silver crucifix, a complete rosary (white metal with beads of black glass), an unidentified saint's medal, a hinge from a cast-iron pew kneeler, and many fragments of stained flat glass (presumably from the replacement of stained-glass windows in the adjacent convent).

Also unsurprising is the presence of artifacts attesting to the educational mission of the order. As we have previously mentioned, the sisters founded boys' and girls' schools shortly after their arrival in Fort Smith. A total of 212 artifacts were coded in the "personal, writing and desk" category—including 144 writing slate fragments, 41 slate pencil fragments, and a number of ink bottles and ink-bottle fragments. Given the large number of this artifact class, the authors feel there is a clear link to the nearby educational institutions and the sisters' educational work.

Also present are artifacts confirming that the sisters did indeed use this building as a laundry building (as it is labeled on the previously discussed Sanborn Fire Insurance maps). Several bottles (both whole and fragmentary) containing laundry bluing (whitening) agents were recovered, as well as boot polish and a zinc washboard.

But other, subtler, artifact patterns shed further light on the sisters' activities and beliefs. For instance, of the 825 (14,814.8 g) fragments of ceramic recovered, the vast majority (almost 60%) were undecorated ironstone. This was distantly followed by undecorated whiteware (N=142; 17%). Thus, less than 5% of the assemblage (41 sherds) bore decoration. Moreover, these decorated sherds were mostly very small fragments with very few matching patterns. Likewise, porcelain makes up a very small percentage of the tableware assemblage (N=38; less than 5%).

The first observation, that the ceramic assemblage is largely plain and cheap, probably speaks to the ideology of the Sisters of Mercy. The Sisters of Mercy take a vow of poverty, and thus should strive to eschew worldly goods. The communal, institutional, plain and cheap character of the overall ceramic assemblage points toward this vow.

The second observation about the ceramic assemblage, that it contains a number of very small plate and platter fragments from differently decorated sets of tableware, may point to social reciprocity directed at the Sisters of Mercy. One of the authors (Hilliard) has elsewhere interpreted a similar artifact pattern at a Northwest Arkansas Presbyterian Church as evidence of "dinner on the grounds" or "church dinner" traditions still popular today (Hilliard 2008:59). This is indicative of food being prepared elsewhere and platters and plates from various

Figure 6.5. Artifacts recovered from the Sisters of Mercy Complex.

households being brought to the church for communal dinners. On the rare occasion that a plate or platter is broken, the large pieces are cleaned up, leaving an assemblage of small, differently decorated sherds to enter the archaeological record. In the case of the Sisters of Mercy, however, we may be looking as covered dishes being brought to the convent as reciprocal "payment" for their good deeds and community service. These small artifacts may be tangible evidence of the sisters' vows of service.

Of the 2,263 fragments (12,350 g) of vessel glass and whole bottles recovered from these six excavation units, 30% (N=3,706) could not be classified by function. Of the identifiable glass vessel fragments and whole bottles 36% (N=3097) were classified under the "foodways" category, and less than 3% (N=273) were classified as consumer goods. But it is the staggering 61% (N=5,273) that were classified under the "personal, health" that catches the attention of the careful analyst. Most of these specimens are patent medicine bottles—including a number of whole or reconstructable examples (Figure 6.5). The large quantity of patent medicine bottles certainly speak to the Sister's long tradition of ministering to the ill—although they certainly chose poorly.

Of course, the sisters were not alone. "Patent medicine" is a term used to describe any number of concoctions sold in the late-19th and early-20th centuries to cure all types of aliments—without a prescription, of course (Fike 1987:3). They were widely popular with the public as they could be purchased without a visit to the doctor, and prior to 1900 "shrewd opportunists took advantage of the lack of federal drug controls" and made outlandish claims for their products that often contained little, if any, actual medicine (Fike 1987:3). For instance, several of the bottles recovered at 3SB1088 once held the very products that caused Samuel Hopkins Adams to write The Great American Fraud (1905) exposing the patent medicine industry in the early 20th century. Liquizone, shown in Figure 5 in two bottle sizes recovered from excavations, was labeled as a cure for everything from dysentery to dandruff (Fike 1987:68), but could actually be quite harmful as it was 99% water and 1% hydrochloric acid. Similarly, several whole and partially reconstructable examples of Dr. J. Hostetters Stomach Bitters bottles were recovered from the excavations. Hostetters was a common, popular bitters that could contain up to 47% alcohol (in the same range as whiskey; Fike 1987:36) but otherwise contained like to "cure" its patients. Of course, the sisters may have been using products such as Dr. Hostetters Stomach Bitters to consume alcohol in a socially acceptable manner, but he number of these artifacts suggest more than personal use by the sisters—they clearly point toward their established practice of ministering to the poor and sick.

Finally, one of the more interesting (and unexpected) classes of artifacts to be encountered at 3SB1088 was ammunition for firearms. From the six excavation units a total of four artifacts related to firearms were recovered. These include a piece of lead shot and two .22 caliber cartridges. The most fascinating piece of ammunition recovered was a fired .44 caliber Webley center fire cartridge. Introduced in 1868, the .44 Webley round was used in the Webley RIC revolver— the standard service weapon of the Royal Irish Constabulary (Barnes 1972:170) These small, snub-nosed guns were known as pocket revolvers and were widely copied. Popular models were known as the British Bull Dog, or sometimes, more appropriately in this case, the Ulster Bulldog. This .44 Webley cartridge holds a number of important interpretive resonances for the sisters. Not only is it directly connected to Ireland, but the Webley would have been the perfect concealable, protective sidearm for a woman of the cloth on the frontier. This was practical as Fort Smith was a frontier known for its dangerous, violent, male-dominated character.

Hidden Diversity in Fort Smith: Remembering the Sisters of Mercy

One of the intriguing aspects of this project came not from the archae-ology, but from the realm of cultural memory. Everyone we had talked to had mentioned this chimney in connection with Zachary Taylor, but none—not even the Deacon and other members of the Immaculate Con-ception congregation—had mentioned that that this same building had been the first convent of the Sisters of Mercy in Fort Smith (Church of the Immaculate Conception 1999:18–19).

When we came across this fact during our archival research, we were astonished. The story of nuns and at least eight families transplanted directly from Ireland to what was then the very edge of the western world—the frontier border with Indian Territory—seemed like an im-portant piece of history. Not to mention that, unlike Zachary Taylor who was only in Fort Smith for four years, The Sisters of Mercy had a long-term and lasting impact on Fort Smith. They founded St. Anne's Academy and St. Edward's Hospital, and educated many generations of Fort Smith's Catholic youth.

Because of its entanglements with other operational constructs, the definition of cultural memory is remarkably hard to parse. It is "not the retrieval of stored information, but the putting together of a claim about past states of affairs by means of a framework of shared cultural understanding" (Radley 1990:46). Cultural memory can be seen as a piecemeal integration of various different personal pasts into a single common past(s) that members of a larger community come to identify with and remember collectively (Misztal 2003:11). It is a "collective project that is crucial to the consolidation or construction of group, community or national identities," but it's also (and we often do not talk about this aspect as much) "a site of hegemonic struggle, as a fluid ideological terrain" (Swedenburg 2003:xxix).

In the case of Fort Smith, several factors work in multiple ways to favor General Taylor over the sisters in the town's cultural memory. First there is the historical trope of the frontier. To most in the region the idea of historical Fort Smith conjures up pictures of bands of outlaws, the menace of attacks from the Indian territory, "hanging" Judge Parker and his infamous gallows, and, of course, Belle Starr and her other "ladies of the evening" housed in Fort Smith's notorious brothels. This rough, rowdy, lawless portrait of the frontier leaves little room for the formal education and piety represented by the Sisters of Mercy.

Zachary Taylor, on the other hand, was nicknamed Old Rough and Ready, and spent much of his career policing the frontier and battling with Native American groups. The sisters, of course, fit in to aspects of this trope better than one might think as they has a reputation for ministering to prostitutes in the urban slums of Ireland, but that is lost under the weight of popular ideas about the city's frontier past.

Anti-Catholic sentiment is another very likely factor in the suppression of the Sisters of Mercy in Fort Smith's cultural memory. In the 1840s, anti-Catholic factions in the Fort Smith area filed a lawsuit in an attempt to keep Bishop Byrne from purchasing old Camp Belknap for his Irish colony, and anti-papist rhetoric played a major part in discourses of many southern and rural political movements in the late 19th century (as well as the first half of the 20th century). I can't help but suspect that this may be the explanation for large silences in several published Fort Smith histories—such as omission of St. Anne's Academy from the chapter on schools and education in one such history published in the 1960s (Maples 1965:56–61) despite the fact that St. Anne's was the second school to be chartered in the whole state of Arkansas and didn't close its doors until 1973 (Sisters of Mercy 1989:191).

Despite all of these factors that work to mitigate the Sisters of Mercy's presence in Fort Smith's history, this lone chimney and the artifacts recovered from our excavations, have provided us with a glimpse through the haze of cultural memory to their definite and important presence and works. These archaeological excavations have shed a little light on the hidden diversity present on Fort Smith's—and the state of Arkansas's—history.

REFERENCES

Adams, Samuel Hopkins
1905   *The Great American Fraud*. Press of the American Medical Association, New York, New York.
Barnes, Frank C.
1972   ".44 Webley/.44 R.I.C.", in *Cartridges of the World*, Pp. 170 & 177. Northfield, IL: DBI Books.
Bauer, K. Jack
1985   *Zachary Taylor: Soldier, Planter, Statesman of the Old Southwest*. Louisiana State University Press: Baton Rouge, LA.
Church of the Immaculate Conception
1999   *From the Foundation Up: The Story of a Frontier Parish*. August House.
Dyer, Brainerd
1946   *Zachary Taylor*. Louisiana State University Press: Baton Rouge.
Faulk, Odie B. and Billy Mac Jones
1983   *Fort Smith: An Illustrated History*. Western Heritage Books, Muskogee, OK.

Fry, J. Reese
1848   *A Life of Gen. Zachary Taylor: Comprising a Narrative of Events Connected with his Professional Career, Derived from Public Documents and Private Correspondence.* Grigg, Elliot and Company: Philadelphia, PA.
Hamilton, Holman
1941   *Zachary Taylor: Soldier of the Republic.* Bobbs-Merrill Company: Indianapolis, IN.
Hilliard, Jerry E.
2008   An Antebellum Ozark Community and the Civil War: The Archeology of the Second Mount Comfort Church (3WA880), Washington, County, Arkansas. Arkansas Archeological Survey Research Series No. 63.
Mapes, Ruth B.
1965   *Old Fort Smith: Cultural Center on the Southwestern Frontier.* Pioneer Books, Little Rock, AR.
Misztal, Barbara A.
2003   *Theories of Social Remembering.* Open University Press, Maidenhead, Berkshire, England.
Nuttall, Thomas
1999   [1821] *A Journal of the Travels into the Arkansas Territory During the Year 1819.* (edited by Savoie Lottinville). University of Arkansas Press, Fayetteville.
Patton, J. Fred
1992   *History of Fort Smith, Arkansas: 1817–1992.* Heritage Press, Little Rock, Arkansas.
Radley, Alan
1990   Artifacts, Memory, and a Sense of Place. In *Collective Remembering*, David Middleton and Derek Edwards, editors, Pp. 45–59. Sage Publications, London, England.
Sisters of Mercy with Jane Ramos
1989   *Arkansas Frontiers of Mercy: The Sisters of Mercy in Arkansas.* St. Edwards Press: Fort Smith, AR.
Swedenburg, Ted
2003   *Memories of Revolt: The 1936–1939 Rebellion and the Palestinian National Past.* University of Arkansas Press, Fayetteville, Arkansas.

7

UNCOVERING THE PAST

The Lewis Log Home and Its Place in Ozark History

Eric Proebsting

Log architecture is an important part of American culture.[1] Even though the above-ground remains of log buildings are disappearing from the present landscape, memories associated with these structures still capture our collective imagination by drawing on notions of pioneer settlement and rugged self-sufficiency. Myths have grown around these structures over the years, including the idea that log architecture represents a building tradition unique to America (Shurtleff 1939). Proven false by several generations of architectural historians, it is clear that similar traditions existed elsewhere in northern Europe, Germany, and parts of the British Isles when colonists immigrated to the New World in the 17th and 18th centuries (Kimball 1922; Mercer 1927a, 1927b; Wertenbaker 1938; Kniffen and Glassie 1966; Jordan 1985; Jordan and Kaups 1989; as cited in Johnson 1997:57–60). While there have been stylistic changes over time, the basic methods of log construction—like many other cultural traditions—were carried by immigrants to America from overseas during the colonial period.

A second set of myths has intertwined log buildings with American politics. Starting in the 19th century, the idea of leaders rising from humble beginnings to assume political office became a common theme, especially during election years. In presidential politics, this concept came to the forefront during the Log Cabin Campaign of 1840, which carried William Henry Harrison to office behind frontier-based images of log buildings, plows, and hard cider (Gunderson 1957; Roberts et al. 2012). Although scholars have shown this image to be more fiction than reality, among the handful of presidents who truly were born into humble circumstances, none embodies this ideal more completely than Abraham Lincoln (Pessen 1984; Weslager 1969:261–315). The son of a backcountry farmer, Lincoln, like his neighbors, lived in log homes throughout his childhood. His nickname "rail splitter" came to represent these rough-hewn beginnings during the election of 1860; however, as discussed in more detail near the conclusion of this essay, it was only years after his death that Lincoln's image came to be associated with log cabins (Donald 1995:19–37, 244–245; Pitcaithley 2001:240–242; Weslager 1969:291–298).

While the use of log buildings to represent, preserve, and commemorate American heritage has a long and complex history, this chapter has the modest goal of uncovering the history of a single log home located in the Ozark Mountains of northwest Arkansas. Built in 1841, the Lewis log house was among the oldest buildings standing in the state when it was dismantled and moved to the Shiloh Museum of Ozark History in 1989.[2] Permanent exhibits on the region's pioneer past now use portions of this structure to convey the heritage of the region. An unfortunate result is that the memories of more recent family history and the creation of an imagined Ozark landscape have covered over the true pioneer period history of this structure, and the story of the Lewis family who built it.[3] Through the research methods, materials, and perspectives of historical archaeology, it is possible to reconnect the Lewis log home with its original owners and surrounding landscape. The result is a complex story that brings to light the rich historical record that can exist for this period of Arkansas history, even for a seemingly straightforward archaeological site, such as an Ozark Mountain farmstead.

Research Approach, Methods, and Materials

Contextual approaches have grown in importance in historical archaeology over the past twenty years (Beaudry et al. 1991; De Cunzo and Herman 1996; Heath 1999; Barile and Brandon 2004; Hicks and Beaudry 2006; Majewski and Gaimster 2009; Lee 2011). As presented in Mary Beaudry's essay, "Reinventing Historical Archaeology," this program of research seeks to focus research directly on people, by showing them as active agents who are engaged in shaping their world. In this way, the details of everyday life are as important as the broader themes of human history (Beaudry 1996:480–481, 483). As a result, contextual archaeology provides a compelling way to challenge historical myths, requiring a shift away from making "totalizing generalizations" about the past toward studying the actual lives of individual people and the communities in which they lived (Beaudry 1996:494–496).

This approach to historical archaeology uses diverse lines of historical evidence to examine the past (Hicks and Beaudry 2006). A classic definition by James Deetz states that the materials available for archaeologists to study can include anything found within "that segment of [our] physical environment which is purposely shaped . . . according to culturally dictated plans" (Deetz 1977a:10; see also Deetz 1977b:24–25, 1996:35–37). In this spirit, the material culture drawn on for this chapter is broadly defined and includes census records, local history, family photographs, oral accounts, household ceramics, and architectural remains. While there are many ways to use these sources to answer questions about the past, the key is to draw on the strengths that are inherent to each strand of data. Using an analytical approach, both qualitative and quantitative evidence can be woven together to create new information about past people and their cultures that would otherwise remain out of reach (Barber and Berdan 1998:247–273).

In addition, this chapter seeks to contribute toward the research design proposed to historical archaeologists by Mark Groover in his book entitled *The Archaeology of North American Farmsteads* (2008). In particular, Groover stresses the need to develop detailed stories of individual farmsteads, which are placed within the larger communities and regions that surrounded them (Groover 2008:18, 25). In this way, examining the Lewis farmstead on its own terms provides a compelling description of life as it existed on this portion of the Arkansas frontier from the outset of American settlement. This is significant, as other archaeologists have noted little has been done to examine Ozark farmsteads from the first half of the 19th century (Sabo 1990; Stewart-Abernathy 1999; Wettstaed 2003). These farmsteads, and the people who created them, deserve our attention. Farmsteads were the fundamental form of American settlement and their social, economic, and environmental practices continue to shape the character of the region.

American Settlement and Northwest Arkansas

Arkansas, on the southwestern frontier of the United States, came open to American settlement following the Louisiana Purchase in 1803. Free individuals and their families took advantage of this chance by traveling to Arkansas Territory in search of new economic opportunities. Enslaved

African Americans were an important part of this westward movement, as were the displaced groups of Native Americans who were driven from their homelands (Bolton 1993, 1998; McNeilly 2000; Williams et al. 2005).

Northwest Arkansas was contested ground from the outset of American settlement. At this time, northwest Arkansas was occupied by several different groups of Native Americans, largely the Osage and the Cherokee. Tempers ran high as these two tribes struggled to gain hold over the region's rich hunting grounds. To lessen these tensions, William Lovely, a government agent, persuaded the Osage to cede their land claims to the Cherokee in 1816. Known as Lovely's Purchase, these lands were intended as a peaceful buffer between the two groups. Instead, they became a battleground. The result was that northwest Arkansas was left largely uninhabited until the Cherokee were removed westward to Indian Territory, and the region was officially opened to American settlement in 1828 (Key 2000:136–137).

Washington County was created by the Arkansas Territorial legislature in 1828. At first, the county was much larger than today, but became smaller in size as it filled with American settlers until reaching its present size and shape in 1836 (Goodspeed 1889:36, 142). The population of Washington County grew quickly, and by 1840, it was the largest in the state. Most of these settlers were farmers, and census records show Washington County still led the state in the production of livestock, wheat, oats, and corn in 1850 (Smith 1995:48; U.S. Census 1841, 1853).

While the majority of these settlers did not own slaves, slavery played an important part in the county's settlement, politics, and economy throughout the antebellum period.[4] In general, most slaveholdings were small compared with the large cotton plantations established in southern Arkansas. This reality meant that slaves living in Washington County often lived and worked in close proximity to their owners. Regardless of these different working conditions, research has shown that the institution of slavery could be just as brutal a reality for those living under its lash in the uplands of Washington County as it was for those living in the lowlands of southern Arkansas and elsewhere across the state (Hughes 2009; Proebsting 2009:189–190; Smith 1995).

The Local Community

Finding the boundaries of a farming community can be difficult. This is especially true in the antebellum South where these settlements were more dispersed and divided along racial lines than their contemporaries in the in the northeastern United States (Burton and McMath 1982:xi–xii; see also Burton 2002). In the broadest sense, for a community to exist, its individuals need to share something in common, which can include such things as shared interests, experiences, identities, or geographies. For the purpose of the present research, the community surrounding the Lewis Farmstead is defined by the historic boundaries of its political township.[5]

White River Township was established in the southwestern portion of Washington County in 1837 (Baker 2003:189) (Figure 7.1). Within the community's boundaries was an interesting mix of terrain. The most prominent geographic feature was its namesake, the White River, which flowed as two separate branches through the community with a fertile band of soil along its banks. Most of the community's bottomlands bordered the White River. These lowlands attracted the many farmers who settled this portion of the Ozarks. The White River could be used for fishing and transportation, and its soils were deeper and more fertile than could be found along the rugged hills that lined the sides of the valley (Harnish 1978:31; Harper et al. 1969; Featherstonhaugh 1835:57). In the northern section of the community, these river bottoms were covered in trees at the outset of American settlement, which gave way to gently rolling prairies with occasional clusters of oak trees dotting the landscape. In the southern half of the community, the ground rose upward toward the Boston Mountains. Here, the headwaters of the White River were surrounded by stonier upland soils, which were covered by mature, oak-hickory forests (Lesquereux 1860:337; Harper et al. 1969; Miller 1972; Chaney 1990).

Since nearly all of the households who settled this portion of northwest Arkansas were farmers, it is not surprising that the more desirable bottomlands were the first portion of the community to be settled. According to the occupations recorded in the federal census, 143 of the 148 free adult men (96.6%) residing in White River Township in 1840 had agriculture listed as their main occupation. The rest of the township's residents were focused on skilled trades or manufactures. Even though census takers did not name specific trades in 1840, White River Township's 1850 Census suggests these settlers could have been blacksmiths, carpenters, millers, stone workers, and wagon makers (Proebsting 2009:340–353). As the community grew in size, the local economy became more diverse. This meant that in 1850, about 10% of township's 146 free adult men 16 years of age or older were primarily involved in skilled trades, education, or ministry. Nevertheless, even for

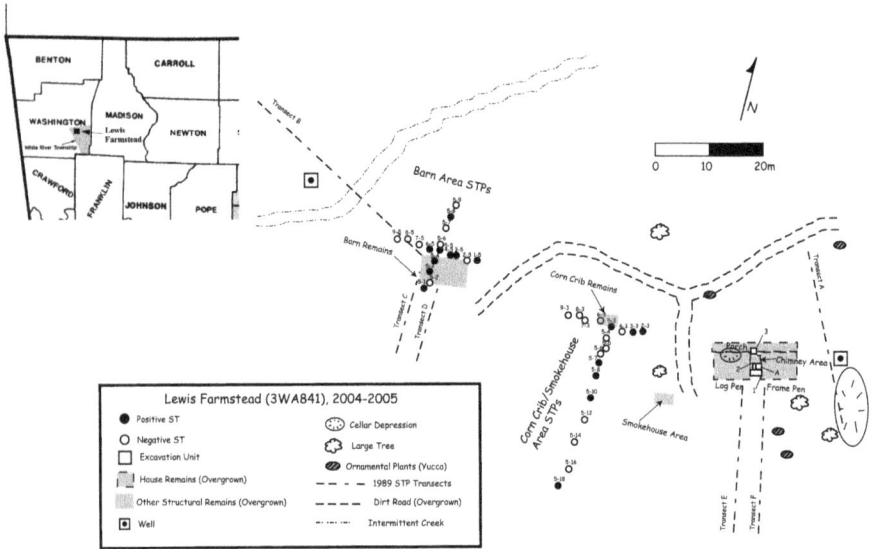

Figure 7.1. Overview of northwest Arkansas showing the location of Washington County, White River Township, and the Lewis Farmstead (inset); Site map of the Lewis Farmstead as recorded during archaeological investigations.

these individuals, the seasonal routines of raising crops and tending live-stock likely remained at the center of daily life (Proebsting 2009:151).

Most of those who immigrated to White River Township began their lives in the Upper South (79.0%). In 1850, this included the slavehold-ing states of Kentucky, Tennessee, Arkansas, Virginia, North Carolina, Missouri, and Maryland. The other settlers hailed from the Lower South (12.7%) and the Lower North (8.0%), with one individual born in England (Proebsting 2009:150). These settlers were not isolated pio-neers. Their most intimate connections were at home, where households depended on each other to make their new farms a success. Extended families and neighbors provided another line of support for tasks, such as house raising, corn shucking, quilting, log rolling, rail splitting, and hog killing (Van Benbrook 1941). Help from extended family members was often a significant part of daily life. In fact, as Mark Hackbarth's research has shown, some settlers in Washington County chose less productive soils in favor of living closer to their kin (Hackbarth 1980:48–49).

Trade was another connection between the settlers of White River Township and the outside world. Fayetteville served as the county seat and economic center of Washington County throughout the antebellum period. Local roads and trails connected residents of White River Township to Fayetteville, while regional thoroughfares facilitated a steady flow of goods, people, and produce in and out of Washington County (Cleek 2013:135–138). The most important of these roads ran from St. Louis, Missouri, through Fayetteville on its way to Van Buren, a town on the banks of the Arkansas River. Hiram Rumfield traveled this route between Fayetteville and Van Buren as an agent for John Butterfield's Overland Mail Company in 1860. In a letter to his wife, he described his noisy stagecoach ride "along the mountain sides [and over] masses of broken rock . . . in fearful proximity to precipitous ravines of unknown depth" (Rumfield 1929:238; see also Greene 1994).

It could be a frightening trip, as speeding stagecoaches and plodding wagons made their way along this path throughout the antebellum period. For the residents of northwest Arkansas, this was because the Arkansas River offered their most convenient, reasonable, and reliable connection with the outside world. As early as the 1810s, settlers used the river, taking flatboats and keelboats to this portion of Arkansas Territory (Goodspeed 1889:143–144; Worley 1952). As steamboats began making their way to Van Buren in the 1820s, a steady supply of goods flowed up the Arkansas River into northwest Arkansas.

For many settlers, raising crops and livestock was the primary means to purchase goods and provide for their families. While the farming economy was built upon mixed-grain agriculture, corn was the most important crop. There was an enormous increase in the amount of corn produced by farmers living across White River Township and the rest of Washington County during the antebellum period (Proebsting 2009:166–167). This corn was not only grown to supply the basic needs of free and enslaved settlers; it was also bartered and sold to purchase goods and services from the local market in Fayetteville (Musgrave 1929:53).

One way to see these purchasing practices is to apply historical geographer Sam Hilliard's subsistence index to the corn yields listed for farmsteads in the United States Census (Hilliard 1972). Developed from antebellum period sources, Hilliard's index estimates the amount of corn required for each person and animal living in agricultural households across the Old South.[6] As such, it provides a good starting point for researching mid-19th century rural economies in Arkansas, and has been used by historians and historical archaeologists working in the region over the past thirty years (Bolton 1993; Otto 1980; Proebsting 2009). The estimated 25,000 extra bushels of corn raised in White River Township in 1850 would have been, in the words of local historian Ted Smith, "as good as gold" on the market of Washington County (Proebsting 2009:167; Smith 1995:40–41). As a result, the acres increased, which led travelers such as Hiram Rumfield to marvel as they passed along the road at the valleys of southern Washington County "covered" with "one or two thousand acres" of corn by the end of antebellum period (Rumfield 1929:238).

While a wide variety of livestock were raised, hogs were the most common type in White River Township throughout the antebellum period. By 1850, there were over four hogs for every person in the community. Many of these hogs were rounded up in the fall and butchered to provide meat for the family during the winter months (Musgrave 1929:52–53; Proebsting 2009:174; Schrock 1992:176–182). Other animals were raised as investments. Sam Hilliard's subsistence index provides an estimate for the number of hogs needed each year to provide for the basic necessities of each household. In 1850, an estimated 70% of the 2,864 hogs owned in White River Township were raised beyond these settlers' basic food requirements (Proebsting 2009:174). As sources of wealth, hogs were sold or bartered to merchants in nearby Fayetteville and across the surrounding countryside. For example, the account books of Stephen K. Stone show that pork and its products—lard, bacon, shoulders, and hams—were taken as credit at his Fayetteville store toward a wide variety of goods during the 1850s (Musgrave 1929:53–54, 72–75).

The Lewis Farmstead

Hugh Lewis and his brother Joseph were among the first American settlers to migrate to northwest Arkansas after it was acquired by the United States from the Cherokee in the Treaty of 1828. For the Lewis family, moving westward was a tradition that began when their grandfather emigrated from Ireland to North Carolina in the 1700s. Their father, John Lewis, continued this westward migration by moving his family from North Carolina to Kentucky where Joseph was born in 1802. Soon after, the family moved once again; this time to Washington County, Missouri, just before Hugh's birth in 1804 (Goodspeed 1889:141,973).

After the brothers were grown, family history claims that 20-year-old Joseph set out on horseback to explore Arkansas in 1822. Traveling south from Missouri, he began his trek in Lawrence County, which was located in the territory's northeast corner and included the recently established town of Davidsonville. He then made his way down the Southwest Trail, staying in Pulaski County, which included the small settlement of Little Rock, before reaching Hempstead County in the southwest corner of Arkansas. Here he most likely spent at least some time in the new frontier town of Washington (Goodspeed 1889:973–974).

It may be that the Lewis brothers reunited in Hempstead County. Here Joseph met his wife, whose family had come to southwest Arkansas from Virginia in the first decades of the 19th century. It is also possible that Hugh met his wife Harriet in Hempstead County. She was from Georgia, but had settled in Arkansas by the time the couple's first child, John, was born in 1829 (U.S. Census 1850; Goodspeed 1889:973–974). After several years, family history suggests Hugh and Joseph traveled to northwest Arkansas in 1831. While Joseph's family stayed behind and waited until his farmstead was established in 1836, it is unknown whether Hugh's wife and young son took part in the initial trip. However, they most likely would have stayed behind as well, since Harriet was pregnant with their second child (U.S. Census 1850; Goodspeed 1889:973–974).

Upon reaching Washington County, Hugh's farmstead was established in White River Township, along the headwaters of the White River valley (Figure 7.1). The remains of three log buildings were found on this site when researchers from the University of Arkansas and Arkansas Archeological Survey examined the Lewis farmstead in the spring of 1989. Efforts were made to map, photograph, and sample these structures for the purpose of tree-ring dating and architectural analysis (Hilliard and Thomson 1998).

Since the late 1970s, dendrochronology has been an important tool to study historic log buildings located across Arkansas (see Stahle 1978, 1979; Stahle and Wolfman 1985). This research seeks to combine dendrochroology with other types of historic evidence whenever possible, such as written records, architectural information, and archaeological remains. Together, this research creates detailed histories by using cutting and construction dates for the building timbers.

Adding to this growing body of research, a Master's thesis examining the building remains of the Lewis farmstead was written by Kerr Thomson (1990) under the direction of Malcolm Cleaveland and David Stahle of the Tree Ring Laboratory at the University of Arkansas. A total of 42 wood samples were collected, processed, and analyzed. The Lewis house was by far the most intact of the buildings studied, and 31 samples were taken from its original log pen. In addition, four samples were taken from the home's timber frame addition; five from the remnants of a log corncrib; and one from a badly decayed double-pen log barn (Hilliard and Thomson 1998:61; Thomson 1990). Results of this analysis provide remarkable insight into the process of establishing the Lewis farmstead and the architectural changes that took place within the house over time.

At least three separate building episodes took place as part of the Lewis family's occupation of the site. The first included the construction of the log corncrib, which dendrochronology suggests was built in the winter of 1834–1835 (Thomson 1990:48). This building would have been a crucial part of establishing the farmstead, providing a place to store the crop over the winter after the initial clearing and cultivating. A log barn may have also been built during this period of settlement. Unfortunately, the barn's remaining timbers were too decayed to produce a conclusive construction date (Thomson 1990:46–48). In addition to these two outbuildings, Hugh built an initial cabin for shelter, and perhaps a smokehouse to cure and store meat. While creating these buildings was important, most efforts would have been focused on establishing fields and raising livestock. These priorities are suggested in local tax assessments, which show Hugh first acquired 80 acres of bottomland in 1836. This purchase was three years before he acquired the less fertile land that overlooked these fields and included the family's first home and associated outbuildings, which had already been established (Hilliard Thomson 1998:63).

By 1840, the Lewis farmstead had grown to 240 acres. Aside from the 80 acre of bottomland, most of this additional land was higher ground that was left as "unimproved" woodlands, which could have been used for cutting timber, grazing livestock, and hunting game. The household grew alongside the farm, with Cornelius, Calvin, and Ella born during this time; making the Lewis' a family of seven by 1840 (U.S. Census 1850). This prompted a second period of building. Dendrochronology shows that construction began on a new single-pen log home in the late winter or early summer of 1841 (Figure 7.2). The home measured 24x16ft, had a hearth and chimney on its east gable that provided a place for cooking and a source of warmth, and included a half-story in the upstairs loft as additional sleeping space (Hilliard and Thomson 1998:64–65). After the new home was built, the family grew yet again, with Rebecca, Rachel, and Susan born in 1843, 1845, and 1849 respectively. Tragically, Calvin died from a horse kick on April 10, 1846 and was buried on the property, where a dressed and lettered sandstone marker still marks his grave. This made the household a family of nine by 1850, with an additional

WEST ELEVATION   EAST ELEVATION

FRONT OR NORTH ELEVATION

Log Pen 1841 Construction

Frame Pen 1851 Construction

BACK OR SOUTH ELEVATION

Log Pen 1841 Construction

Frame Pen 1851 Construction

■ End of Second Floor Joists
■ Log Mortice for Porch

⌊2 ft⌋

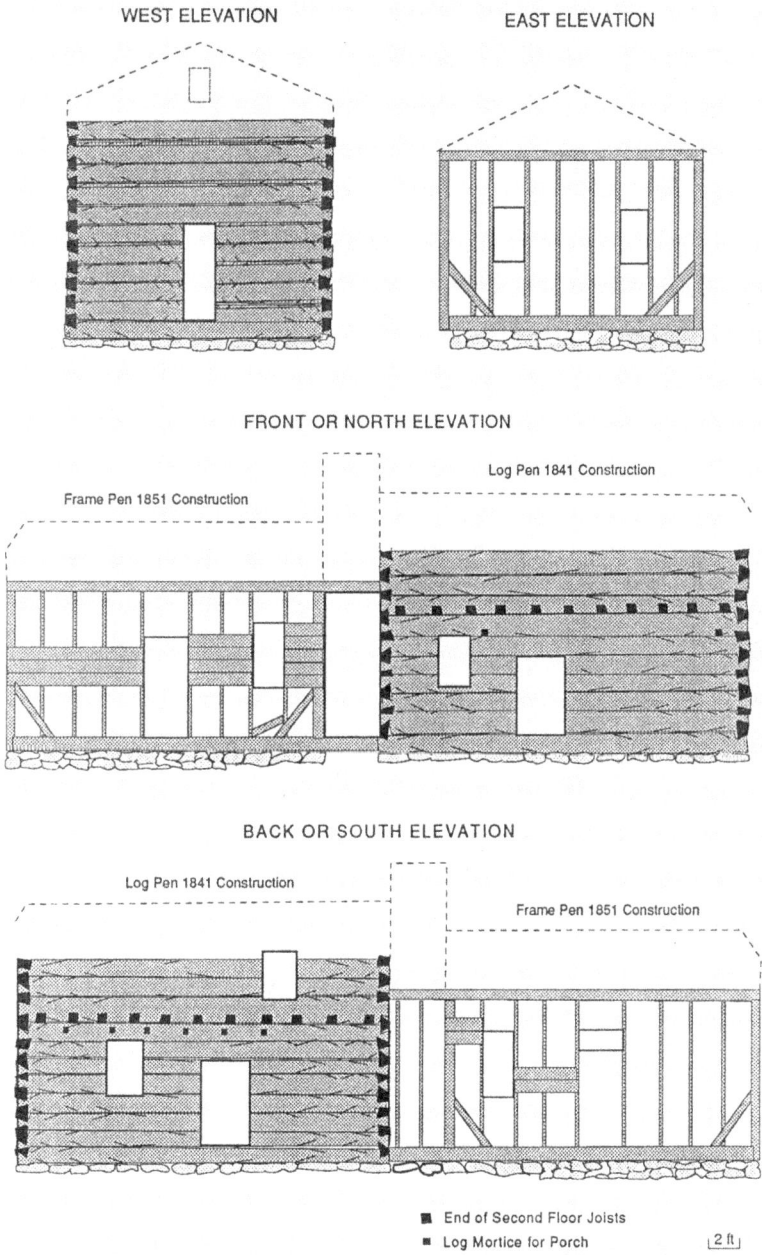

Figure 7.2. Drawings of front, back, and sides of the Lewis House as it appeared prior to its removal to Shiloh Museum. Drawing courtesy of Jerry Hilliard (Hilliard and Thomson 1998:59).

24-year-old free laborer named James West living with them as a farmer when the census was taken (U.S. Census 1850).

Lewis did not own slaves. Nevertheless, based on property value and agricultural production, the Lewis farmstead was among the most successful farms in White River Township in 1850. The family held 260 acres and raised a variety of crops on 80 acres of cultivated land. The corncrib would have held a portion of the family's 1,200 bushels harvested that year. In addition, Hugh's household held 17 horses and 10 oxen—the most in the community. These animals along with 11 milk cows, 20 beef cattle, 54 sheep, and 50 hogs contributed to the Lewis family's livestock having the highest value in White River Township. Since it was open range, these animals could have foraged for mast on the farm's 180 unimproved acres and grazed elsewhere in the surrounding landscape (Proebsting 2009:355; U.S. Census 1850).

There is no doubt that Hugh held a surplus of corn and livestock in 1850. Compared to the number of adults living in the household and the livestock holdings of surrounding farmsteads, it is clear that the Lewis family held more horses and oxen than were needed for everyday use. Applying Sam Hilliard's subsistence index also shows both corn and hogs raised in large enough numbers to be sold and traded on the local market. An estimated 769 extra bushels of corn were produced above the family's basic needs for food and fodder, while 32 hogs were produced beyond simple subsistence (Hilliard 1972; Proebsting 2009:355; U.S. Census 1850).

Along with historic documents, archaeological remains provide evidence of the economic ties that once connected the Lewis farmstead with local and more distant communities. As has been found for farmsteads located elsewhere in the Upland South, well-preserved archaeological deposits are often few and far between, especially when earlier agricultural landscapes have been altered over the course of several periods of land use and ownership. In these circumstances, standing historic structures often provide the best hope for locating preserved archaeological remains in sealed archaeological contexts (Joseph and Reed 1997:86, 94).

This is certainly the case for the Lewis Farmstead, where an intact archaeological feature was discovered beneath the hearth and south sill of the home's frame addition. This timber-framed pen was added in the summer of 1851 (Figure 7.2). It measured 24x16ft and was joined to the east side of the log pen by a 4ft wide space for storage at the front and back of the house, and a large stone chimney at the center (Hilliard and Thomson 1998:58, 61) (Figure 7.3). Discovered by Jerry Hilliard in 1989 as part

Figure 7.3. An early 20th century image of the saddlebag-style home built by the Lewis family in 1851. The Reed family who resided in the house when the photograph was taken is standing in the foreground. Courtesy Shiloh Museum of Ozark History, Ruth Morris Collection (S-90-32-82).

of his archaeological assessment, this small deposit of mid-19th century artifacts was found after the chimney and portions of the house were removed from the property. Excavations revealed a handful of mid-19th century English ceramics, including sponge and shell-edge tablewares as well as transfer-printed patterns and hand-painted floral designs (Hilliard and Thomson 1998:66; Proebsting 2009:160–162, 259–262).

While small in number, these artifacts are emblematic of the broader range of everyday goods used by the Lewis family during the antebellum period. Edge-decorated ceramics, such as those used by the Lewis family, were found on tables all across America (Miller 1991; Miller and Hunter 1990; Ward 1997). Excavations located across Arkansas suggest these relatively inexpensive plates and platters made their way to every corner of the state from the outset of American settlement (Cande et al. 2008; Martin 1978; Proebsting 2009; Stewart-Abernathy 1988). This is certainly true for northwest Arkansas. Like elsewhere, the cost of these goods depended on supply and demand.

Markets were quite fluid during the early years of settlement. For example, when writing his memoirs in the 1870s, John Billingsley recalled paying "$4 for the first set of tea cups and saucers [he had] ever owned and $2 for a green-edged dish worth now about 5 cents." This price was paid to French traders from Arkansas Post who rowed their canoes up the Arkansas River in the late 1810s to sell cloth, "earthing ware," and other items to settlers living near the present town of Van Buren (Worley 1952:329). Even with the advent of steamboats, which dramatically increased the amount of goods arriving in northwest Arkansas, low water and flooding had the potential to cause periodic rises and falls in local prices for settlers living in White River Township and the rest of Washington County during the antebellum period.

Nevertheless, the presence of these tablewares on archaeological sites located across Washington County suggests they were readily available and easily purchased by many households across the region (Bruce 2005; Hilliard 2008; Lafferty et al. 1997; Martin 1972). As shown in Leslie Stewart-Abernathy's research related to the Moser Farmstead, Ozark residents were "independent but not isolated" by the late 19th century. This argument runs against the hillbilly stereotype that dominates the popular perception of the Ozark Mountains, and is strongly supported by material culture (Stewart-Abernathy 1986, 1987, 1992).[7] The Lewis farmstead and other sites across the region show that this principle applies to the antebellum period as well. Although the details vary over time and space, there is no doubt that settlers had a wide variety of social, economic, and cultural connections tying them to their communities and the larger world around them (see Brandon 2004; Brandon and Davidson 2005; Jordan-Bychkov 2003:44; Proebsting 2009).

The Lewis Log House

While "small things forgotten" comprise much of the materials studied by historical archaeologists, larger artifacts, such as historic buildings, also reveal a great deal about the past (Deetz 1977b, 1996). As a result, these larger parts of the cultural landscape have been examined by generations of scholars working in historical archaeology and related disciplines, such as architectural history, folklore, and cultural geography (Carter and Cromley 2005:105–118; Hicks and Horning 2006; Jordan-Bychkov 2003:22; Lounsbury 2010). One goal of this work is to better understand the lives, environments, and traditions of the people who created these buildings. Careful study of the construction materials, practices, and form used in the Lewis house provides additional insight into the daily lives of the Lewis family members as well as the larger history of this portion of the Arkansas Ozarks.

What was it made of?

Local building materials were used to create the Lewis home. The sandstone used to construct the foundation stones, hearth, and chimney was most likely procured on the farmstead (Hilliard and Thomson 1998:65; Sizemore 1994:162). In addition, white oak was selected for building the home and outbuildings. Oak was a principle part of the forests that covered the sandstone foothills of the White River valley when settlers such as Lewis established their farmsteads in the 1830s (Chaney 1990; Miller 1972:36). American settlers chose white oak for construction purposes beginning in colonial times. Larger trees were especially useful, since they provided durable heartwood that could be applied to all manner of construction (Cronon 1983:111–113; Lincoln 1986:189; Sizemore 1994:150). Tree ring analysis of the house and corncrib shows that Lewis selected mature trees for building. Subtracting the cutting dates of these logs from their innermost rings reveals an average age of 153 years old, with their first years of growth ranging in date from AD 1624 to 1761.[8]

These trees were part of the mature forests that surrounded the Lewis farmstead. Cutting dates also reveal that most of these logs were set aside to season before building. Seasoning allowed the timber to become lighter in weight and easier to work during the construction process. This period of drying allowed moisture to release from the logs and helped avoid the settling and shrinking that happens when green timbers are joined together (Lincoln 1986:189; McRaven 1978:10).

For the first pen, most of the logs were cut during the fall and winter of 1840. In addition, one log was cut during the summer of 1841, perhaps as the structure was being built. The building also incorporated timber from an earlier structure, with two logs cut in the early 1830s. It may be that these timbers were originally used as part of the farmstead's first dwelling house, and then reused in the walls of the 1841 log home. A similar pattern of cutting and seasoning was also present in the timber frame addition. Of the four logs sampled, three were cut during the fall and winter of 1850, while the fourth was cut by the summer of 1851 (Thomson 1990:49–54).

The lumber used in this addition would have been milled at one of the handful of local sawmills established in northwest Arkansas at that time (Valentino 2006:148–154). The most famous of these sawmills was placed by Peter Van Winkle on a large tract of pine-covered land about 30 miles north of White River Township around 1851 (Brandon and Davidson 2005:114). Oral history suggests that Van Winkle's Mill created the pine clapboards that covered the Lewis house soon after the timber frame addition was complete (Courtney 1976:2; Hilliard and Thomson 1998:58). Unfortunately, little is known about the early history of Van Winkle's Mill. However, it seems that if these boards were cut there, it would have been done so using a horse or oxen-powered sawmill, rather than the larger steam-powered operation that was run using enslaved and free laborers on the eve of the Civil War (Brandon 2004:61; Valentino 2006:2–3, 21–23).

Who built it?

Before discussing who built the Lewis home, it is necessary to first set aside a common myth about log architecture. Often, this kind of building is automatically linked to notions of self-sufficiency. American historians have wrestled with this concept, especially as it relates to the idea of self-sufficient farming, since the 1950s. Many historians had concluded by the early 1980s that the vast majority of 18th and 19th century farming families did not live isolated from each other (Pruitt 1984:333; Shammas 1982). Instead of being lone pioneers, these farmers were socially, economically, and culturally connected in many different ways to both local and more distant communities. By the 1990s, the debate reached the point where Wilma Dunaway's book on the southern Appalachians entitled *The First American Frontier* dismissed self-sufficiency as a meaningless term. She convincingly argues that it was impossible for farming households to be entirely self-sufficient, since they were inevitably connected with others at some point during the lives of their residents (Dunaway 1996:123).

Nevertheless, the link between log architecture and self-sufficient lifestyles is present in the scholarship related to the Arkansas Ozarks. Jean Sizemore's study of *Ozark Vernacular Houses* describes the 19th and early 20th century Ozarks as being filled with "self-sufficient" family farmsteads (Sizemore 1994:190). She suggests the preference for log, rather than frame, brick, or stone houses is a good indication that "subsistence farming" began in the region with American settlement, persisted through the Civil War, and continued well into the 1880s (Sizemore 1994:155).

Despite these passing generalizations, more in-depth research suggests that only a few of these structures would have been built by a single, self-sufficient individual or household. Warren Roberts shows that a single person or household did not create the vast majority of log homes built in Indiana during the first half of the 19th century. Instead, these buildings were state-of-the-art structures that required additional labor, specialized knowledge, and as many as 70 tools to complete (Roberts 1986; as cited in Sizemore 1994:154). Henry Glassie's research into vernacular architecture supports these conclusions. As he elegantly explains, the "work was divided by specialization. Different people filled different roles in a single process, as actors in a drama" (Glassie 2000:39).

So, instead of demonstrating self-sufficiency, often log homes provide testimony to the involvement of the extended family and other members of the local community. These buildings required neighbors to share tools and donate labor. Log homes could also require the specialized skills of paid craftsmen, such as carpenters and stone masons (see Hutslar 1992; Roberts 1986). Therefore, Hugh had help building his home and outbuildings. It is possible that his brother assisted during the first years of settlement. Other members of the community might have also lent a hand. These early structures were often built as quickly as possible. This was because of the sparse nature of early settlement and the need to focus on establishing crops and livestock.

First homes were typically log cabins. As Donald Hustlar has found for log structures built in Ohio from 1750–1850, these initial habitations were often crudely made. They were characterized by early 19th century observers as having unhewn logs, plank roofs, and poorly chinked walls. These buildings stood in stark contrast to the more permanent log homes that replaced them several years later with their hewn log walls, neatly shingled roofs, and tightly insulated cracks (Hutslar 1992:76–80).

While the appearance of the first Lewis family dwelling is unknown, it was obviously a temporary structure, since it was replaced by a more substantial, single pen log home less than a decade later. Other clues related to its construction include relatively rough hewing marks found on two logs from the early 1830s that were incorporated into the 1841 home (Thomson 1990:49). This suggests that less time, labor, and crafts-manship went into the first structures built on the Lewis Farmstead.

When the new home was built in 1841, members of the Lewis' im-mediate family could have helped. Besides Hugh and Harriet, the 1840 census shows that the household had five children. The oldest child, John, would have been about 11 years old when the first pen was built, and able to assist in some of the less strenuous work. By the time the timber frame addition was added in 1851, seven children were living in the Lewis household. Two of their sons, John and Cornelius, and their oldest daughter, Nancy, were over the age of 15. This made them adults within their farming community and more than able to help with the home's construction. As mentioned before, a 24-year-old man named James West was also living with the family and could have helped with the frame addition (U.S. Census 1840, 1850).

In addition to household members, neighbors may have helped the Lewis family. Community support during house construction often came during house raisings. One of the few primary source materials that document this practice for antebellum Arkansas is the Early Settlers' Personal Histories taken by Works Progress Administration (WPA) employees from 1936 to 1941. Like other WPA interviewing projects, the purpose of these personal histories was to record the experiences of ordinary people. In this case, WPA workers collected the memories of longtime Arkansas residents (Cantrell 2004:50). Interviewers asked their elderly informants 60 standard questions, which ranged from asking the informant's age, name, and place of birth to asking about childhood memories, such as details related to construction of log homes (Cantrell 2004:54–66). The answers to these questions give a rough gauge regarding whether or not the community was involved in the construction of homes in the vicinity of the Lewis Farmstead.

To supplement the small sample of interviews for Washington County (n=5), additional interviews were added from adjoining Madison County (n=11). Eight of the 16 individuals interviewed for these counties remembered house raisings as important aspects of community life. Even more significant is the fact that all of the lifelong residents of Washington and Madison County who were born during the antebellum period remembered witnessing house raisings when they were young (Washington County WPA; Madison County WPA). Hosea Van Bennbrook was one of the lifelong residents of Washington County, born in 1846 within a few miles of the Lewis Farmstead. His interview gives insight into to how house raisings took place. He explained, "logs were brought to the place where the house was to be erected, then a house raising was given." During the event, "neighbors came together" and work was "always followed with a dance in which all took part and had a good time" (Van Bennbrook 1941).

In addition to volunteer labor, skilled craftsmen could have been hired to complete portions of the new home. Federal census records and county tax records both suggest that Lewis was on firm financial footing when the log home was built in 1841 and the frame addition was made in 1851 (Hilliard and Thomson 1998:63–65; Proebsting 2009:160, 354–356). His steady finances could have allowed him to invest in his home using professional builders. The 1850 population census shows two professional carpenters and one stonemason lived within White River Township. By 1860, the number of these craftsmen had grown to four carpenters and two stonemasons (U.S. Census 1850, 1860). And, of course, there were other professional and semi-professional craftsmen living in the surrounding area. Some individuals even chose to hire-out their skills as they moved across the countryside. For example, Clark Ward recounted that his father, a carpenter by trade, built log homes and outbuildings to support his family as they moved across Arkansas Territory in the late 1810s, and continued building for several more decades after settling in southwest Arkansas (McIver 1958).

The use of slave labor is another possibility. Even though census records show that Hugh Lewis did not own slaves himself, others did. Eleven members of the township held slaves in 1840, and nine households owned slaves in 1850 (Proebsting 2009:157). Hugh's brother also owned seven slaves during the antebellum period (Hilliard and Thomson 1998:63). Even though they lived over 15 miles apart, it is possible that Joseph could have sent laborers to help his brother during the building process. At that time, it would have also been common to hire slaves for various work-related tasks, including enslaved craftsmen who were living and working in Washington County (Hughes 2009:22–35; Smith 1995:73, 76).

What form did it take?

Regardless of whether Hugh built his home with his own hands or had help from others, the Lewis family guided the form of their house. The 1841 log house had a rectangular floor plan, measuring 16x24ft wide and one-and-a-half stories high. Based on surviving historic structures recorded in America and abroad, some scholars suggest rectangular homes are associated with Scotch-Irish or German traditions, while square homes reflect an English style of architecture. Since Hugh's grandfather emigrated from Ireland in the 1700s, it is possible Hugh inherited this building tradition from his family (Jordan 1985:23–25; Sizemore 1994:51; Goodspeed 1889:973).

The half-dovetail notches used to join the timbers of the Lewis log home are another interesting detail related to the form of the building. In his book *The Upland South*, Terry Jordan argues the half-dovetail notch was likely developed in the Virginia backcountry during the 18th century. This new invention made dovetail notches easier to fashion. It also improved their ability to channel rainwater away from the joint, which extended the life of the structure. As a result, the technique quickly spread across the region, becoming the most prevalent form of notch used across the Upland South. This was true for northwest Arkansas and the greater Ozark region, with at least 10 examples of this type of construction recorded for Washington County alone (Jordan-Bychlkov 2003:26–27; see also Sizemore 1994:150–153).

Before continuing, it should be noted that while building with logs had advantages, especially when trees were plentiful during the early years of settlement, log-based architecture also had significant constraints. Physical limits related to the length and weight of the logs made it much more common for homes to expand horizontally by adding another pen, rather than growing upward by adding another story. There were several different configurations that these new additions took, and scholars have carefully recorded their distribution to gain insight into broader cultural changes that took place across the American landscape over time (Johnson 1997:67–68; Kniffen 1965).

The Lewis home became a saddlebag-style house after the second pen was added in 1851 (Figure 7.3). The name saddlebag is a vernacular term used to describe what appeared to be two saddlebags in the form of building pens balanced on either side of a horse, which took the form of a central chimney (Rehder 2012:64–65). There is a great deal of debate about the origin of the saddlebag house in America. Some argue that it was first brought over from Britain to the Chesapeake tidewater and the Georgia and South Carolina low country during the colonial period. It was then adapted to notched-log architecture when it reached the piedmont in the 18th century (Jordan-Bychkov 2003:34).

Another explanation for the saddlebag house is that it was a variation on the Georgian style of architecture that made its way to the American colonies from England in the 1700s. Similar to the Georgian style, the two pens of a saddlebag structure are symmetrically balanced. But unlike Georgian designs, saddlebag houses followed an earlier medieval style, which gave guests access to both private and public portions of the home (Brown 1992:117–119; Glassie 2000:141; see also Deetz 1996:153–164). While this notion of an ordered shift in mindset is intriguing, such strict, structuralist readings of material culture have been criticized for lacking the historic context needed to support such broad claims about people in the past (see Johnson 1993; Orser 2002:561–562; Stewart-Abernathy 1992:114). From a practical standpoint, Hugh and Harriet had seven children ranging in age from one to 21 years old, and perhaps an additional 24-year-old man living under their roof in 1851 (U.S. Census 1850). Investing in their home by attaching a second room to the central chimney would have provided another place for cooking and heating, while also doubling the size of the home and providing additional opportunities for privacy and storage within the household.

The Production of Heritage

Hugh and Harriett Lewis sold their property to George Goodridge in 1853. It was then bought by Ambrose and Selena Clark in 1862, and Alexander and Elizabeth Reed in 1866. From that time on, the Reed family occupied the home until it was deeded to Alexander and Elizabeth's grandchildren in 1958 (Figure 7.4) (Courtney 1976:4–10; Hilliard 1989:7B).

In 1989, Elizabeth's granddaughter, Ruth Morris, agreed for the log portion of the house and sandstone chimney to be dismantled and moved to the Shiloh Museum of Ozark History in downtown Springdale, Arkansas. The Shiloh Museum was established in the 1960s to develop an understanding and appreciation of the history of this portion of Northwest Arkansas through the collection, preservation, exhibition, and interpretation of material culture related to the history of the region. Today these activities support its broader mission to "serve the public by providing resources for finding meaning, enjoyment, and inspiration in the exploration of the Arkansas Ozarks" (Shiloh Museum 2006).

Since moving to the museum, the house has been used to represent the heritage of northwest Arkansas in several ways. As part of a permanent display on pioneer history, the Shiloh Museum has used a portion of the 1841 log house to transmit what the interior of a typical pioneer log cabin once looked like (Shiloh Museum 2015). The room is mostly furnished by family heirlooms donated by Ruth Morris, which occupied the home during her childhood. The house also goes by the name of McGarrah-Reed, which is the maiden and married name of Ruth's grandmother (Figure 7.4). There is, however, no mention of the Lewis family who built and occupied the home in the 1840s and 1850s during the pioneer period of American settlement in the Ozarks.

The Lewis house has also been incorporated into an outdoor exhibit located on the grounds of Shiloh Museum (Figure 7.5). Its chimney stones were used in the restoration of the Ritter-McDonald Cabin, which is one of five buildings that were lifted from their original landscapes and reconstructed on the museum's grounds in the 1980s and 1990s. Other buildings include a barn, doctor's office, cabin, outhouse, and general store ranging in date from the 1850s to the 1930s (Neal 1989:121–122;

Figure 7.4. Ruth Morris (standing) and Elizabeth McGarrah Reed in front the home, circa 1932. Courtesy Shiloh Museum of Ozark History / Ruth Morris Collection (S-2003-2-582).

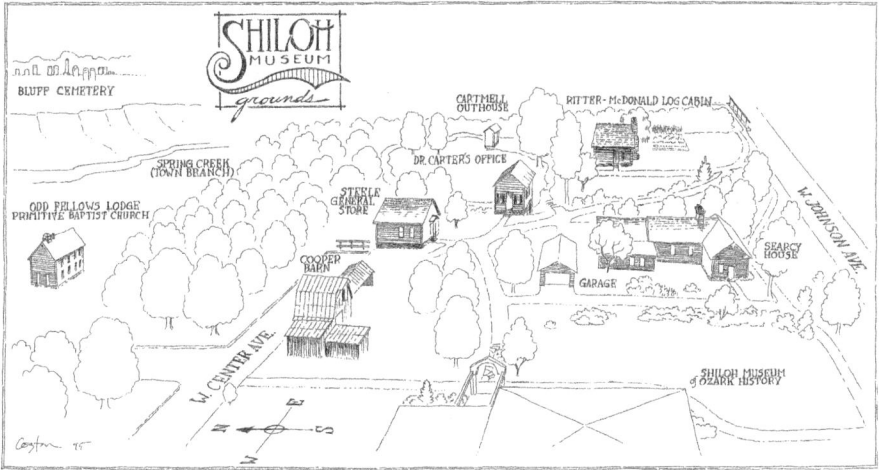

Figure 7.5. Map of the Shiloh Museum grounds. Courtesy Shiloh Museum of Ozark History.

Young 2011). Together, this mythic community of vernacular buildings contributes to the museum's overall desire to help foster and preserve a collective heritage for northwest Arkansas.

As introduced earlier in this chapter, the site that has come to be known as Abraham Lincoln's Birthplace Cabin was created near Hodgenville, Kentucky at the request of a New York-based entrepreneur at the turn of the 20th century. Undeterred by the fact that Lincoln's actual birth home had long been destroyed, a replica was built of logs taken from a nearby farm. Popularized as the "Lincoln Birthplace Cabin," it was nationally portrayed as an authentic connection to the president's pioneer past. In 1906, preservationists acquired the cabin, and after the completion of a stately stone memorial, the cabin was miniaturized to better fit its new home. Today thousands of visitors come each year to pay their respects, thus living on as an iconic symbol of our national heritage (see Pitcaithley 2001; Weslager 1969:288–297).

As historian Dwight Pithcaithley explains, constructing heritage at places like Lincoln Farm and Shiloh Museum often displays buildings and other artifacts out of their original context. Sometimes, the contexts that are created at these heritage sites reflect the "memories of the commemorators" more than "historical reality." As a result, they portray a history that is distinct from the original time and place in which the objects on display once occupied and are prone to overlook, misrepresent, and even replace the past with idealized versions of history (Pitcaithley 2001:240–241).

Conclusion

The methods and perspectives of historical archaeology shed light on the history of the Lewis home. Placing the home back within its historic context also provides an important window into the everyday lives and landscapes of the families who came to this portion of the Arkansas Ozarks during the antebellum period. The memories of more recent family history and the myths of an imagined Ozark landscape had covered over much of this history. In this respect, the Lewis log home joins a long list of cases where myth and memory have played a significant role in the portrayal of history at historic sites located in the Ozarks and elsewhere across America (see Brandon 2004; Eichstedt and Small 2002; Fitzhugh 2000; Handler and Gable 1997; Shackel 2001; Yentsch 1988).

Over the past decade, Shiloh Museum has consistently worked toward improving and expanding the museums exhibits and programs to better connect with the local community. Updating their permanent exhibits on pioneer history to include the Lewis family and their early- to mid-19th century agricultural community would build on these efforts. A discussion of the labor, materials, and other resources that went into creating the home and surrounding farmstead would also add to the history portrayed at the museum by tying the Lewis log home much more closely to its place in Ozark history. An updated exhibit could incorporate artifacts recovered during the archaeological excavations of the Lewis Farmstead. These objects might include the remains of ceramic vessels to represent a few of the everyday items used by the Lewis' in the 1840s. In doing so, these pieces provide material evidence of the connections that existed between the Lewis family and their larger world during the antebellum period. The result would be a tangible example of how new perspectives provided by historical archaeology can create a more complete, contextually-oriented presentation of the past, which allows for a deeper historic understanding of the Arkansas Ozarks.

Acknowledgments

I would like to thank Carl Drexler and David Markus for bringing this volume to completion and Alicia Valentino for all of her previous efforts. I am also grateful to Skip Stewart-Abernathy and George Sabo for their comments on conference and classroom versions of this paper. Together they have provided me and so many others with the methods, mindset, and inspiration needed to successfully explore the historical archaeology of Arkansas. My sincere appreciation to Jamie Brandon whose research and teaching inspired me to pursue topics related to historical myth and memory. I would also like to thank Jerry Hilliard who first guided me to the McGarrah-Reed Site. Over the years, he has generously shared his time, talent, and advice with me as I built on his previous research into the history of the Lewis farmstead. I would like to also thank members of the Historical Archaeology Working Group (HAWG) and Grace Church of Northwest Arkansas who assisted in the 2004 and 2005 excavations of the Lewis Farmstead as well as John Morris who gave us permission to excavate. Jeannie Whayne has provided me with direction, guidance, and encouragement throughout my journey into Arkansas history. Jennifer Ogborne and Lori Lee have offered many useful suggestions and revisions for this chapter. And finally, I would like to thank the Shiloh Museum of Ozark History and the University of Arkansas Special Collections for the use of their archives.

NOTES

1. As Henry Glassie suggested in his presentation on vernacular architecture at the University of Arkansas entitled, "The Architecture of American Regionalism," it is not merely a coincidence that in American Sign Language the representation of interlocking logs swirled in the shape of a melting pot has become the symbol for "America" (Glassie 2005).

2. Note that in previous research, this structure has been referred to as the McGarrah-Reed House and the associated archaeological site has been referred to as the McGarrah-Reed Site (Courtney 1976; Hilliard and Thomson 1998; Thomson 1990). These names belong to the family who owned the property in the years following the Lewis family's occupation.

3. Scholars define the pioneer period of American settlement for the Ozarks as occurring from 1803–1860, between the Louisiana Purchase and the outbreak of the Civil War. *Arkansas: A Narrative History* provides an excellent overview of this time period as it relates to the state as a whole (Whayne et al. 2002:75–165). In addition, Blevins provides a historical summary as it relates to the Arkansas Ozarks (Blevins 2002:11–29). For a good archaeological overview, see Sabo's "Historic Europeans and Americans" (Sabo 1990:136–156). Rafferty's research also provides insight into the historical geography of this first phase of American settlement in the Ozarks (Rafferty 1996, 2001:41–61).

4. The antebellum period of American history, as discussed in this chapter, begins with the Missouri Compromise in 1820 and ends in 1860 on the eve of the Civil War.

5. Political townships in Arkansas were established at the outset of settlement for administrative purposes to allow county officials to hold elections, maintain public roads, and collect taxes more easily. Settlers living within these townships provide a good cross-section of the local community. This is particularly true by the mid-19th century, when federal census records were being collected to record detailed information about free and enslaved residents as well as agricultural and industrial production. As a result, the township provides a snapshot of antebellum Arkansas

that is large enough to gain insights beyond a single farmstead or neighborhood, yet small enough to develop a reasonably detailed image of community life.

6. Central to these estimates is Sam Hilliard's concept of "consuming units." Free and enslaved adults from each household are each given 1 consuming unit, while children less than 15 years old are given .5 consuming unit. To determine extra corn bushels, the total bushels of corn annually produced by each farm is subtracted by 13 bushels for each adult, 7.5 bushels for each child, 4 bushels for each hog, and 7.5 bushels for each horse or mule listed in the agricultural census. To determine the extra hogs produced for each farm, each household's consuming units are multiplied by the estimated amount of pork eaten by each adult (2.2 hogs) per year, which is then subtracted from the total number of hogs listed for the household in the agricultural census (Hilliard 1972: 104–106, 157–158, 261).

7. See Harkins' *Hillbilly* (2004) for a discussion of how the hillbilly stereotype relates to American culture. As for how this image relates to Arkansas history, see Blevins' *Hill Folk* (2002) and *Arkansas/Arkansaw* (2009). Brandon's dissertation *Mountain Modernity, Cultural Memory and Historical Archaeology in the Arkansas Ozarks* (2004) provides an excellent anthropological discussion of how the hillbilly sterotype relates to the history of northwest Arkansas. In addition to Stewart-Abernathy's (1986, 1987, 1992) ground-breaking work conducted on this topic in the 1980s, Otto's "Reconsidering the Southern 'Hillbilly'" (1985) provides another historical archaeologist's perspective on this subject as it relates to the Ozark region.

8. This number was calculated using a total of 19 logs that had pith or near pith dates and measurable cutting dates present. The pith date represents the first year of tree growth for the height at which the dendrochronology sample was taken (Thomson 1990:40–45).

REFERENCES

Barile, Kerri S. and Jamie C. Brandon
2004   *Household Chores and Household Choices: Theorizing the Domestic Sphere in Historical Archaeology*. University of Alabama Press, Tuscaloosa.

Baker, Russell P.
2003   *Arkansas Township Atlas, 1819–1930*. Revised and Enlarged Edition. Arkansas Genealogical Society, Little Rock, AR.

Barber, Russell J. and Frances F. Berdan
1998   *The Emperor's Mirror: Understanding Cultures through Primary Sources*. University of Arizona Press, Tucson.

Beaudry, Mary
1996   Reinventing Historical Archaeology. In *Historical Archaeology and the Study of American Culture*, Lu Ann De Cunzo and Bernard Herman, eds., Pp. 473–497. University of Tennessee Press, Knoxville.

Beaudry, Mary, Lauren Cook, and Stephen Mrozowski
1991   Artifacts and Active Voices: Material Culture and Social Discourse. In *The Archaeology of Inequality*, Randall H. McGuire and Robert Paynter, eds., Pp. 150–191. B. Blackwell, Oxford, UK.

Blevins, Brooks
2002   *Hill Folks: A History of Arkansas Ozarkers and their Image*. University of North Carolina Press, Chapel Hill.

2009   *Arkansas/Arkansaw: How Bear Hunters, Hillbillies, and Good Ol' Boys Defined a State.* University of Arkansas Press, Fayetteville.

Bolton, S. Charles

1993   *Territorial Ambition: Land and Society in Arkansas, 1800–1840.* University of Arkansas Press, Fayetteville.

1998   *Arkansas, 1800–1860: Remote and Restless.* University of Arkansas Press, Fayetteville.

Brandon, Jamie C.

2004   *Mountain Modernity, Cultural Memory and Historical Archaeology in the Arkansas Ozarks.* Doctoral dissertation, University of Texas. University Microfilms, Ann Arbor.

Brandon, Jamie C., and James Davidson

2005   The Landscape of Van Winkle's Mill: Identity, Myth, and Modernity in the Ozark Upland South. *Historical Archaeology* 39(3):113–131.

Brown, Sarah

1999   Folk Architecture in Arkansas. In W.K. McNeil and William M. Clements, eds., *An Arkansas Folklore Sourcebook*, Pp. 107–154. University of Arkansas Press, Fayetteville.

Bruce, Theresa K.

2005   Fitzgerald's Station, Springdale, Arkansas, on the Butterfield Trail: History and Archaeology. Master's thesis, University of Arkansas, Fayetteville.

Burton, Orville Vernon

2002   Reaping What We Sow: Community and Rural History. *Agricultural History* 76(4):631–658.

Burton, Orville Vernon and Robert C. McMath, Jr. (editors)

1982   *Class, Conflict, and Consensus: Antebellum Southern Community Studies.* Greenwood Press, Westport, CT.

Cande, Kathleen H., Jared S. Pebworth, Aden Jenkins, and Michael Evans

2008   Muffins, Chimneys and Clinkers: Expanding Public Interpretation at Old Davidsonville State Park, Randolph County, Arkansas. Report submitted to the Arkansas Natural and Cultural Resources Council by the Arkansas Archeological Survey Sponsored Research Program. Arkansas Archeological Survey, Fayetteville.

Cantrell, Andrea

2004   WPA Sources for African-American Oral History in Arkansas: Ex-Slave Narratives and Early Settlers' Personal Histories. *Arkansas Historical Quarterly* 63(1):44–68.

Carter, Thomas, and Elizabeth Collins Cromley

2005   *Invitation to Vernacular Architecture: A Guide to the Study of Ordinary Buildings and Landscapes.* University of Tennessee Press, Knoxville.

Chaney, Phillip L.

1990   Geographic Analysis of the Presettlement Vegetation of the Middle Fork of the White River, Arkansas: A GIS Approach. Master's thesis, University of Arkansas, Fayetteville.

Cleek, Katherine

2013   *"An Ample Provision for our Posterity": Transportation, Ceramic Diversity and Trade in Historic Arkansas, 1800–1930.* Doctoral dissertation, University of Arkansas. University Microfilms, Ann Arbor, MI.

Courtney, Stephen E.
1976   The McGarrah-Reed House—Elkins Vicinity, Arkansas. Term paper for Historic Architecture taught by Dr. Cyrus Sutherland. On file in Special Collections at the University of Arkansas, Fayetteville.

Cronon, William
1983   *Changes in the Land: Indians, Colonists, and the Ecology of New England.* Hill and Wang, New York.

De Cunzo, Lu Ann and Bernard Herman (editors)
1996   *Historical Archaeology and the Study of American Culture.* University of Tennessee Press, Knoxville.

Deetz, James
1977a   Material Culture and Archaeology—What's the Difference? In *Historical Archaeology and the Importance of Material Things*, Leland Ferguson, ed., Pp. 9–12. The Society for Historical Archaeology, Special Publications Series, Number 2.
1977b   *In Small Things Forgotten: An Archaeology of Early American Life.* Anchor Press, Garden City, NY.
1996   *In Small Things Forgotten: An Archaeology of Early American Life.* Revised Edition. Anchor Books, New York.

Donald, David Herbert
1995   *Lincoln.* Simon and Schuster, New York.

Dunaway, Wilma A.
1996   *The First American Frontier: Transition to Capitalism in Southern Appalachia, 1700–1860.* University of North Carolina Press, Chapel Hill.

Eichstedt, Jennifer L. and Stephen Small
2002   *Representations of Slavery: Race and Ideology in Southern Plantation Museums.* Smithsonian Institution, Washington, DC.

Featherstonhaugh, George W.
1835   *Geological Report of an Examination Made in 1834 of the Elevated Country between the Missouri and Red Rivers.* Gales and Seaton, Washington, DC.

Fitzhugh, Brundage W. (editor)
2000   *Where these Memories Grow: History, Memory, and Southern Identity.* University of North Carolina Press, Chapel Hill.

Glassie, Henry
2000   *Vernacular Architecture.* Indiana University Press, Bloomington.
2005   The Architecture of American Regionalism. Presentation given April 7 at the Reynolds Center Auditorium, University of Arkansas, Fayetteville.

Goodspeed Publishing Company
1889   *Goodspeed's History of Benton, Washington, Carroll, Madison, Crawford, Franklin and Sebastian Counties, Arkansas.* Goodspeed Publishing Company, Philadelphia.

Greene, A. C.
1994   *900 Miles on the Butterfield Trail.* University of North Texas Press, Denton.

Groover, Mark D.
2008   *The Archaeology of North American Farmsteads.* University Press of Florida, Gainesville.

Gunderson, Robert Gray
1957   *The Log Cabin Campaign.* University of Kentucky Press, Lexington.

Hackbarth, Mark

1980   The Effect of Kinship on Land Choice in Washington County, Arkansas, 1830–1850. Master's thesis, University of Arkansas, Fayetteville.

Handler, Richard and Eric Gable

1997   *The New History in an Old Museum: Creating the Past at Colonial Williamsburg.* Duke University Press, Durham, NC.

Harkins, Anthony

2004   *Hillbilly: A Cultural History of an American Icon.* Oxford University Press, New York.

Harnish, Harry E.

1978   Historical Geography of the Upper White River Valley. Master's thesis, University of Arkansas, Fayetteville.

Harper, M. Dean, William W. Phillips, and George J. Haley

1969   *Soil Survey of Washington County, Arkansas.* Department of Agriculture Soil Conservation Service, Washington, DC.

Heath, Barbara

1999   *Hidden Lives: The Archaeology of Slave Life at Thomas Jefferson's Poplar Forest.* University Press of Virginia, Charlottesville.

Hicks, Dan and Mary C. Beaudry (editors)

2006   *The Cambridge Companion to Historical Archaeology.* Cambridge University Press, Cambridge, UK.

Hicks, Dan and Audrey Horning

2006   Historical Archaeology and Buildings. In *The Cambridge Companion to Historical Archaeology*, Dan Hicks and Audrey Horning, eds., Pp. 273–292. Cambridge University Press, Cambridge, UK.

Hilliard, Jerry E.

1989   McGarrah-Reed House. Site Survey Form on file at the Arkansas Archeological Survey, Fayetteville.

2008   *An Antebellum Ozark Community and the Civil War: The Archeology of the Second Mount Comfort Church (3WA880), Washington County, Arkansas (1840–ca.1865).* Arkansas Archeological Survey Research Series Number 63. Arkansas Archeological Survey, Fayetteville.

Hilliard, Jerry E. and Kerr J. Thomson

2005   Tree-Ring Dating and Archaeology of an Ozark Pioneer Period Farmstead: The McGarrah-Reed Site (3WA841). *The Arkansas Archaeologist* 39:57–68.

Hilliard, Sam B.

1972   *Hog Meat and Hoecake: Food Supply in the Old South, 1840–1860.* Southern Illinois University Press, Carbondale.

Hughes, Jenny L.

2009   *The Development and Decline of a Slave System, Washington County, Arkansas.* Master's thesis, University of Arkansas. University Microfilms, Ann Arbor.

Hutslar, Donald A.

1992   *Log Construction in the Ohio Country, 1750–1850.* Ohio University Press, Athens.

Johnson, Jerah

1997   Vernacular Architecture of the South. In *Plain Folk of the South Revisited*, Samuel C. Hyde, Jr., ed., Pp. 46–72. Louisiana State University Press, Baton Rouge.

Johnson, Matthew
1993   *Housing Culture: Traditional Architecture in an English Landscape.* ULC Press, London.
Jordan, Terry G.
1985   *American Log Buildings: An Old World Heritage.* University of North Carolina Press, Chapel Hill.
Jordan, Terry G. and Matti Kaups
1989   *The American Backwoods Frontier: An Ethnic and Ecological Interpretation.* John Hopkins University Press, Baltimore, MD.
Jordan-Bychkov, Terry G.
2003   *The Upland South: The Making of an American Folk Region and Landscape.* Center for American Places, Santa Fe, NM.
Key, Joseph Patrick
2000   *Indians and Ecological Conflict in Territorial Arkansas.* Arkansas Historical Quarterly 59(2):127–146.
Kimball, Fiske
1922   *Domestic Architecture of the American Colonies and of the Early Republic.* Charles Scribner's Sons, New York.
Kniffen, Fred B.
1965   Folk Housing: Key to Diffusion. *Annals of the Association of American Geographers* 55(4):549–577.
Kniffen, Fred B. and Henry Glassie
1966   Building in Wood in the Eastern United States: A Time-Place Perspective. *Geography Review* 56(1):40–66.
Lafferty, Robert H., Robert F. Cande, and John Arnold
1997   Archaeological Investigations at Waxhaws. MCRA Report 97–104. Prepared by Mid-Continental Research Associates, Inc. for the City of Fayetteville, AR. Arkansas Archeological Survey, Fayetteville.
Lee, Lori
2011   Beads, Coins, and Charms at a Poplar Forest Slave Cabin (1833–1858). *Northeast Historical Archaeology* 40:104–122.
Lesquereux, M. Leo
1860   Recent Botany and General Distribution of the Plants of Arkansas. In *Second Report of a Geological Reconnaissance of the Middle and Southern Counties of Arkansas, Made During the Years 1859 and 1860,* Richard Owen, ed., Pp.320–345. C. Sherman and Son, Philadelphia, PA.
Lincoln, William A.
1986   *World Woods in Color.* Linden Publishing Company, Fresno, CA.
Lounsbury, Carl R.
2010   Architecture and Cultural History. In *The Oxford Handbook of Material Culture Studies,* Dan Hicks and Mary C. Beaudry, eds., Pp. 484–501. Oxford University Press, Oxford, UK.
Madison County Works Progress Administration (WPA)
[1936–   Arkansas Early Settlers' Personal History Questionnaires. United States
1941]   WPA Historic Records Survey Collection, Special Collections, University of Arkansas Libraries, Fayetteville.
Majewski, Teresita and David Gaimster (editors)
2009   *International Handbook of Historical Archaeology.* Springer, New York.

Martin, Patrick E.

1972   Archeological Investigations at the Ridge House-3WA209. Arkansas Archeological Survey, Fayetteville.

1978   *An Inquiry into the Locations and Characteristics of Jacob Bright's Trading House and William Montgomery's Tavern.* Arkansas Archeological Survey Research Series Number 11. Arkansas Archeological Survey, Fayetteville

McIver, H. M.

Reminiscences of an Arkansas Pioneer as Recorded in 1890. *Arkansas Historical Quarterly* 17(1):56–67.

McNeilly, Donald P.

2000   *The Old South Frontier Cotton Plantations and the Formation of Arkansas Society, 1819–1861.* University of Arkansas Press, Fayetteville.

McRaven, Charles

1978   *Building the Hewn Log House.* Arkansas College Folklore Monograph Series No. 1. Mountain Publishing Services, Hollister, MO.

Mercer, Henry C.

1927a   The Origin of Log Houses in the United States. *Old-Time New England* XVIII (July):2–20.

1927b   The Origin of Log Houses in the United States. *Old-Time New England* XVIII (July):51–63.

Miller, George L.

1991   A Revised Set of CC Index Values for Classification and Economic Scaling of English Ceramics from 1787 to 1880. *Historical Archaeology* 25(1):1–25.

Miller, George L. and Robert R. Hunter Jr.

1990   English Shell Edged Earthenware: Alias Leeds Ware, Alias Feather Edge. In *Proceedings of the 35th Annual Wedgwood International Seminar*, Pp. 107–136. Birmingham Institute of Art, Birmingham, AL.

Miller, Henry M.

A Vegetal Reconstruction of Early Historic Northwest Arkansas. Undergraduate honors thesis, University of Arkansas, Fayetteville.

Musgrave, Bonita

1929   A Study of the Home and Local Crafts of the Pioneers of Washington County, Arkansas. Master's thesis, University of Arkansas, Fayetteville.

Neal, Joseph C. (editor)

1989   History of Washington County Arkansas. Shiloh Museum, Springdale, AR.

Orser, Charles

2002   Vernacular Architecture. In *Encyclopedia of Historical Archaeology*, Charles E. Orser, ed., Pp.559–562. Routledge, London.

Otto, John S.

1980   Slavery in the Mountains: Yell County, Arkansas 1840–1860. *Arkansas Historical Quarterly* 39(1):35–52.

1985   Reconsidering the Southern "Hillbilly": Appalachia and the Ozarks. *Appalachian Journal* 12(4):324–331.

Pessen, Edward

1984   *The Log Cabin Myth: The Social Backgrounds of the Presidents.* Yale University Press, New Haven, CT.

Pitcaithley, Dwight T.
2001   Abraham Lincoln's Birthplace Cabin: The Making of an American Icon.
        In Paul A. Shackel, ed., *Myth, Memory, and the Making of the American
        Landscape*, Pp. 240–254. University Press of Florida, Gainesville.

Proebsting, Eric
2009   *Economy and Ecology on the Edge of America: The Historical Archaeology
        of Three Farming Communities in the Arkansas Landscape*. Doctoral
        dissertation, University of Arkansas. University Microfilms, Ann Arbor.

Pruitt, Bettye Hobbs
1984   Self-Sufficiency and the Agricultural Economy of Eighteenth-Century
        Massachusetts. *The William and Mary Quarterly* 41(3):333–364.

Rafferty, Milton D.
1996   *Rude Pursuits and Rugged Peaks: Schoolcraft's Ozark Journal, 1818–1819*.
        University of Arkansas Press, Fayetteville.
2001   *The Ozarks: Land and Life*. Second Edition. University of Arkansas Press,
        Fayetteville.

Rehder, John B.
2012   *Tennessee Log Buildings: A Folk Tradition*. University of Tennessee Press,
        Knoxville.

Roberts, Robert North, Scott John Hammond, and Valerie A. Sulfaro
2012   *Presidential Campaigns, Slogans, Issues, and Platforms: The Complete
        Encyclopedia*. Greenwood, Santa Barbara, CA.

Roberts, Warren E.
1986   The Tools Used in Building Log Houses in Indiana. In Dell Upton and John
        Michael Vlach, eds., *Common Places: Readings in American Vernacular
        Architecture*, Pp. 182–203. University of Georgia Press, Athens.

Rumfield, Hiram S.
1929   Letters of an Overland Mail Agent in Utah. In *Proceedings of the American
        Antiquarian Society*, Archer Butler Hulbert, ed., Pp.227–302. Davis Press,
        Worcester, MA.

Sabo, George, III
1990   Historic Europeans and Americans. In *Human Adaptations in the Ozark
        and Ouachita Mountains*, George Sabo III, Ann M. Early, Jerome C. Rose,
        Barbara A. Burnett, Louis Vogele, Jr., and James P. Harcourt, eds., Pp. 135–
        170. Arkansas Archeological Survey Research Series Number 31. Arkansas
        Archeological Survey, Fayetteville.

Schrock, Earl F., Jr.
1992   *Traditional Arkansas Foodways*. In An Arkansas Folklore Sourcebook, W.K.
        McNeil and William M. Clements, eds., Pp. 173–211. University of Arkansas
        Press, Fayetteville.

Shiloh Museum of Ozark History (Shiloh Museum)
2006   Mission Statement, Adopted by Board of Trustees on July 13, 2006, www.
        shilohmuseum.org. Accessed March 22, 2015.
2015   Wagons and Log Cabins, www.shilohmuseum.org. Accessed March 22,
        2015.

Sizemore, Jean
1994   *Ozark Vernacular Houses: A Study of Rural Homeplaces in the Arkansas
        Ozarks, 1830–1930*. University of Arkansas Press, Fayetteville.

Shackel, Paul A. (editor)
2001   Myth, Memory, and the Making of the American Landscape. University Press of Florida, Gainesville.

Shammas, Carole
1982   How Self-Sufficient Was Early America? Journal of Interdisciplinary History 13(2):247–272.

Shurtleff, Harold R.
1939   The Log Cabin Myth: A Study of the Early Dwellings of the English Colonists in North America. Harvard University Press, Cambridge, MA.

Smith, Ted J.
1995   Slavery in Washington County, Arkansas, 1828–1860. Master's thesis, University of Arkansas. University Microfilms, Ann Arbor.

Stahle, David W.
1978   Tree Ring Dating of Selected Arkansas Log Buildings. Master's thesis, University of Arkansas, Fayetteville.

1979   Tree-Dating of Historical Buildings in Arkansas. Tree-Ring Bulletin 39:1–28.

Stahle, David W. and D. Wolfman
1985   The Potential for Archaeological Tree–Ring Dating in Eastern North America. In Advances in Archaeological Method and Theory, Vol. 8. Michael B. Schiffer, ed., Pp. 279–302. Academic Press, New York.

Stewart-Abernathy, Leslie C.
1986   The Moser Farmstead: Independent But Not Isolated: The Archaeology of a Late Nineteenth Century Ozark Farmstead. Arkansas Archeological Survey Research Series No. 26. Arkansas Archeological Survey, Fayetteville.

1987   From Memories and from the Ground: Historical Archaeology at the Moser Farmstead in the Arkansas Ozarks. In Visions and Revisions: Ethnohistoric Perspectives on Southern Cultures, George Sabo III and William M. Schneider, eds., Pp. 98–113. University of Georgia Press, Athens.

1988   Queensware from a Southern Store: Perspectives on the Antebellum Ceramics Trade from a Merchant Family's Trash in Washington, Arkansas. Paper presented at Society for Historical Archaeology Conference, Reno, NV. Southwest Arkansas Regional Archives, Arkansas History Commission, Washington, AR.

1992   Industrial Goods in the Service of Tradition: Consumption and Cognition on an Ozark Farmstead Before the Great War. In The Art and Mystery of Historical Archaeology: Essays in Honor of James Deetz, Anne Yentsch and Mary Beaudry, eds., Pp. 101–126. CRC Press, Boca Raton, FL.

1999   From Famous Forts to Forgotten Farmsteads: Historical Archaeology in the Mid-South. In Arkansas Archaeology: Essays in Honor of Dan and Phyllis Morse, Robert C. Mainfort and Marvin Jeter, eds., pp225–244. University of Arkansas Press, Fayetteville.

Thomson, Kerr James
1990   Tree-Ring Dating of the McGarrah-Reed Farmstead, Washington County, Arkansas. Master's thesis, University of Arkansas, Fayetteville.

United States Bureau of the Census (U.S. Census)
1840   United States Manuscript Census: 1840. Washington, DC.

1841   Compendium of the Enumeration of the Inhabitants and Statistics of the United States. Department of State, Washington, DC.

1850   United States Manuscript Census: 1850. Washington, DC.
1853   The Seventh Census of the United States: 1850. An Appendix, Embracing
        Notes Upon the Tables of Each of the States, Etc. Robert Armstrong, Public
        Printer, Washington, DC.
1860   United States Manuscript Census: 1860. Washington, DC.
Valentino, Alicia
2006   The Dynamics of Industry as Seen from Van Winkle's Mill, Arkansas.
        Doctoral dissertation, University of Arkansas. University Microfilms, Ann
        Arbor, MI.
Van Bennbrook, Hosea
1941   WPA Early Settlers' Personal History Questionnaires, Washington County,
        Arkansas. Interviewed by Virgil C. Erwin. Special Collections, University of
        Arkansas, Fayetteville.
Ward, Rufus, Jr.
1987   Shell-Edge Decorated Ceramics. Mississippi Archaeology 32(1):27–39.
Washington County Works Progress Administration (WPA)
[1936– Arkansas Early Settlers' Personal History Questionnaires. United States
1941]   WPA Historic Records Survey Collection, Special Collections, University of
        Arkansas Libraries, Fayetteville.
Wertenbaker, Thomas Jefferson
1938   The Founding of American Civilization: The Middle Colonies. Scribner's,
        New York.
Weslager, C. A.
1969   The Log Cabin in America: From Pioneer Days to the Present. Rutgers
        University Press, New Brunswick, NJ.
Wettstaed, James R.
2003   Perspectives on the Early-Nineteenth-Century Frontier Occupations of the
        Missouri Ozarks. Historical Archaeology 37(4):97–114.
Whayne, Jeannie M., Thomas A. DeBlack, George Sabo III, and Morris S. Arnold
2002   Arkansas: A Narrative History. University of Arkansas Press, Fayetteville.
Williams, Patrick, S. Charles Bolton, and Jeannie M. Whayne (editors)
2005   A Whole Country in Commotion: The Louisiana Purchase and the American
        Southwest. University of Arkansas Press, Fayetteville.
Worley, Ted (editor)
1952   Letters from an Early Arkansas Settler. The Arkansas Historical Quarterly
        11(4):327–330.
Yentsch, Anne
1988   Legends, Houses, Families, and Myths: Relationships between Material
        Culture and American Ideology. In Mary C. Beaudry, ed., Documentary
        Archaeology in the New World, Pp. 5–19. Cambridge University Press,
        Cambridge, UK.
Young, Susan
2011   Shiloh Museum of Ozark History. In the Encyclopedia of Arkansas History
        and Culture, www.encyclopediaofarkansas.net/. Accessed February 19, 2014.

8

THUNDER IN THE HOLLOW
The Archaeology of Missouri State Guard Artillery at the Battle of Pea Ridge

Carl G. Drexler

Arkansas has long been a contested land. The earliest written records pertaining to the state, the chronicles of the Hernando De Soto expedition, record battles between the Spanish explorers and Native Americans (Clayton et al. 1993). European powers fought over it in the American Revolution, violent clashes surrounded the expulsion of Native American communities along the Red River in the 1830s, and several notorious instances of violent encounters between African Americans and European Americans have marred the state's past. None of these surpass the American Civil War for the divisions created amongst Arkansans, and the kinds of strife and pain brought home during those four long years of war.

These and other conflicts involved Arkansans in other ways. When the specter of combat did not flit through the Ozark hollows or the Delta's marshes, the people of Arkansas volunteered to serve on the front lines and organized to produce food, clothing, weapons, and other military necessities. Mobilization of Arkansas's people, infrastructure, and resources produced lasting changes on the state's built environment, many of which we live with today. For instance, Southern Arkansas University Tech, in East Camden, occupies the buildings of the former Shumaker Naval Ammunition Depot, a World War II-era production and development facility whose former bunker field still houses a booming private rocket research and development facility.

The state's conflict heritage helps support its growing tourist industry. Arkansas has three national parks, Pea Ridge National Military Park, Fort Smith National Monument, and Arkansas Post National Memorial, along with five state parks, including the battlefields at Prairie Grove and Poison Spring, which are connected to its war-related history.

Other parks, such as Historic Washington State Park, in southwest Arkansas, owe at least a portion of their significance to their ties to periods of conflict. Washington, in addition to being the early market center of southwest Arkansas, was the state's Confederate capital after the U.S. Army took Little Rock, and was an armed camp through much of the later stages of the war (Medearis 1976). Recent excavations in its market district recovered Civil War-related finds, including Confederate buttons.

Conflict archaeology in Arkansas has been a major theme through the past 40 years, though not one that has usually involved a specialist in the field. Some of the first historical archaeology in the state focused on military sites (see introduction), as has some of the most recent (Carlson-Drexler, Scott, and Roeker 2008; Drexler 2013).

This chapter has several different aims. It opens with an overview of the history of conflict archaeology in the state, as this is a diverse history with many interesting facets. The main purpose of the chapter, though, is a study of small finds recovered by the National Park Service at Pea Ridge National Military Park in the early 2000s. The ability of historical archaeologists to recover the detritus of the military's footprint has repeatedly challenged historically-based understandings of the past and provided a unique window on conflict, often based on relatively few finds. A scattering of a few dozen bullets or shell fragments can tell us much about how fighters distributed themselves across and utilized the landscape, how they moved, what kinds of weapons and accouterments they carried, and, occasionally, where they died and how they were treated after death (Scott and McFeaters 2011). Few other areas of specialization within historic archaeology can derive so much information from such small assemblages as can conflict archaeology.

That being said, though we frequently deal with smaller assemblages than our colleagues, we rarely deal with single or a few artifacts. Conflict archaeology, particularly when it focuses on battlefields, has historically dealt primarily with artifacts as an aggregation, not in isolation. From the Little Bighorn (Scott et al. 1989) to Chalmette (Cornelison and Cooper 2002), from Olynthos (Lee 2001) to Isandlwana (Pollard 2007), it is the patterning of numerous artifacts that has intrigued us more than the idiosyncratic isolated find.

Though aggregate patterns have been one of conflict archaeology's strengths, this chapter presents a case where three artifacts highlighted a controversy about the battle. These artifacts, three bits of iron amongst the thousands recovered at the site, challenge historically-based interpretations of the battle into question our understanding about who participated in the battle, and how the combatants were equipped. These ferrous orbs stand to alter not just our interpretation of the battle, but the way in which the engagement and its memorialization is structured for the public and the way in which visitors to the site connect with the past.

Conflict Archaeology in Arkansas

As part of the purpose of this volume is to take stock of historical archaeology in Arkansas, and part of that stock-taking includes a look back at the progress made, I would like to open with a brief overview of conflict archaeology in the Natural State before addressing the Pea Ridge finds. This is in keeping with a recent trend towards reflection in other areas of conflict archaeology, such as battlefield archaeology (Scott and McFeaters 2011) and warfare in general (Bleed and Scott 2011).

To properly frame this history, I feel it necessary to clarify what I mean by the term "conflict archaeology." Though there is now a regular conference series devoted to the subject, and an online discussion forum (The Conflict Archaeology Information and Research Network, or CAIRN), we are still honing the parameters of the term. Conflict archaeology, as it is becoming increasingly widely used, includes archaeological research on sites associated with some form of armed, organized conflict. This would obviously include, but not be limited to, battlefields, fortifications, prisoner of war camps, and other military sites. Indeed, "military sites archaeology" was one of the terms originally offered to describe the field. Schofield (2009), among others, cast the net wider, including the sites of anti-war protests and other places that owed their existence to or were fundamentally altered by conflict. Orr (1994) once suggested "the archaeology of trauma," to cover much the same ground, but the term never gathered a following. I see conflict archaeology as encompassing any site to which a direct and clear link to a period of organized warfare or preparation therefore might be drawn, and whose links to that conflict are a central part of the research. This would include battlefields, fortifications, arsenals, military industrial facilities, and the other places and facilities needed to carry on a conflict. I would also include under this rubric civilian sites with a compelling link to a period of conflict, a dimension I have explored in my recent dissertation research (Drexler 2013).

Fortifications

As the introductory chapter makes clear, some of the first historical archaeology in Arkansas concerned sites that have some conflict dimension. Arkansas Post, the site of the first historical archaeological research in the state, was attacked by English-friendly Native Americans in 1783, thus making it the only Revolutionary War battle in Arkansas. Though the 18th century battlefield has not been identified archaeologically, Walker (1971) later excavated the bank at Arkansas Post, finding many traces of the site's Civil War phase, when it was used first as a hospital by Confederate soldiers and then its reduced during the January, 1863 assault by U.S. Army troops during the reduction and capture of the fort.

Though the bulk of the archaeological work at Arkansas Post focused on identifying the early colonial period, the interpretation of the park itself emphasizes the Civil War battle as well. The focus of the U.S. Navy's bombardment of the position, an earthwork known as Fort Hindman, has since eroded into the Arkansas River, but much of the battlefield remains intact and open to archaeological investigation.

More directly, Clyde Dollar's research at Fort Smith focused on a point that was a garrison and buffer between settlers and Indians, and a point that was crucial to military control of the frontier during the decades before the Civil War. It was one of the bastions of early settlement, and Dollar's excavation helped to relocate and interpret the early military footprint on Arkansas (Dollar 1960; Dollar 1966). As mentioned in the introduction, Dollar's views on historical archaeology, which formed part of a dialog crucial to the development of the discipline, were formed during his research at Fort Smith.

Over on the Mississippi River, the city of Helena has used archaeology as part of the basis for the revitalization of the former cotton port as a heritage tourism center, focusing on the city's Civil War past and the emergence of blues music in the Mississippi Delta. In 1968, Burney McClurkan, of the Arkansas Archeological Survey, undertook to locate the remains of Fort Curtis, one of the main points of defense for the Union forces holding the city (McClurkan 1968). McClurkan's excavation results were inconclusive, but Fort Curtis remained a point of interest for local historians and boosters, who recently commissioned a scale reconstruction of the fort to be built on a full city block in downtown Helena. In recent years, Kim and Stephen Mcbride (personal communication, 2011) worked to locate the remains of Battery C, another part of the Union defenses of Helena, as part of the city's efforts to promote visitation and to revitalize its downtown. John House, successor to Burney McClurkan, excavated a mass grave at Battery C in 2003 (personal communication 2012). House recovered portions of 4–5 individuals that had been disturbed during tree removal on the site. Given their disorderly arrangement in the ground, House believed them to have been Confederate soldiers hastily buried by Union soldiers, who held the field after the battle.

Research at Dooley's Ferry, in southwest Arkansas, dealt with fortifications crowning the bluffs overlooking the Red River there. Unlike Arkansas Post and Helena, these fortifications were never tested in battle. Built as the last line of defense against a federal advance on east Texas that never materialized, they also served as a sign of Confederate governmental authority in a situation where social stability was much in question.

Other fortifications exist around the state, including those at Elkins Ferry, Tate's Bluff, and around the city of Camden on the Ouachita River, that await further scrutiny. Notable amongst these last are Fort Southerland (actually Fort Diamond) and Fort Lookout, both of which either have been or are planned to be, at the time of this writing, developed as heritage sites. Analyses of any or all of these works in historical, tactical, and strategic context would be valuable additions to conflict archaeology.

Battlefields

Battlefields were long seen as a challenge to historical archaeologists. Noël Hume (1969) famously (or infamously) wrote that their shallow stratigraphy and dispersed nature made them nearly impossible to gather adequate data from, and too many examples exist of research that found that shovel testing and other forms of archaeological survey were ineffective on battlefields. In 1984, however, the National Park Service and University of South Dakota pioneered a metal detector-based methodology for battlefield survey at the site of the 1876 Battle of the Little Bighorn. This survey established a model that has been pursued in many places in many different countries (Scott et al. 1989).

Arkansas ranks among those places. Between 2001 and 2003, the National Park Service's Midwest Archeological Center conducted a large-scale metal detector sweep of large portions of the battlefield at

Pea Ridge, in the northwest corner of the state. The fieldwork at Pea Ridge resulted in the recovery of 2,700 battle-related finds and produced a number of studies in addition to the final report (Carlson-Drexler, Scott, and Roeker 2008; Coles 2003; Coles 2004; Drexler 2004; Volf 2003). This was conducted at the same time as a parallel survey at Wilson's Creek National Battlefield, outside of Springfield, Missouri (Scott, Roeker, and Carlson-Drexler 2008). The research at Pea Ridge located artifacts directly associable with certain units, helped establish the patterning of the battle on the local landscape, and provided material for the park's visitor's center that adds to its interpretation. This was also the project that gave rise to this chapter.

The other major battlefield in northwest Arkansas, Prairie Grove, has also been studied archaeologically, but not with the wide-area metal detector survey that Pea Ridge received. Using historical accounts of the battle, Williamson (1993) created a predictive model for artillery artifact distribution as a thesis for the University of Arkansas. The Arkansas Archeological Survey recently completed excavations and geophysical surveys at the sites of several houses associated with the battle, helping the park to improve its interpretation through identifying these points on the landscape and learning something of their layout.

The four batteries at Helena, site of the siege and July 4, 1863, battle, were documented along with Fort Curtis, an earthwork now under a church in downtown Helena-West Helena. McClurkan's early research (see above), while not directly recovering evidence of the battlefield, found the corner of one of the brick magazines, which played a role in the engagement. The aforementioned Confederate dead excavated at Battery D in 2003 are likewise tied into the battle. The service of African Americans at Helena and other eastern Arkansas battlefields have been a basis for the development of heritage tourism around Helena-West Helena, which features "Freedom Park," interpreting the transition from slavery to freedom for many Arkansans and Mississippians during the war, and their defense of the Little Rock Road during the battle.

The Arkansas Archeological Survey is currently working to locate the site of the Action at Wallace's Ferry, a July 1864 engagement notable for being one of the few engagements during the war where the Union forces, for the bulk of the battle, were entirely African American. Locating the battlefield will not only allow for the commemoration of the event, it will add to the heritage tourist effort currently underway in nearby Helena-West Helena.

Camps

Two military camps have been studied, both in the northwest part of the state. The site of Camp Benjamin, in Cross Hollows north of Fayetteville, was surveyed by the Arkansas Archeological Survey in the early 2000s. Though much of the camp has been lost under Beaver Lake, impounded in the 1960s, the survey did identify a satellite camp and artillery emplacement guarding the Telegraph Road, and a number of rifle pits associated with the use of the hollow as a defensive point during the war (Hilliard et al. 2008). At around the same time, Camp Babcock, a Union encampment on Lindsey's Prairie occupied just before the battle of Prairie Grove, was surveyed with metal detectors, though the site would need more fieldwork to characterize the camp and locate its various portions.

Bridging the gap between military camps and the home front are the host of World War II-era camps constructed in Arkansas, some of which are gaining attention from archaeologists. Jodi Barnes recently initiated a mapping and metal detection project at Camp Monticello, a camp for Italian prisoners outside of the eponymous city. C. Andrew Buchner, working for Panamerican Consultants, has written on the Japanese-American internment camps at Jerome and Rohwer, in the Arkansas Delta. These offer great prospect for future research, and the presence of numerous other camps, including a camp for conscientious objectors outside of Magnolia in southern Arkansas.

The Home Front

Hilliard (2004) investigated one of the idiosyncratic pieces of Arkansas's conflict past. In the latter half of the Civil War, a guerilla war raged across the Ozarks that federal authorities were hard-pressed to contain. One of the novel approaches taken to combatting the problem was the brainchild of Colonel M. LaRue Harrison of the 3rd Arkansas Cavalry (US). Harrison organized unionist farmers into "post colonies" scattered across the hollows surrounding Fayetteville. Ideally, these colonies would be able to defend themselves against pro-Confederates. Hilliard's excavations at Old Mount Comfort Church directly addressed the period when it was a post colony, finding evidence of the site's use as a hospital and its destruction by fire at the end of the war.

The main focus of my own recent research at Dooley's Ferry, in Hempstead County on the Red River, has been the civilian community surrounded during the Civil War by Confederate trenches in expectation of a Federal move against east Texas. As an important hub of the transportation networks that brought in goods and people to support the Confederate war effort, it was one of the main conduits for the passage of Confederate troops to the front and Federal troops to the rear in the Trans-Mississippi, and was one of the places where the increasingly feeble Confederate supply lines stretched into Arkansas. Understanding the home front war in the Confederate-held portions of southwest Arkansas requires the consideration of civilian sites like Dooley's Ferry.

A state as remote and cut off as Arkansas was had to work hard to ameliorate the shortfalls produced by its isolation. In Arkansas, the city of Arkadelphia was one of the major centers of wartime production. The Confederate government established various faculties there, including a "chemical factory," munitions factory, arsenal, and other establishments. The city remained an important facility until 1863, when concerns over the federal occupation of Little Rock caused the Confederates to evacuate the facilities to Texas. Don Ross (1995) surveyed a section of the Mill Creek valley on the north side of Arkadelphia for evidence of the powder mill. He found evidence for a burned structure dating as early as 1840 and possibly wartime, but was not ready to declare the site to be that of the powder mill, which exploded in 1863.

These are the major studies in the history of conflict archaeology in Arkansas. There are thousands of other sites in the Arkansas Archeological Survey's site files. The bulk of these have been diligently recorded by the Survey staff and by volunteers from the Arkansas Archeological Society. This is truly a wide open field, as most of those recorded sites have not had extensive research conducted on them. Given the salience of the Civil War to Arkansas's past and the passion with which so many follow its history, it comes as no surprise that conflict sites associated with other wars in other places have not been as extensively studied.

Small Finds in Conflict Archaeology

To return to the focus of this chapter, I must point out that what follows is somewhat out of keeping with most of the publications in conflict archaeology. As stated before, conflict archaeologists studying battlefields typically focus on artifacts in the aggregate, looking at either dynamic or gross patterning to reveal information about the engagement (Fox and Scott 1991). This entails sifting through information on dozens if not hundreds or thousands of artifacts at once. While this provides the basis for some truly fascinating research (Lee 2001; Scott et al. 1989), this chapter follows a different route, looking at small finds (one or two artifacts, only). This alternative route yields different information and different results, and I hope to show can be just as salient to our understanding of the past, and at times more poignant, as the more expansive analyses.

Of course, other conflict archaeologists have published small finds research before. I would like to mention a few prominent examples such work to show what kinds of information can be garnered. Several studies focus on using artifacts to establish the identity of human remains found on a battlefield, which makes it possible to re-bury the individual in a named grave.

Occasionally, small finds have greater implications. Whitford and Pollard (2009) used an Australian "Alberton Medallion" to establish the presence of the remains of Private Henry Victor Willis of the 31st Battalion, Australian Imperial Force, in a mass grave at the World War I Battle of Fromelles, Belgium. Though not associable with a particular set of remains, the medallion helped prove to the Australian government that the context of the find was one of six mass graves of Australian soldiers made by German forces at the close of the battle. As a result, the graves were subsequently excavated and the remains of approximately 250 soldiers prepared for reburial in individual graves in a nearby Commonwealth Graves Commission cemetery. DNA comparisons with surviving relatives will hopefully allow these soldiers to lie in graves marked with their actual names.

Pearson and Connah (2009) recently took a single battlefield artifact, albeit a rather large one, and used documentary information to historicize what had been a de-contextualized museum exhibition piece. This artifact, a World War II German 88mm anti-aircraft/anti-tank gun had been captured somewhere in North Africa in 1942 and subsequently put on display in the Royal Australian Armoured Corps Museum. Other details surrounding its acquisition and the identities of the Australian soldiers who captured it were forgotten, robbing it of its historical context. Archaeologists compared extant damage to the gun with photographs of similar kinds of artillery captured in North Africa and were able to identify it conclusively. Once a photographic link was made, the lost story surrounding its capture could be reconstructed from documents. Pearson and Connah establish where and when it was captured, narrowed the list of candidates for the German unit the gun belonged to down to a few, identified the unit that captured it, and even who was responsible for shipping it to Australia. Rebuilding the story surrounding the piece fundamentally altered the nature of its display, taking it from being a generic example of the famed 88mm gun to an artifact with a full story to tell.

To me, one of the most poignant small finds reported during an archaeological investigation of a battlefield is a silver-plated brass wedding ring recovered from the area of the South Skirmish Line, at the Little Bighorn battlefield, in 1984. When Scott et al (1989:93) recovered the ring, it still encircled one of the finger bones of the man who had worn it. It is a sharp, tangible reminder of the ties broken by conflict and the ramifications that events on the battlefield hold for families of soldiers, whose loved one was not coming home.

Though not so poignant, the subject finds of this study carry their own kinds of instructive context. Before we delve into them, though, we need to know something of the context of their deposition and recovery, as both condition how we see them as artifacts and how we understand their wider significance.

The Battle of Pea Ridge

This small find study focuses on three artifacts recovered from the battlefield of Pea Ridge, in northwest Arkansas. Once dubbed the "Gettysburg of the West" for its severity and strategic importance, the battle cemented Federal control over northern Arkansas and secured St. Louis from Confederate capture, allowing it to be used as a base of operations for expeditions down the Mississippi River (Brown 1956; Shea and Hess 1992). To paint it with the broadest of brushes, the battle was an overly-ambitious attempt by the Confederate Army and Missouri State Guard (the Show-Me State's pro-Confederate militia) to flank the U.S. Army force dug in on the bluffs overlooking Little Sugar Creek, sever its communications and supply lines, and then force it to destroy itself in an eventual attempt to break through Southern lines, trying to escape.

Long-running rancor between the commanders of the Confederate forces west of the Mississippi River, Confederate Major General Ben McCulloch, and Missouri State Guard commander Sterling Price, necessitated the assignment of an overall commander to the region, a post given to Major General Earl Van Dorn. His appointment occurred as the Union force in Missouri under Major General Samuel R. Curtis chased the Missouri State Guard into Arkansas. Now united, the Southern forces were camped in the Boston Mountains around Van Buren and Fort Smith when Van Dorn arrived at the end of January 1862 (Shea and Hess 1992).

Well known for his impetuosity, a characteristic forged commanding small cavalry forces on the plains before the war, Van Dorn ordered an immediate move against the federals when he arrived at the Southern camps around Van Buren. Though they outnumbered the federals, the long march to Pea Ridge exhausted the Southerner foot soldiers. By the time they approached the Federal lines along Little Sugar Creek on March 6, the Southern soldiers needed a rest.

They would not receive one. Van Dorn instead ordered a night march around the Federal flank on a road known as the Bentonville Detour, intending to strike the Telegraph Road north of Elkhorn Tavern and descend on the federal rear. By dawn, the tired Southerners had split into two columns. The leading column, the Missouri State Guard, reached the Telegraph Road and turned south near dawn on the 7th. The Confederates, lagging behind, turned onto a road, Ford Road, which ran south of Big Mountain, intending to cut some distance from their march and rendezvous with the Missourians at Elkhorn Tavern. This did not come to pass. Both portions of the Southern forces were pulled into separate engagements with small groups of Federal troops, sent to investigate reports of Confederates moving around the Federal rear. The Confederate troops were drawn into a fight in Oberson's and Foster's fields, near Leetown while the Missouri State Guard ran into opposition in the hollows north of Elkhorn Tavern.

The battle around Leetown quickly became a shambles for the Confederates. Ben McCulloch, scouting Oberson's Field in preparation for an attack, was shot dead by Federal skirmishers. His next in command died a few minutes later, leading a cavalry charge. The third in line, Col. Louis Hebert, had been sent to the left to launch an attack through Morgan's Woods, and was unreachable. The fourth in command, Albert Pike, waffled for hours before ordering a retreat. Most of the Confederate forces around Leetown, including all but one artillery battery, never engaged. This allowed the Federals, who slowly realized that the Confederates were in their rear and not their front, to feed units into the Leetown fight, enabling them to repel Hebert's advance and to hold onto Leetown.

The Missouri State Guard, meanwhile, made slow progress through the hollows north of Elkhorn Tavern, facing artillery and small arms fire from their front. As at Leetown, Federal reinforcements gradually bolstered U.S. strength. Their lines bent instead of breaking. Confederates pushed south through the hollow, threw a Union force out of Sharp's Field, and drove to the north edge of Cox's and Ruddick's field before nightfall put an end to the fighting. During the night, the rest of the Federal forces from Little Sugar Creek and those that had been engaged at

Leetown arrived. When dawn broke on March 8, 1862, the entire Union force was drawn up in the fields south of Elkhorn Tavern, presenting a solid front to the Confederates and commanding high ground, upon which they massed artillery.

The second day of battle started with a massive artillery duel, sparked by Tull's Missouri Battery, in Ruddick's Field. The firing soon spread, with every cannon on the field taking part. The duel soon became one-sided, however, as Confederate gunners found that the Van Dorn had neglected to order supply wagons with extra ammunition forward two nights before. Their limbers quickly emptied, and gun-by-gun, battery-by-battery, the Southern cannons fell silent. This freed the Union artillerists from focusing on counterbattery fire, allowing them to hammer Southern infantrymen up and down the line, including at the toe of Big Mountain, where soldiers crouching in a flint outcrop found themselves being sliced to pieces by shards of splintered stone. Exhausted, unfed, unable to return fire, and pounded by relentless Federal fire, the Southern forces started to quit the field in small groups. A final push from Union infantry claimed the field for the Federals.

The Missouri State Guard subsequently transferred to Confederate service and served, along with the rest of Van Dorn's troops, in Tennessee and Mississippi. Union troops later marched across southern Missouri and descended eastern Arkansas, taking and fortifying Helena on the Mississippi River in July. The federals held on to northwest Arkansas throughout the rest of the war, though the Ozarks around Pea Ridge gained notoriety for the vicious guerilla conflict that swirled through its hollows.

Archaeology at Pea Ridge

The National Park Service created Pea Ridge National Military Park in 1965 to mark the battle's location. During those first few years, in aid of the park's interpretive mission, Rex Wilson conducted excavations that helped to relocate the site of Leetown. These also identified a number of features that were likely battlefield graves of U.S. soldiers, re-excavated in the years after the war when the burials were shifted to Fayetteville National Cemetery (Wilson 1965).

Between 2001 and 2003, the U.S. National Park Service's Midwest Archeological Center (MWAC) undertook several wide-area controlled metal detector surveys over large portions of the park as part of the NPS's Systemwide Archeological Inventory Program (SAIP). Over the course

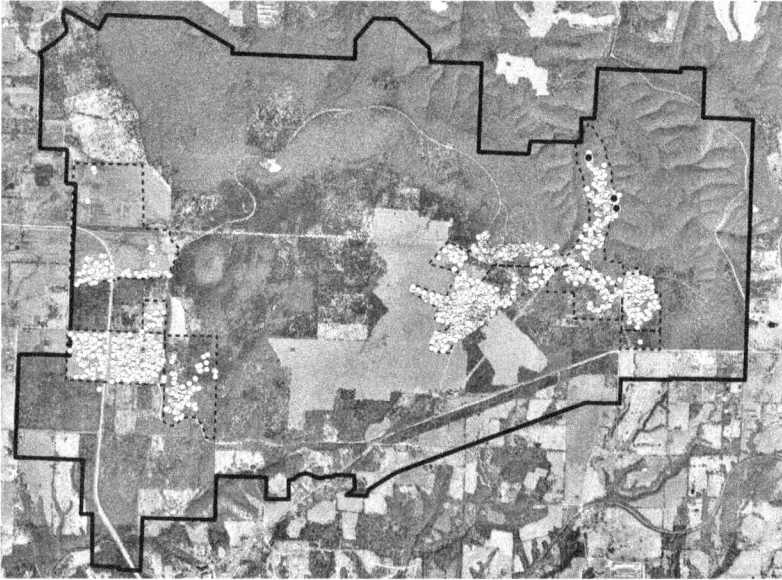

Figure 8.1. Pea Ridge National Military Park (solid outline), showing surveyed areas (dashed outline), and artifact coverage (white dots) and artifacts subject of this chapter (black dots).

of three years, a crew of NPS archaeologists, park staff, and volunteers expert in the use of metal detectors swept 592 acres of the park property, recovering over 2,700 battle-related artifacts (Figure 8.1). Most of these were small arms and artillery ammunition, but also included personal items, weapons parts, and pieces of military equipment (Carlson-Drexler, Scott, and Roeker 2008). A parallel project at nearby Wilson's Creek National Battlefield, Missouri, occurred simultaneously, also under the auspices of the SAIP (Scott, Roeker, and Carlson-Drexler 2008).

The SAIP project covered large swaths of the most significant portions of the battle, including Foster's and Oberson's Fields and Morgan's Woods, near Leetown, and Sharp's and Cox's Fields, near Elkhorn Tavern, all major points contested during the battle. Archaeologists and volunteers worked in waves, allowing rapid coverage and careful, systematic documentation and curation of identified finds.

At the outset, a NPS archaeologist marked off search corridors with pin flags, providing guides for the metal detector crews. Metal detector operators were primarily volunteers skilled in the use of metal detectors, who would sweep the corridors systematically, working next to each other in as consistent a fashion as was practicable. Each hit identified by the metal detector would be marked with a pin flag and left for an excavator crew.

Excavators dug each hit and, provided the artifact was not patently of recent origin, would leave it next to the flag for documentation. Finally, a collection crew of one to two people bagged, assigned a field specimen number to, and piece-plotted each artifact. Spatial and artifact data were collected using a Trimble GeoXT global positioning system (GPS) using a data dictionary customized for collecting battlefield finds. This approach was pioneered at the Little Bighorn project in the mid-1980s, and employed during subsequent work by Doug Scott at Monroe's Crossroads, North Carolina, before being applied to the Pea Ridge and Wilson's Creek projects, among many others.

The artillery-related artifacts consisted of both long-range and short-range ammunition. Long-range ammunition, used primarily at ranges over 400 yards, consisted of shell fragments and rotating band (sabot) pieces (Gibbon 1860; Griffith 1987). All but one model of field cannon used during the war were muzzle-loaders. Rifled guns, as many on both sides at Pea Ridge were, required ammunition that was elongated (bullet-shaped) and yet small enough in diameter to be loaded by being rammed down the bore. Such ammunition would be fitted with lead or brass rotating bands that, when the gun discharged, expanded into the gun's rifling and imparted spin, increasing range and accuracy. Smoothbore guns and howitzers could fire either elongated or spherical rounds, the latter being the prototypical round cannonball.

Long-range ammunition, both elongated and spherical, was designed to explode in the air above an enemy formation, showering the surrounding area with iron shards. Some such rounds, known as "case shot," were packed with lead or iron balls, slightly under 3/4 of an inch in diameter, which increased the shrapnel distributed by the round's explosion, thereby upping its lethality. These rounds were incredibly destructive when employed against the massed infantry formations used during the war, including at Pea Ridge.

Short range cannon ammunition consisted primarily of "canister." Canister consisted of a large iron can packed with iron balls, stabilized inside the round with sawdust (Thomas 1985). When loaded into the cannon, the round acted much like a very large shotgun round, scattering a cluster of shot downrange. In cases of extreme urgency, Civil War gunners would double-load their guns with canister, throwing a devastating amount of shot at oncoming enemies. Canister employed against the massed infantry formations typical of the Civil War was simply frightful in its effectiveness, tearing gaping holes in battle lines, destroying lives and breaking bodies.

Canister Ammunition Design

Despite the very rudimentary concept behind canister, the ammunition was carefully designed and precisely produced in order to maximize its lethality on the battlefield. It is tempting to think of this ammunition as simply iron balls poured into a can, but such an assessment belies the careful thought that went into the planning and construction of every round. The key to the design was the size of the balls employed. For every caliber of gun to which a round of canister would be fitted, there was a carefully prescribed diameter for the contained balls. This allowed them to be packed evenly, in layers, inside the can, minimizing empty (wasted) space and maximizing the number of balls in each round. This maximized the number of projectiles dispersed with each round fired, thereby upping the potential destructive force and killing capacity of the round.

Period ordnance manuals, such as John Gibbon's (1860) *The Artillerist's Manual*, set out the dimensions of different canister balls to be used with each caliber of field gun. Gibbon also states "the exterior diameter of each canister ball should be verified with the maximum shot gauge," suggesting that quality control was a concern and consistence of ball sizing was something period ordnance manufacturers paid attention to (Gibbon 1860:346). Analysis of the canister balls recovered from Pea Ridge found that these different size balls were readily identifiable in the archaeological record, and that they largely fit the specifications laid out in the manuals of the day (Drexler 2004).

At Pea Ridge, the bulk of canister ammunition fragments recovered were designed for use with 6 and 12 pound field pieces. These caliber designations are based on the weight of a solid iron shot fitted to that particular weapon. A 6-pounder's bore diameter measured 3.43 inches, while a 12-pounder's was 4.32 inches (Gibbon 1860). During the Civil War, inch-based caliber definitions were also used, though for large naval and siege guns, which ranged up to 20 inches in diameter, or newly-developed rifled field guns, such as the three inch ordnance rifle (Thomas 1985). Artillery pieces included guns, which fired on flat trajectory over a long range, howitzers, firing on a shorter, arching path, and mortars, which lofted shells short distances on very high trajectories. Though useful for firing over earthwork walls, their weight and performance characteristics kept mortars from being used widely during the Civil War. Six and 12-pounder guns and 12-pounder howitzers, along with the newly-developed 1857 gun-howitzer (commonly known as "the Napoleon"), dominated the battlefield (Thomas 1985).

Our small finds in question stand out amongst all the hundreds of artillery-related artifacts in that they were designed for use with a weapon little used on Civil War battlefields. Unlike the 6 and 12-pounder ammunition that dominates the canister assemblage, the NPS fieldwork also recovered three pieces of 24-pounder canister ammunition. This would have been fired by the 24-pounder field howitzer, a bronze gun with a short barrel and large (5.4 inch) bore. These pieces of 24-pounder howitzer ammunition stood out for the simple fact that historians assert (repeatedly) that there were no 24-pounder howitzers at Pea Ridge.

The Finds

The four troublesome pieces of iron consist of two balls and one case shot fragment. The balls, three in number, were recovered from the hollows north of Elkhorn Tavern. Cataloged as FS2377, FS2399, and FS2434, these three balls were recognized based on their diameter, ranging within the 1.84–1.87 inches (Figure 8.2 is an example) prescribed by period ordnance manuals, markedly larger than other canister balls recovered during the project.

In addition, the final analysis of the artifacts recovered from Pea Ridge located another piece of evidence, which makes it certain that there was a 24-pounder howitzer on the field at Pea Ridge. This is FS2651. It is, like the canister rounds, a piece of artillery ammunition. Found near Elkhorn Tavern, in the area where the Missouri State Guard was engaged, FS2651 is a fragment of 24-pounder spherical case shot. Case shot rounds consisted of an iron ball packed with small lead or iron balls and a bursting charge of black powder.

Fitted with a fuse that would light when the artillery piece discharged, the case shot would, ideally, explode over an enemy formation at range, showering it with shrapnel. Both case shot and canister were anti-personnel weapons. Case shot was for engaging an enemy at long range, typically over 400 yards away, while canister would be used at shorter ranges.

Deploying Howitzers at Pea Ridge

Historians have offered several detailed analyses of the composition of the forces engaged at Pea Ridge. In addition to Shea and Hess's (1996)

Figure 8.2. 24-pounder canister ball (2 views).

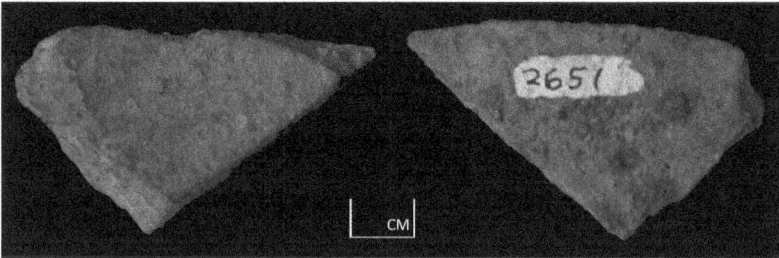

Figure 8.3. 24-pounder canister case shot fragment (2 views).

keystone history of the battle, the National Park Service maintains an online order of battle for both sides, and Bearss (1962) wrote a detailed analysis of artillery units involved during the battle's centennial. Between these sources, we have a good understanding of the units involved and, for the artillery, the kinds of weapons they fielded.

The order of battle for the Union Army of the Southwest shows no unit as fielding a 24-pounder howitzer. Welfley's Independent Missouri Battery, the 1st Missouri Flying Battery, the 2nd Ohio Independent Battery, Battery A of the 2nd Illinois Light Artillery, the 1st Iowa Independent Light Artillery Battery, and the 3rd Iowa Independent Light Artillery all fielded the smaller 12-pounder howitzers, but these could not fire ammunition for the larger-bore 24-pounders (Shea and Hess 1992). These units also typically featured guns alongside their howitzers, and several other Union batteries, not equipped with howitzers, fought at Pea Ridge.

On the Southern side, several batteries brought howitzers to the battle. Three Confederate units, Provence's and Gaines's Arkansas batteries, and Capt. John J. Good's Texas battery all had 12-pounder howitzers. With the Missouri State Guard, Wade's, Guibor's, and Mcdonald's batteries were likewise equipped (Shea and Hess 1992:331–339).

Many of these units, north and south, conformed to a Mexican War-era approach to equipping artillery batteries. These units would typically field two howitzers and four guns, giving the battery the ability to both batter an opponent with rounds fired on a flat trajectory from the guns, as well as loft shells over earthworks and fortification walls using the howitzers.

One unit only, on either side, is known to have been equipped with 24-pounder howitzers. Formed at Springfield, Missouri, two months before the battle, this battery was known by the name of its commander, Captain John C. Landis. Along with a section (two pieces) of 24-pounder howitzers, Landis's Battery included a section of 12-pounder howitzers, making it the only all-howitzer unit in either army (Bearss 1962:47). Knowing the identity of the battery that likely fired the recovered rounds offers a unique opportunity to associate artifact to unit. Indeed, no other kind of artillery ammunition recovered at Pea Ridge is so directly associable with a distinct unit.

At this point, there is a temptation to start writing the conclusion and declare this analysis complete, as it makes for a nice artifact-oriented story that effectively links finds to the past. However, recent historical work casts doubt on Landis's role in the engagement, to the point of questioning whether or not the unit was within one hundred miles of the battle. While refereeing the historical record is not the most intellectually stimulating activity, the larger implications of this debate make it necessary to acknowledge and understand this historical disagreement en route to trumping it with the archaeological record to establish grounds for repatriating one of Landis's howitzers to Pea Ridge National Military Park, an act that would profoundly change the way in which the National Park Service helps connect visitors to the past.

Historians Comment on the Role of Landis's Battery

The proposal that the 24-pounder ammunition could be directly connected to Landis's Battery has met resistance from historians interested in the Civil War in the Trans-Mississippi. A large number of them maintain that Landis's Battery did not take part in the fight, and that it likely was not even at the battle, arriving in Arkansas just after the battle, while the Southern forces regrouped around Van Buren on the Arkansas River. To appreciate their argument, which is well grounded in the historical record, I feel it necessary to review the historical debate on the role (or lack thereof) of Landis's Battery at Pea Ridge.

There are two entries from *the Official Records of the War of the Rebellion* relating to Landis's Battery during the period surrounding the Pea Ridge Campaign. The earlier of the two is a general order issued to the Missouri State Guard on January 23, 1862, establishing an organization for Guard troops (Brand 1880:740). This order formed the Guard into two brigades, the second of which, under Brigadier General William Y. Slack, included "Captain Landis' squad of artillery." This suggests that some portion of the battery was already with the army as early as January of 1862. That it was referred to as a "squad," when Captain William Wade's artillery unit is termed a battery, suggests that the full complement was not on hand at the time.

The latter was a similar order issued immediately after the battle, when the Southern forces re-grouped around Van Buren. General Van Dorn worked to reorganize both the Confederate and Missouri soldiers, who were transitioning to national service, into a serviceable, unified force. Landis's Battery, consisting of four howitzers (calibers not mentioned) joined its peers in an artillery brigade commanded by Brigadier General David M. Frost (Van Dorn 1880). This order clearly states that Landis was on hand with four pieces, suggesting that the battery was complete (regulations called for six-gun batteries, but four-gun batteries were quite common during the war) and present. These two documents, both dating to the time of the battle, allow us to infer that Landis's Battery was with the Missouri State Guard before and after Pea Ridge, and before the army regrouped at Van Buren.

Other primary documents related to Landis's Battery are in short supply. To date, two diaries written by men who served in Landis's battery have been published. Samuel Dunlap (2006) and his brother, Robert Caldwell Dunlap (2005), served with Landis throughout most of the war, and both participated in the battle of Pea Ridge. Unfortunately for our purposes, both men served in infantry units elsewhere in the Missouri State Guard during the battle, transferring to Landis's unit after the battle, as the Missouri State Guard reorganized following the debacle. Neither man commented on the battery's role at Pea Ridge. Robert Dunlap did recall, in a diary entry on March 22, 1862, that the battery consisted of two 12-pounder and two 24-pounder howitzers when the brothers joined, but that the "company [was] not thoroughly organized, not having a sufficient number of men to elect officers" (Dunlap 2005:40). Samuel corroborates the 22nd as the date of their enrollment with Landis, but offers no comment on the unit's previous service, though he writes about the unit as though it were a new formation (Dunlap 2006:76–77).

While General Orders No. 26 suggests the presence of at least a portion of Landis's Battery at Pea Ridge, none of the primary document can be said to unequivocally state that the unit, or any part thereof, took part in the battle. None of the after-action reports mention Landis's unit. Brigadier General Slack died at Pea Ridge, so Colonel Thomas Rosser, his replacement on the field, wrote the brigade's report (Rosser 1880). Rosser mentions only Captain William Lucas's battery when discussing the conduct of the brigade's artillery, noting that it was detached from the brigade throughout the conflict.

For secondary sources, the earliest history of Landis's Battery was that written by its commander, Captain John C. Landis. Capt. Landis penned a short history of the battery for the *Missouri Republic*, of St. Louis, in 1895 (Landis 1895). In it, he states that the battery was equipped in Tennessee and arrived in Arkansas *after* Pea Ridge, when the Confederate Army (now including the Missouri State Guard, which had been transferred to national service) camped at Van Buren. Landis clearly means that the unit not only did not engage at Pea Ridge, it was hundreds of miles from the fight. This is the strongest piece of evidence for the unit not participating in the fight. Given that it was written by the battery commander, a man who would know better than anyone the service record of the unit, it is a source that should be respected and heeded. Indeed, McGhee's (2008) recent *Guide to Missouri Confederate Units, 1861–1865* cites Landis in its unit history for the battery, which recapitulates Landis's chain of events.

The authoritative historical work on the Battle of Pea Ridge, William Shea and Earl Hess's (1992) *Pea Ridge: Civil War Campaign in the West* is mute on Landis's involvement. They do mention it in the Order of Battle for the Missouri State Guard, noting its assignment to General brigade (Shea and Hess 1992:337). If it were with Slack during the battle, it would have been it would have been in the vicinity of Elkhorn Tavern and fought alongside its fellow Missouri State Guard units, particularly Lucas's gunners. This would place Landis's unit in the area where we found the canister ammunition in question.

We know of one soldier who served with Landis and who left a memoir of his wartime experiences. George Bent, son of Colorado fur trader William Bent, served with the Missouri State Guard at Pea Ridge, and used his personal correspondence to write his memoirs in the 1910s. George Hyde, of Omaha, Nebraska, saw the manuscript to publication half a century later (Bent and Hyde 1968). Though he enlisted with the First Missouri Cavalry, he transferred to Landis's Battery before the battle when the Missouri State Guard tried to change his unit into infantry (Halaas and Masich 2004:85–86). Bent's account of this period of the war largely recounts the service of Albert Pike, a white officer commanding Native American troops. For Pea Ridge, Bent wrote "I saw [Pike's] Indians in action on that field; but the warriors did not understand the white man's method of fighting, all standing up in a row in the open, and they had no liking for the big guns" (Bent and Hyde 1968:116). The action Bent describes is the charge of Pike's troops against two companies of the 3rd Iowa Cavalry on the first day of the battle (Shea and Hess 1992:101). Curiously, this is at Leetown, not Elkhorn Tavern, where the Missouri troops were engaged.

Subsequent research by Halaas and Masich (2004) places him in Landis's Battery at the time of the battle, and places Landis's Battery in the thick of the fighting at Pea Ridge, though the cursory attention given to the engagement does not make this a reliable source (Halaas and Masich 2004:85–86). Bent went on to lead an extraordinary life, growing disgusted with the war and joining his mother's Cheyenne people in camp at Sand Creek, Colorado. He was there when the camp was attacked by U.S. soldiers under Col. John Chivington in 1864 (Halaas and Masich 2004:113–153), and later joined the Dog Soldiers, perhaps the most illustrious Cheyenne warrior society of the period. In his later life, he served as an interpreter and liaison between the Army and several plains tribes (Bent and Hyde 1968; Halaas and Masich 2004).

With contemporary documentation being vague, at best, and postwar documentation and secondary sources, notably Landis's account, pointing to the battery not being on the field, our historical understanding of the role these Missourians did or did not play in the engagement is, at best, nebulous. In contrast to the muddled historical picture, the archaeological record seems rather clear. Two pieces of 24-pounder canister and one 24-pounder shell fragment suggest that such a weapon was on the field and took some part in the fighting around Elkhorn Tavern. There are three possible explanations for the divide between historical, historiographical, and archaeological datasets. I present them here in no particular order, though, as I have made clear and will return to in future, I have my conclusions.

First, and most in line with what I believe the archaeological research and some (enough) historical data suggest, Landis's Battery did receive its howitzers in time to participate in the battle, marched with the rest of the Missouri State Guard to Pea Ridge, and fired on U.S. soldiers around Elkhorn Tavern. As they are the only unit in the area known to have 24-pounders, this would be a reasonable explanation. The entirety of the battery may not have been on hand, and it is possible that Capt. Landis was with a portion that had not yet arrived. This would explain his recollection that the unit did not participate in the fight while simultaneously supporting the references in the *Official Records* indicating Landis's Battery as being present. Of course, Landis (1895) did not make such a distinction, and unequivocally recalled the entirety of the unit as arriving after the battle.

Second, some other battery at Pea Ridge had at least one 24-pounder in operation for which there is no record. This would account for the ammunition being found at Pea Ridge while McGhee and Landis have the battery being elsewhere. If we have been focusing myopically on Landis's Battery when some other unit was fielding the same weapon, this debate has been rendered moot. The obvious counter-argument against this is that neither Army, despite being well covered with adjutants, clerks, and diary- and memoir-writers, report any other unit as fielding a 24-pounder howitzer in the engagement. Neither the *Official Records* nor Shea and Hess (1992), Bearss (1962), or any other historian, identified any such unit.

There is a third explanation to consider as well. At the same time as the Pea Ridge project, MWAC undertook a similar survey of Wilson's Creek National Battlefield, near Springfield, Missouri. Like Pea Ridge, Wilson's Creek was an early war, Trans-Mississippi battle that featured many of the units, particularly on the Southern side, that fought at Pea Ridge.

Prior to Wilson's Creek, we know that the Missouri State Guard made expedient canister ammunition by cold-cutting iron bars into small pieces and placing them in cloth bags (Patrick 1997). MWAC fieldwork at Wilson's Creek found many of these pieces of expedient canister (Scott, Roeker, and Carlson-Drexler 2008). We found a few pieces at Pea Ridge, too, indicating that the Missourians still had some on hand (Carlson-Drexler, Scott, and Roeker 2008). It is conceivable that if the Confederates had broken up some old 24-pounder canister ammunition and used the balls for expedient canister, firing them from smaller-caliber cannon instead.

Period accounts do not indicate that this was the case, and we do not know whether the main sources of Missouri State Guard artillery ammunition, the captured federal stockpiles at Liberty and Lexington,

Missouri, even contained such rounds. Yet, this last would only explain the recovery of the canister rounds. FS2651, the shell fragment, however, means that a 24-pounder had to be on the field. A 5.4 inch iron ball cannot be forced into a 4.2 (12-pounder) or 3.4 (6-pounder) gun, and no larger caliber weapon was used at Pea Ridge. In order for a 24-pounder case shot round to be used at Pea Ridge, a 24-pounder had to have been there to fire it. In the absence of there being any unit on either side fielding such a weapon at any time near the battle, the recovery of 24-pounder howitzer ammunition at Pea Ridge means Landis's Missouri Battery was there to fire it.

Returning Landis to Pea Ridge

But, so what? Why take the time to unravel the historiography of Landis's Battery and its relationship to Pea Ridge, and why spill ink over a point of historical minutia? The ramifications of this research are greater than a pithy academic debate for two reasons. First, there is a need to properly mark and commemorate the wartime experiences of soldiers and civilians who endured our nation's conflict(ed) history. If Landis's Battery was caught in the maelstrom of the fighting around Elkhorn Tavern on the battle's first day, we should recognize that fact, both in print and in interpretation to the public.

Second, in the years since the fieldwork took place, Steve Black, former chief ranger and historian at Pea Ridge, located the barrel of one of Landis's howitzers, mounted as a display piece (along with numerous others) at Petersburg National Battlefield, Virginia. At the time, there was some interest in organizing an exchange of cannons, trading one of Pea Ridge's Napoleons for the Landis howitzer. The effort flagged when the debate about Landis's presence, predicated significantly on John Landis's unit history from 1895 and furthered by McGhee's (2008) recent research, suggested that the battery had missed the battle.

In writing this chapter, I hope to have accurately laid out the sides in the debate (hence the extended historiographical discussion) as well as to have made a strong counterclaim to this recent historical interpretation. Archaeological evidence insists that Landis's Battery had a presence at the battle, and the repatriation of the howitzer barrel from Petersburg would be a valuable addition to the park and an unusually powerful interpretive device.

Archaeologists routinely talk and write about how artifacts can serve as bridges to the past, connecting the modern observer with the people who made, used, and deposited the detritus of everyday life decades, centuries, and millennia ago. The poignancy of battlefield finds, such as the wedding ring mentioned above, makes these artifacts particularly powerful bridges to the past. A bullet is not just a bullet. It was fired by a person at another person, each of whom may have been thrilled at the experience of combat or scared out of his mind (or both together). Buttons, torn from the clothes of the wounded or popped from the tunics of the dead, bespeak the pain incurred during these hours of struggle. We have literally thousands of artifacts from the battle of Pea Ridge, yet the Landis howitzer, if brought back to Arkansas, would assume a degree of import beyond that of the other battlefield finds. This is due to the manner in which soldiers then (and, to a marked degree, today) relate to different pieces of military equipment in different ways. Not everything issued is equally important, and this fact is something we should bear in mind when interpreting the archaeological record of conflict.

Bullets and artillery shells, though vital to the conduct of battle, are fundamentally expendable. They are designed to be gotten rid of, preferably into the body of an enemy. There is no real attachment to them outside of the want of more when the battle drags on and supplies run low. The weapons that fire them, however, are a different manner. It is the weapon that makes a soldier of value in a fight, and to lose one's weapon is a censurable offense. This is particularly true for cannons. Teams of soldiers worked each artillery piece, and while it was common for crews to abandon ammunition wagons in moments of crisis, losing the cannon itself was the acme of embarrassment for an artillery crew. Conversely, capturing a piece was sure to be noted in any report, and could mean medals and promotion for those who captured it. During the war, the U.S. Army awarded more than a dozen Congressional Medals of Honor to soldiers who either captured or saved cannons from capture. Indeed, the German 88mm gun mentioned above (Pearson and Connah 2009) was shipped halfway around the world to stand as a war prize in recognition of its captors. Some cannons were even given names, according them a measure of celebrity. Captain Hiram Bledsoe's battery in the Missouri State Guard featured a cannon, captured during the Mexican War, affectionately known throughout the Guard as "Old Sacramento."

As Nora (1989) made popular the concept of the *lieu de memoire* to describe places with great memorial significance, such a howitzer would become a thing of great memorial significance, a *chose de memoire*. Bringing the Landis cannon from Petersburg would be a powerful addition to the site and could become a fixture of the park's interpretation of the battle to the public. The value placed on artillery pieces in the past, and the magnetic draw that cannons have for visitors make them particularly compelling connections between the present and the past. The continuity of place and event inherent in a howitzer from Landis's Battery, a veteran of the battle, being on display at Pea Ridge National Military Park would be a uniquely powerful bridge to the eponymous battle.

Acknowledgments

I would like to thank Troy Banzhaf, ranger and historian at Pea Ridge National Military Park, for his discussion of the background of the Landis debate. Douglas Scott, who directed the research at Pea Ridge, also pointed out the Bent memoir and reminded me about the shell fragment, FS2651. The field research could not have happened without a large number of volunteers and NPS staff, both at Pea Ridge and at the Midwest Archeological Center. I thank them all, and direct the reader to the acknowledgments section of the report on the investigations for a comprehensive list.

REFERENCES

Bearss, Edwin C.
1962   Artillery at Pea Ridge. Manuscript on file, USDI/NPS/Midwest Archeological Center, Lincoln, Nebraska.
Bent, George, and George E. Hyde
1968   *Life of George Bent: Written from His Letters*. University of Oklahoma Press, Norman.
Bleed, Peter, and Douglas D. Scott
2011   Contexts for Conflict: Conceptual Tools for Interpreting Archaeological Reflections of Warfare. *Journal of Conflict Archaeology* 6(1): 42–64.
Brand, William H.
1880   General Orders No. 26. In The War of the Rebellion: A Compilation of the Official Records of the Union and Confederate Armies, Series 1, Volume 8, Part 1 (Pea Ridge), Chapter 18: Correspondence, Etc.—Confederate pp. 739–741. Government Printing Office, Washington, DC.
Brown, Walter L.
1956   Pea Ridge: Gettysburg of the West. *The Arkansas Historical Quarterly* 15: 15–16.
Carlson-Drexler, Carl G., Douglas D. Scott, and Harold Roeker
2008   "The Battle Raged... With Terrible Fury:" Battlefield Archaeology of Pea Ridge National Military Park. Technical Report No. 112. USDI/NPS Midwest Archeological Center, Lincoln, Nebraska.
Clayton, Lawrence A., Vernon J. Knight, Edward C. Moore, and Jay I. Kislak
1993   *The De Soto Chronicles: The Expedition of Hernando de Soto to North America in 1539–1543*. University of Alabama Press, Tuscaloosa.

Coles, Alicia L.
2003   Metallurgical Analysis of Shell and Case Shot Artillery from the Civil War Battles of Pea Ridge and Wilson's Creek (PERI and WICR). Manuscript on file, USDI/NPS/Midwest Archeological Center, Lincoln, Nebraska.
2004   Fracture Mechanics: Analysis of Shell and Case Shot Artillery from the Civil War Battles of Pea Ridge and Wilson's Creek. Paper presented at the 37th Annual Meeting of the Society for Historical Archaeology, St. Louis.

Cornelison, John E., and Tammy D. Cooper
2002   An Archeological Survey of the Chalmette Battlefield at Jean Lafitte Historical Park and Preserve. USDI/NPS Southeast Archaeological Center, Tallahassee, Florida.

Dollar, Clyde D.
1960   Interim Report, Old Fort Smith Project. Fort Smith National Historic Site, Fort Smith, Arkansas.
1966   The First Fort Smith Report. Fort Smith National Historic Site, Fort Smith, Arkansas.

Van Dorn, Earl
1880   General Orders No. 24. In The War of the Rebellion: A Compilation of the Official Records of the Union and Confederate Armies, Series 1, Volume 8, Part 1 (Pea Ridge): Operations in Mo., Ark., Kans., and Ind. T. P. 788. Government Printing Office, Washington, D.C.

Drexler, Carl G.
2004   Identifying Culturally-Based Variability in Artillery Ammunition Fragments Recovered from the Battlefield of Pea Ridge, Arkansas. Master's thesis, Department of Anthropology, University of Nebraska, Lincoln.
2013   Dooley's Ferry: The Archaeology of a Civilian Community in Wartime. Doctoral dissertation, Department of Anthropology, The College of William & Mary, Williamsburg, Virginia.

Dunlap, Robert Caldwell
2005   As the Mockingbird Sang: Civil War Diary of Pvt. Robert Caldwell Dunlap, C.S.A. Platte Purchase Publishers Civil War Series. Platte Purchase Publishers, St. Joseph, Missouri.

Dunlap, Samuel Baldwin
2006   Fishing on Deep River: Civil War Memoir of Pvt. Samuel Baldwin Dunlap, C.S.A. Platte Purchase Publishers, St. Joseph, Missouri.

Fox, Richard A., and Douglas D. Scott
1991   The Post-Civil War Battlefield Pattern: An Example from the Custer Battlefield. Historical Archaeology 25(2): 92–103.

Gibbon, John
1860   The Artillerist's Manual: Compiled from Various Sources and Adapted to the Service of the United States. D. Van Nostrand, New York, New York.

Griffith, Paddy
1987   Battle Tactics of the Civil War. Yale University Press, New Haven, Connecticut.

Halaas, David F., and Andrew E. Masich
2004   Halfbreed: The Remarkable True Story of George Bent: Caught between the Worlds of the Indian and the White Man. Da Capo Press, Cambridge, Massachusetts.

Hilliard, Jerry E.
2004   An Antebellum Ozark Community and the Civil War: The Archaeology
        of the Second Mount Comfort Church (3WA880), Washington County,
        Arkansas (1840–Ca. 1865). Research Series No. 63. Arkansas Archeological
        Survey, Fayetteville.
Hilliard, Jerry E., Mike Evans, Jared Pebworth, and Carl G. Carlson-Drexler
2008   A Confederate Encampment at Cross Hollow, Benton County, Arkansas.
        The Arkansas Historical Quarterly 67(4): 359–374.
Landis, John C.
1895   The Landis Battery. *St. Louis Republic* 12 May. St. Louis, Missouri.
Lee, John W.I.
2001   Urban Combat at Olynthos, 348BC. In *Fields of Conflict: Progress and
        Prospect in Battlefield Archaeology.* P. W. M. Freeman and A. Pollard, eds.
        Pp. 11–22. BAR International Series. Archaeopress, Oxford, UK.
McClurkan, Burney
1968   Archeological Investigation at Fort Curtis, Helena, Arkansas. *Phillips County
        Historical Quarterly* 6(3): 2–8.
McGhee, James E.
2008   *Guide to Missouri Confederate Units, 1861–1865.* University of Arkansas
        Press, Fayetteville.
Medearis, Mary
1976   *Washington, Arkansas: History on the Southwest Trail.* Etter Printing
        Company, Hope, Arkansas.
Noël Hume, Ivor
1969   *Historical Archaeology.* Alfred A. Knopf, New York.
Nora, Pierre
1989   Between Memory and History: Les Lieux de Mémoire. *Representations* 26:
        7–24.
Orr, David G.
1994   The Archaeology of Trauma: An Introduction to the Historical Archaeology
        of the American Civil War. In *Look to the Earth: Historical Archaeology
        and the American Civil War.* Clarence R. Geier and Susan E. Winter, eds.
        Pp. 21–36. University of Tennessee Press, Knoxville.
Patrick, Jeffrey L.
1997   Remembering the Missouri Campaign of 1861: The Memoirs of Lieutenant
        William P. Barlow, Guibor's Battery, Missouri State Guard. *Civil War
        Regiments* 5(4): 20–60.
Pearson, David, and Graham Connah
2009   Battlefield Casualty: The Archaeology of a Captured Gun. *Journal of Conflict
        Archaeology* 5(1): 231–256.
Pollard, Tony
2007   Looking for the Thin Red Line. *Skirmish Magazine* (October): 6–8.
Ross, Don
1995   A Confederate Armament Works in Arkadelphia (3CL283). *The Arkansas
        Archeologist: Bulletin of the Arkansas Archeological Society* 34: 83–91.
Rosser, Thomas H.
1880   Report of Colonel Thomas H. Rosser, Commanding Second Brigade,
        Confederate Cavalry. In The War of the Rebellion: A Compilation of the

Official Records of the Union and Confederate Armies, Series 1, Volume 8, Part 1 (Pea Ridge): Operations in Mo., Ark., Kans., and Ind. T. Pp. 312–313. Government Printing Office, Washington, D.C.

Schofield, John

2009   *Aftermath: Readings in the Archaeology of Recent Conflict.* Springer, New York, New York.

Scott, Douglas D., Richard A. Fox, Melissa A. Connor, and Dick Harmon

1989   *Archaeological Perspectives on the Battle of the Little Bighorn.* University of Oklahoma Press, Norman.

Scott, Douglas D., and Andrew P. McFeaters

2011   The Archaeology of Historic Battlefields: A History and Theoretical Development in Conflict Archaeology. *Journal of Archaeological Research* 19: 103–132.

Scott, Douglas D., Harold Roeker, and Carl G. Carlson-Drexler

2008   "The Fire Upon Us Was Terrific:" Battlefield Archaeology of Wilson's Creek National Battlefield, Missouri. Technical Report No. 109. USDI/NPS Midwest Archeological Center, Lincoln, Nebraska.

Shea, William L.

1996   *War in the West: Pea Ridge and Prairie Grove.* Ryan Place, Fort Worth, Texas.

Shea, William L., and Earl J. Hess

1992   *Pea Ridge: Civil War Campaign in the West.* Chappell Hill: University of North Carolina Press.

Thomas, Dean S.

1985   *Cannons: An Introduction to Civil War Artillery.* Thomas Publications, Gettysburg, Pennsylvania.

Volf, William J.

2003   Geophysical Resistance Surveys at the Elkhorn Tavern and Leetown Locations within Pea Ridge National Military Park, Pea Ridge, Arkansas. USDI/NPS/Midwest Archeological Center, Lincoln, Nebraska.

Walker, John W.

1971   Excavation of the Arkansas Post Branch of the Bank of the State of Arkansas, Arkansas Post National Memorial. USDI/NPS/Southeast Archeological Center, Tallahassee, Florida.

Whitford, Tim, and Tony Pollard

2009   For Duty Done: A WWI Military Medallion Recovered from the Mass Grave Site at Fromelles, Northern France. *Journal of Conflict Archaeology* 5(1): 201–228.

Williamson, Malcolm

1993   Predictive Modeling of Civil War Artillery Artifact Dispersion Using Geographic Information Systems. Unpublished master's thesis, Department of Anthropology, University of Arkansas, Fayetteville.

Wilson, Rex L.

1965   Archaeological Investigations in Pea Ridge National Military Park. Manuscript on file, USDI/NPS Midwest Archeological Center, Lincoln, Nebraska.

9

THE ARCHAEOLOGY OF JUDAISM, SLAVERY, AND ASSIMILATION ON THE ANTEBELLUM FRONTIER

David M. Markus

Any discussion of the Jewish experience in Arkansas must begin with the first documented Jewish family to immigrate to the state in search of new opportunities. Or in the words of the historian Caroline LeMaster (1994:3) when "Abraham comes to Arkansas." This statement of immigration genesis does not refer to the figure of biblical notoriety but rather the subject of this study, Abraham Block and his family.

As Jews began to populate the Southern and Western states and territories they had to make concessions with regard to their religious tradition in order to provide for their families. Abraham, a merchant by trade, made the conscious decision to forgo a formalized religious infrastructure to provide greater economic stability for his family. To this end, his role as a Southern merchant can be understood.

This, however, provides only one vantage point on the Block family experience in Arkansas. Archaeological investigations at the Block family home in Washington, begun in the early 1980s, have helped to put into context some of the assumptions made about Southern Jewish life. Archaeology can provide new perspectives on the understanding of ethnicity by looking at material culture through time. Research at the Block property provided an opportunity to examine how one family acted within and upon their Jewish traditions and beliefs to create a way of life that held to sacred tenets but also accommodated secular conditions of frontier life.

This chapter seeks to answer three questions about the nature of life on the frontier from the perspective of the Block family and their house lot. *First,* building on the roughly 30 years of excavation at the site, what can more recently uncovered features in the yard space do to alter the interpretation of the Block household? *Second*, what can this new assemblage tell us about Block family? Is there evidence of Jewish lifeways? Or evidence that they were not holding a Jewish household? Is the assemblage similar in composition to previously analyzed assemblages from the site? *Third*, does the new assemblage given any insight into the life of the Block slaves or their relationship to the Block family?

Antebellum Jewry

The antebellum period, defined as beginning with the Missouri Compromise of 1820 and ending just prior to the outbreak of the Civil War in 1860, was a time of great change. The trajectory of Judaism in America during this time is largely no different. Even though small in number, the Jewish community of the early American South was able to socially integrate to the point of intermarriage with non-Jewish populations. This social acceptance into the larger Southern culture did not translate into the development of a strong Jewish community. In fact, the establishment of a synagogue, seen as an important step in creating a Jewish base, did not even garner local interest in New Orleans, the outpost of Judaism in the Old Southwest. The first synagogue in New Orleans, Gates of Mercy, received limited local support from both Jews and non-Jews, including Abraham Block, who joined as a founding member.

Generally speaking, the majority of European immigrant Jews in the 19th century did not come to the South from urban centers such as Paris, Bordeaux (known as a large Sephardic community), or Metz (the center of Jewish life in Alsace-Lorraine) but instead these Jews came from towns and villages dependent on agriculture and landownership. For these Jews the American South was seen as a place with fresh economic prospects. Immigration occurred not only from Europe to the South but also from within the United States Jewish population, as was the case with the Blocks. Jewish businessmen from cities such as New York brought goods and capital to trade and sell in southern towns and cities. Jews of the period tended to change locations and business partners frequently to the surprise of others. The Block family is a prime example of this; with ties to Arkansas, Louisiana and Texas (Kwas 2009a) Abraham Block and his five sons set up shops in a variety of locations including New Orleans, Washington and Fulton, Arkansas and several towns along the railroad heading from Houston to Dallas, Texas. Each son would partner with their father and learn the trade and as each son matured and came in to his own he would give way to the younger brothers and begin his own business either with a brother, or with another merchant. The link to family or even just coreligionists in business contributed to the successes felt by many Jews in the South.

A Brief History of Washington, Arkansas

The antebellum town of Washington in Hempstead County, Arkansas, was established in 1824 on a campsite established by Reverend William Stevenson in 1820 on the hill above Bois D'Arc Creek along the Southwest Trail. The area was still part of the Missouri Territory (Guthrie and Witsell 1985:17). The early pioneers and settlers of the town were a mix of planters, merchants and frontiersmen eager to serve those traveling along the Southwest Trail. As the county seat of the area, Washington soon became a hub for business and law that led to a boom in growth. Cotton was the primary crop for the area and Washington rapidly became the focal point of the associated industries. As a result of its role and location, the population of Washington grew quickly. After subdividing the town into blocks in 1825 it was incorporated in 1830, the first in Arkansas to do so (Kwas 2009b:6). During the 1830s roads and waterways were continually improved to the point that it became an important stop in the regional transportation network—many historical figures came through the town such as James Bowie (1826–1831), Sam Houston (1834), and Davy Crockett (1835), and the state's first Jewish family, the Blocks.

Archaeological Studies of Jewry in the Americas

Despite constituting one of the longest tenured Diasporic communities in the Americas, Jewish sites have received less archaeological study than other groups. While this deficiency has been noted elsewhere (Wesler 2012:210), there are a growing number of Jewish sites across the United States and the Caribbean that have been excavated since the 1980s. In the Caribbean research conducted in Nevis (Terrell 2000; Terrell 2005), St. Eustatius (Barka 1985; Barka 1987; Barka 1988; Gilmore 2006), Jamaica (Allsworth-Jones et al. 1998; Allsworth-Jones et al. 2000; Allsworth-Jones et al. 2003; Wesler 2002), and Barbados (Miller 2010; Miller 2011; Miller 2012a; Miller 2012b) has focused on the larger

Jewish community and the extant synagogues and ritual spaces (such as ritual baths known as *mikvahs*) that serve as reminders of their existence. In the United States archaeological treatments of Jewry have covered a wider variety of site types. In addition, these studies also cover a large number of geographic areas across the expanses of the continental United States. Much like in the Caribbean there have been synagogue and *mikvah* studies conducted in Baltimore, Maryland (Ecker and Jackson 2000; Read 2012), Manhattan, New York (Bergoffen 1997; CITY/SCAPE 2003) and Chesterfield, Connecticut (Acly 2011; Clouette and Harper 2007; Harper 2008; Historical Perspectives, Inc. 2011; Historical Perspectives, Inc. 2012; Horn et al. 2012). Further studies of Jewish landscapes have taken place in Boston, Massachusetts (Spencer-Wood 1999; Spencer-Wood 2010) and throughout the Midwest in the form of cemetery studies (Gradwohl 1993a; Gradwohl 1993b; Gradwohl and Gradwohl 1988).

Arguably the most significant sites excavated relating to the Jewish Diaspora in the Americas are those focused on the households of Jewish families. These studies allow for the investigation of the private lives of individuals outside of their contributions to the landscapes of the communities that they inhabit. There have been several such sites excavated across the United States in Sacramento (Praetzellis 1991), San Francisco (Praetzellis 2009; Yentsch 2009), and Oakland (Praetzellis 2004), California; Five Points (Milne and Crabtree 1998; Milne and Crabtree 2001) and Staten Island (Baugher et al. 1985), New York; Michilimackinac, Michigan (Heldman 1986; Scott 1991; Scott 1992; Scott 2008); and Arkadelphia (Ross 1997) and Washington, Arkansas (Applegate and Markus 2011; Guendling et al. 1999; Guendling et al. 2002; Kwas 2009a; Kwas 2009b; Markus 2011; Markus 2012; Markus and Brandon 2010; Markus et al. 2012; Ruff 1985; Stewart-Abernathy 1985; Stewart-Abernathy and Ruff 1989; Winburn and Markus 2012).

What makes the studies conducted at the Block House especially important is that, along with the Benjamin House in Arkadelphia, Arkansas (Ross 1997), it represents the only site excavated in a Southern state. The Block House also includes an enslaved component that allows for additional questions about the Antebellum Jewish experience to be asked. What follows is an analysis of the Block Family experience in Arkansas that uses archaeological research conducted at their home to understand their experience as Jews and as slave owners on the Southwestern Frontier.

Figure 9.1. Abraham Block (left) and Fanny Block (right), courtesy of Caroline Grey LeMaster.

A History of the Block Family

While the focus of this study is on the Block family during their time in Arkansas it is necessary to take a brief look at the family trajectory prior to their arrival in Arkansas to frame the findings (see Kwas 2009a for a more extensive study of the Block family Genealogy). Abraham Block was born on January 30, 1780 (or in 1781) in Schwihau, Bohemia. The names of his parents are unknown, and little is known of his years in Bohemia. Around the age of twelve, Block immigrated to Richmond, Virginia. He likely traveled to the United States with an older relative or came to live with relatives already in America; these familial relationships, however, are unknown. Despite the details regarding Abraham Block's origins being rather hazy, a bit more is known about the family of his wife, Fanny. (Markus 2011; LeMaster 1994:1–2; Kwas 2009a:42–43)

Frances "Fanny" Isaacs, the eldest child of Isaiah Isaacs, a successful businessman and Jewish pioneer, was born in Charlottesville, Virginia, on February 27, 1797. Fanny's lineage is in strongly Judaic families. Fanny's father died relatively early on in her childhood in April 1806, but his will made several provisions that influenced the trajectory of Fanny's later life. Isaiah's will stipulated that his children be placed "in the families of respectable Jews to the end that they may be brought up in the religion of the forefathers" (Isaacs 1971). While all of Isaiah's property, including the first tavern in Richmond (known as the Bird-In-Hand), were willed to his children he blocked the sale of those properties until the youngest of his children had reached the age of twenty-one

After a brief courtship, fifteen-year-old Fanny and thirty-one-year-old Abraham were married on October 2, 1811. The years that followed were rather eventful for the couple as Abraham served in the War of 1812, earning the title of Captain, all the while building a solid merchant business in Richmond. Seven children—Hester (1813), Simon (1815), Rosina (1816), Isaac (1817), Augustus (1818), Henry (1820), and David (1823)—were born to the Blocks during their married years in Richmond, though there may have been two additional children who died as infants (Kwas 2009a:52). Although they were entrenched in the commercial and religious communities of Richmond, the Blocks made the decision to uproot and move to the Southwestern frontier. The rationale for the move is unknown but by this time Fanny had reach her majority, which would have allowed for such a move. As Kwas (2009a:53) points out the move was not financed by sale of the properties inherited from Isaacs, as the Blocks rented the properties and renewed their insurances as late as 1836. Perhaps their age and the glut of Jewish merchant business competition in the area allowed for the conditions of their departure. In 1822, Abraham, at the age of forty-two and with Fanny expecting their seventh child (David), left for New Orleans. By 1823 Abraham had arrived in Arkansas and by 1825 he had established a business in the new town of Washington.

The Blocks as Merchants

As a result of their choice to pursue new economic opportunities in the west, the family of Abraham and Fanny Block became the first documented Jewish immigrants to the state of Arkansas. This gamble proved fruitful, as Abraham and several of his sons were able to establish successful businesses in a number of locations in the old southwest. Abraham used the first few years in Arkansas traveling between Washington and New Orleans to establish business opportunities. Abraham may have undertaken the quintessentially Jewish male pursuit of the 19th century, peddling, in the interim (Diner 2005), though it did not take long for a store to take root in Washington.

Block engaged in a series of partnerships with more established local, non-Jewish, merchants in his early ventures, likely to establish a level of credibility and lend some reliable capital to the business. Outside of assisting Abraham in gaining a foothold in the Arkansas markets, his alignment with non-Jews fits into the larger pattern of behavior for immigrant Jews of the time (Ashkenazi 1988). In order to accomplish the goal of attaining social acceptance in the xenophobic South, Jews eschewed *all* public performances of faith and foreign born identity; instead mimicking the clothing, speech, activity and ideology of Southern America (Bhanha 2007:338). The mimicry of standard Southern mercantilism through his partnerships with non-Jews may have created a level of comfort for Southerners in dealing with Abraham as a Jew while allowing him to establish a business (at least situationally) free of the stigma of "otherness."

Newspaper advertisements at the time indicate that Block offered a wide variety of goods in his store such as: clothing, dry goods, fancy goods, hardware, glassware and dishes, tools and groceries. Block and his partners also took on the sale of goods, real estate, cattle and slaves for others as part of their consignment business (Kwas 2009a:80). Several sons took on positions as clerks in their father's store. Sons Augustus, Simon, David, and Virginius all were trained in their father's craft. By 1847, Augustus had stepped out on his own—with another brother—under the title of "Block Brothers and Co." Until that same year Abraham ran the business solely in his name, after which he took on his sons as junior partners. First David and the Virginius joined their father's firm forming "Block and Son" and later "Block and Sons." The success of their merchant ventures manifested itself as property and personal wealth for Abraham and his sons, chiefly David and Virginius who remained in Washington. Upon their father's retirement in 1850, David and Virginius took over the business forming "Block Brothers Co." They later incorporated members of the Jett family, who were related by marriage, into the business to form "Block, Jett and Co." (Kwas 2009a:80)

The Blocks in the Business of Slavery

In the southern states during the antebellum period, slavery was a way of life. In keeping with the trend of understanding Southern Jewish mimicry, several leading Jewish scholars such as Bertram Wallace Korn (1969) have found little difference between the patterns of Jews and non-Jews with regard to slavery. Southern Jews were involved in the purchase, sale and owning of slaves just as any other Southerner was. As there is little known of Abraham's early life in Richmond prior to his marriage to Fanny, it is difficult to know whether the relatives that he was living with were engaged in aspects of the slave trade. In the case of Fanny's childhood, the attitude of her father towards slavery is known. Isaiah Isaacs owned several slaves in conjunction with his business partner Jacob Cohen. When their business relationship ended in 1792, he received five slaves. In 1799, Isaacs freed the first of his slaves, a woman by the name of Lucy. In his will from 1803, three years prior to his death, Isaacs outlined the conditions for the release of his slaves from bondage:

Being of opinion that all men are by nature equally free and being possessed of some of those beings who are unfortunate [sic] doomed to slavery, as to them I must enjoin upon my executors a strict observance of the following clause of my will. My slaves hereafter named are to be and they are hereby manumitted and made free so that after the different periods hereafter mentioned they shall enjoy all the privileges and immunities of freed people (Isaacs 1971)

It is readily apparent from that statement that Isaiah was somewhat uncomfortable with the institution of slavery. This did not stop him, however, from benefitting from their labor or transferring their ownership to his children. The property tax records of Abraham Block during his time in Richmond show that he owned between two and three slaves from 1815 to 1824. In 1824, when the inherited property from Isaiah Isaacs was split between Fanny and her brother, only one slave is listed, Matilda (Kwas 2009a:83). Matilda shows up again in public documents in September 1826 where she is listed as the slave of Abraham Block and charged with the theft of: "Carrying off two pound of cheese, valued at 25 cents; 2 ½ pouns [sic] of sugar, valued at 30 cents; one bottle of cordial, $1; and five tumbler, 37 cents, the goods and chattels of Grace Marx. She was found not guilty. For defending her from the charge of stealing $1.62 of property the court allowed her council $10" (Ezekiel and Lichtenstein 1917). Since the Blocks had already left for Arkansas by this time, Matilda, who was slated to be freed at the age of thirty-one per Isaiah Isaacs will, seems to have been left behind in Virginia.

While looking at their time in Virginia is useful, a better indication of the Block attitudes towards slavery is their time in Arkansas. According to the Hempstead County tax records Block owned a single slave in 1839. This number increased through the 1840s to as high as five. There is a drastic increase in the number of slaves in 1850, when the tax records list Block as owning eleven slaves. In the slave schedule of the same year Block is listed as owning thirteen slaves, six of whom were adults (Kwas2009a:83).

The Blocks also dealt with the sale and purchase of slaves as part of their merchant ventures. Linda McDowell (2000) lists the Blocks as purchasing twelve slaves yet selling only one. The majority of these purchases were listed in partnership and three were directly identified as collateral for loans. None of the advertisements of Abraham's various business partnerships lists them as slave dealers and it seems that their transactions were limited to loan collateral.

The number of slaves owned by the Blocks suggests that they owned more than was the norm for an urban setting. Undoubtedly some were used in domestic settings, but the numbers indicate an elevated economic status. Furthermore the Blocks relied heavily of the patronage of the plantation economy surrounding Washington and were deeply ingrained in the slave-based agricultural economy.

The Blocks as Jews

As was the case with Abraham's early business history in Richmond, there is a lack of information about his links to Judaism during his time in Bohemia or in Richmond. Fanny's Jewish upbringing is easier to track. The product of a mixed marriage of her Sephardic mother, Hetty Hays, and her Ashkenazi father, Isaiah Isaacs, she was part of an old line of Sephardic Jewish immigrants. Her father had the foresight to stipulate in his will from 1803 that she be placed in the home of a Jew upon his death as her mother had died in roughly the same year. Where Fanny lived after the death of her parents is difficult to track but Kwas believes that she lived with members of the Hays family in New York (Kwas 2009a:48).

Because little is known of Abraham's early days and Fanny's orphan status it is difficult to pinpoint where they lived or how they met prior to their marriage. What is known is that the couple wed in New York's Shearith Israel Synagogue, the oldest Jewish congregation in America. It is possible that they met in New York where Abraham is listed as a member of Shearith Israel prior to 1820. According to Kwas (2009a:49) one descendant of the Block family claims that Abraham was in New York studying to become a Rabbi. Nevertheless, soon after their wedding the Blocks moved to Richmond to begin their married lives. The strength of the Jewish community meant that they had an active religious and social life during this time.

The Blocks had left the relative comfort of the Jewish community in Richmond and entered into an area in the South that was bereft of a local Jewish community. The community that they were *de facto* members of, New Orleans, had such extreme repression of public expressions of faith that, the establishment of a synagogue, seen as an important step in creating a Jewish base, did not garner local interest until 1828, when Congregation Gates of Mercy was established.

For the rest of the significant milestones in the Jewish life cycle it is difficult to prove the Blocks' participation. The first significant step in the life cycle of Jews is that of circumcision performed within seven days of birth by a *mohel*, a ritual specialist. Of the seven Block boys; five were born during the family's time in Richmond when they had access to a large Jewish community and religious infrastructure. From this we can assume that those five sons were circumcised. For the last two sons born after leaving Richmond, establishing their circumcision is more difficult. Without readily available access to a *mohel*, the nearest congregation was that of Gates of Mercy in New Orleans, the likelihood that these sons were circumcised is minimal despite, as Stewart-Abernathy and Ruff (1989:106) note, the ability to delay the ceremony until a *mohel* is found. In even rarer circumstances a father could perform the ceremony himself with the appropriate training, which Block may have received if his partial rabbinical training is to be believed.

The next step in the Jewish life cycle for males is that of *Bar Mitzvah*, or the rite of passage into manhood undertaken at the age of 13. As none of the Block sons were of that age when the family moved to Washington it is difficult to believe that any of them underwent the ritual. A *Bar Mitzvah* requires a significant amount of training in certain aspects of Jewish life and there would have been no one to teach the necessary information. Again, Abraham could have instructed his sons in this process but they would have had to wait until a trip to New Orleans to have the process completed. For the Block daughters there would have been no rite of passage into womanhood, as the ritual of the *Bat Mitzvah* had not come into existence in the 19th century.

While Abraham and Fanny were able to wed in a traditional Jewish fashion their children would not have been able to do so. Firstly only one of the Block children, Augustus, is known to have married within the faith. After moving to New Orleans, Augustus married into the Jonas family in 1856 (Stewart-Abernathy and Ruff 1989:107). The remaining eleven children married into prominent Christian families in Washington and their marriages could not have been performed in the Jewish tradition as the town lacked a Rabbi or the *Minyan,* or quorum of Jewish males, necessary to make the marriage official. As Jewish law and tradition states that membership in the faith is dictated by maternal line, none of the children of the Block sons, save for the six children of Augustus (Kwas 2009a:98), could have been considered Jewish as they were born to Christian mothers. None of the Block daughters married into Jewish families and although their children would have been considered Jewish by the letter of the law they are not known to have been raised in Jewish households.

The final rituals in the Jewish life cycle are those related to death. Jewish law stipulates how a body must be treated after death and dictates how the living must honor the dead. Upon his death on 1857, Abraham was buried in New Orleans in the Jewish tradition in the second, more conservative, Sephardic rite, congregation of Nefutze Judah, or Dispersed of Judah. When he died several obituaries in both regional and national Jewish newspapers give an indication of his adherence to the faith. *The Occident and American Jewish Advocate* ran a three-page obituary for Block that read, "[He] had time to pray to the God of Israel, and to invoke a blessing upon his children. He died as the good die: with him a moment of preparation was sufficient. He sleeps according to his Cherished wish among his people, in the Portuguese Cemetery, on the Metairie Ridge, in the city" (Anonymous 1857b). While it is to be expected that a national Jewish newspaper would recognize Abraham's faith, the statewide newspaper the *Arkansas Gazette* also makes note of his religion in the April 4, 1857 issue: "Few men have lived to the age of Captain Block, who have left have left more lasting mementoes of a life better spent, with more friends or fewer enemies. His virtues, let us all try to emulate, none can ever hope to excel. The loss to his family and friends is indeed irreparable, but it is a consolation for them to feel, their loss, is his gain, for he passed from earth to immortality. Truly, 'A good man has fallen in Israel'" (Anonymous 1857a). Other than Abraham only Fanny, who died in 1871, and their son Augustus were buried in the Jewish tradition with both joining him at Dispersed of Judah.

The burial locations and obituaries of the remaining Block children give an indication of the loss of faith in the family. The three Block children who died during their childhood, Isaac, Simon and Laura, were all buried in the Pioneer Cemetery in Washington, despite Abraham's link to congregations in New Orleans. Juliet, Hester and David, who all died as adults, are also buried in Washington. Juliet was buried with her siblings in the Pioneer Cemetery and Hester and David were buried in the Washington Presbyterian Cemetery. Hester's obituary mentions "devout Christian faith" which is a good indicator of the conversion within the family as Hester was the oldest child of Abraham and Fanny (Anonymous 1887).

Certainly the alternation and repression of traditional rites of passage had a greater effect on the subsequent generations of Blocks. Rather than an outright abandonment of faith, early Jews of the rural South such as the Blocks chose to practice personal forms of religious expression without the infrastructure to support them, allowing them to blend into American society.

Archaeological Research at the Block House

Initial Excavation

Based on the results of an initial survey conducted in 1980, the Arkansas Archeological Survey and Arkansas Archeological Society conducted excavations at the Block property in 1982 and 1983. Three research priorities were identified; seek architectural evidence of the detached kitchen, delineate the spatial position of the kitchen in relation to other structures on the property and interrogate the lifeways of the household, both secular and sacred, based on the remains of the kitchen complex (Stewart-Abernathy 1982a).

At the conclusion of the 1982 season, a large trash pit (see Figure 9.2) in the interior of the kitchen location was identified as a dark, organic and artifact rich stain in two excavation units (Stewart-Abernathy 1985:9–11). In the following season of 1983 the trash pit was fully excavated and additional units were dug in the surrounding area. This additional work resulted in several new features being identified (Stewart-Abernathy 1985).

Stewart-Abernathy (1985:9–11) summarized the initial findings of the 1982 and 1983 field seasons by indicating that 25,000 artifacts dating from the early 19th century (1820s–1850s) were found. As a result of these artifacts and the associated features, the kitchen is thought to have been constructed in the in the 1830s and demolished

Figure 9.2. 1982 excavations at the Block Family House, courtesy of Arkansas Archeological Survey.

in the by the middle of the 20th century. The trash pit is thought to have been a root cellar under the rear kitchen room and was likely abandoned by the mid 19th century. While the initial research questions included finding evidence of Judaic faith at the site, no artifacts were recovered from the pit feature or the surrounding midden that supported a Jewish household.

Keenly, Stewart-Abernathy used the assemblage from pit feature to look at Jewish identity in the household in absence of any artifactual markers of religious identity. Stewart-Abernathy contracted with Barbara Ruff of the University of Georgia to conduct a faunal analysis on the remains from the pit feature trash pit uncovered in 1982 and 1983. The purpose of this analysis was to determine the dietary patterns of the Block family by looking at a sealed dumping episode, gain insight into general dietary patterns on the southwestern frontier, and determine the Block family's adherence to the system of *kashrut*, or kosher dietary law that governs the consumption of certain animals (Ruff 1985; Stewart-Abernathy and Ruff 1989). The results of Ruff's analysis of the 2625 piece assemblage indicated that the Block diet consisted of cows, fowl, pigs and deer supplemented by fish and small game (Stewart-Abernathy and Ruff 1989:101–102; also see Ruff 1985). This information indicated that

Figure 9.3. Chimney feature from 1999 excavations at the Block Family House, courtesy of Arkansas Archeological Survey.

the Block family did not adhere to the *kashrut* system that forbids the consumption of pork and certain types of fish, such as catfish (Stewart-Abernathy and Ruff 1989:103–104).

In 1998 a series of auger tests, excavation units and backhoe trenches were dug in the backyard and adjacent, previously uninvestigated side yard, to locate features associated with the Block occupation. These excavations revealed a buried 1830s–1840s sheet midden in the side yard as well as a brick feature (see Figure 9.3) that resembled a chimney base or pier in the backyard (Guendling et al. 1999:33–54). Guendling believed that this feature, which was in line with the previously excavated kitchen from the 1982 and 1983 Training Programs, was in fact an end chimney for that structure. Unfortunately a lack of funding did not allow for the complete excavation of the feature at the time and as a result a debate arose as to exactly what the feature represented.

Site Reassessment

In 2010 a series of excavation units were placed surrounding the brick feature uncovered in 1998 with the express purpose of determining the features use (Applegate and Markus 2010; Markus 2011; Markus and Brandon 2010). A rich, ash-laden deposit was contained within the feature that included burned faunal remains. In conjunction with two iron ash pans at the base of the feature, these contents point to a chimney in the vicinity of the feature or that material surrounding a chimney was used to fill the feature. Additionally there is no evidence of burning or fire damage on the bricks of the feature. While the feature is not itself evidence of a remnant chimney it is an indication of a pier likely near a chimney of a structure separate from the kitchen (Markus 2011:42). To further substantiate the evidence that the chimney related feature is representative of a separate structure, the only other hard architectural feature found at the site was re-analyzed (Markus 2011:45). In 1983 a brick feature with a similar construction style was identified as a pier and likely represents an architectural element of the structure (Guendling et al. 2002).

Clearly, this additional structure is not the kitchen, but its exact function must be inferred. It is not difficult to imagine the multiple structures on an "urban farmstead" (cf. Stewart-Abernathy 1986) of this time, as the Blocks would have needed to be largely self-sufficient, given their location on the western edge of America. Stewart-Abernathy (1986:8) gives a listing of the types of outbuildings found on the urban farmstead landscape: "kitchen, wash house, privy, well house, spring house, wood or coal shed, equipment shed, repairing facility, servant quarters, buildings or rooms for poultry, swine, milk cows, and horses, carriage house or wagon shed, harness room, granary, potato house, hay barn, and general storage shed." Though some of these services can be housed in a multiple-use building (Hart 1975:115–36) the list given by Stewart-Abernathy is relatively comprehensive and means that the Abraham Block house lot was likely a crowded place. Given that the kitchen was been identified on the landscape that leaves as many as eighteen structures unaccounted for. Of the buildings listed, only servant quarters and perhaps the washhouse would have needed a chimney. Most of the structures on the urban farmstead landscape were industrial or agricultural in nature and would not have required heating or the removal of smoke.

Archival evidence helps support this inference. A second-hand memory map by an informant named Moss Rowe, drawn sometime in the 20th century in the historian's office of Washington gives a rough sketch map of the arrangement of major structures on the Abraham Block

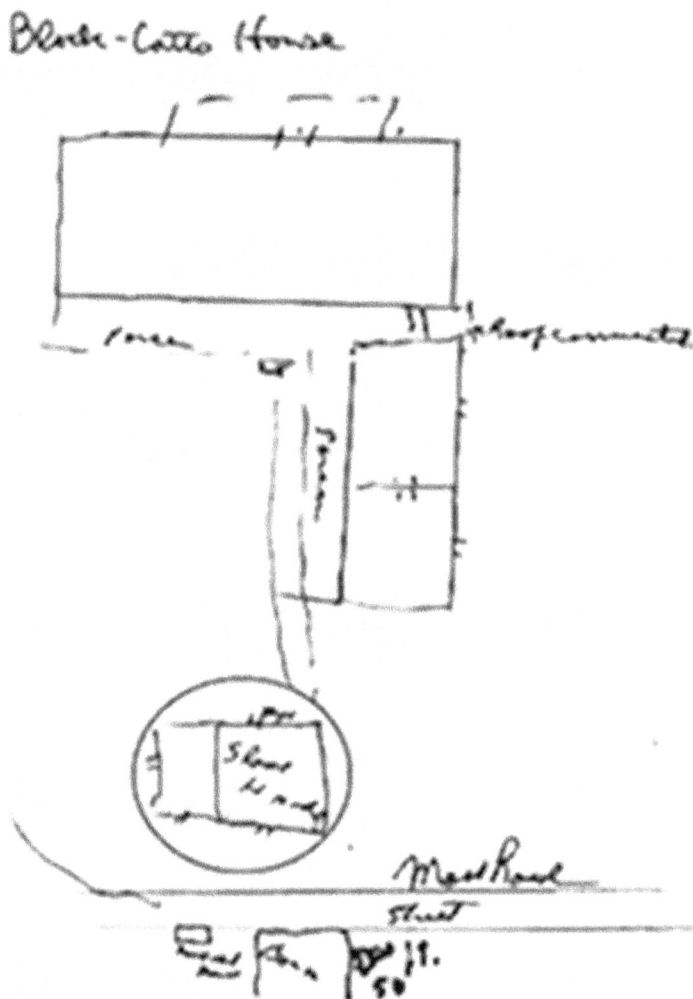

Figure 9.4. Second-hand memory map from informant Moss Rowe with slave quarters marked, courtesy of Historic Washington State Park.

house lot. Rowe lists two structures in the yard behind the main house: a kitchen and a "slave quarters." While a second-hand memory map should not be the entire basis for the interpretation of the structure as a slave quarters, Rowe does get many of the details about the building arrangement on the landscape correct. Rowe places the kitchen on the appropriate side of the main house and notes its detachment from the house by a covered walkway. He also correctly identifies the original back porch (which was not standing) and the location of the additional structure as being exactly on the expected footprint of the building supported by archaeological evidence (see Figure 9.4).

The artifactual evidence also supports the idea that the additional structure was a domestic space. An initial analysis of the faunal remains of the chimney feature shows evidence of butchery and cooking (Markus et al. 2012) and the nature of the rest of the artifact assemblage do not suggest an industrial use (Markus 2011:48). Based on the presence of several artifactual means of dating the site, it is possible to give a rough estimation of the construction of the quarters. Transfer printed ceramics offer the first set of dates for the quarters. Of the 452 transfer printed sherds 42% were of colors other than blue and black (37 brown, 31 green, 24 red and 100 purple) (Markus 2011:48), which were introduced between 1829 and the 1840s (Miller 1991:9). Additionally, two maker's marks were found on undecorated whiteware sherds from the site. Both marks were impressed Davenport anchors dating to 1848 and 1853 (Kowalsky and Kowalsky 1999:167). A single silver seated liberty half dime dating to 1838 was found at the base of the period midden suggesting that it was lost near to the date of the quarters construction (Markus 2011:49). A similar silver dime was found in pit feature during the 1982/1983 excavations that dated to 1831 (Stewart-Abernathy 1988; Guendling et al. 2002).

The clothing portion of the assemblage also supports a similar date range. The presence of Prosser porcelain buttons in high quantity (30% of the total button assemblage) means that the structure likely dates to after 1840 (Albert and Adams 1970:4–5; Sprague 2002:111–118). The presence of two part pant buttons (17%) adds to this as such buttons did not gain traction until after their patent in 1845, although they were available earlier as the patent is described as a refinement of an earlier design (Davidson 2006:175–176).

Using all of these dates it appears that the construction of the slave quarters dates to between 1840 and 1850. This date corresponds well with the increase in the number of slaves in the Block household. As mentioned previously, there were a total of two slaves documented to have been in the Block household during the 1830s. These individuals would have been housed in one of the two rooms in the kitchen without any major space constraints. When the number increases to as many as thirteen in the 1850 slave census there would have had to have been an additional structure to house those individuals. Even in less than ideal conditions, a single room in a two-pen structure could not sufficiently house the six adults and seven children listed on the slave schedule (Kwas 2009a).

Discussion

Artifactual Evidence of Jewry

So how does the interpretation of the Block Household change in light of the new archaeological evidence? The current archaeological excavations do little to reinforce the Block's identity as Jews. Much like both of the previous sets of excavations there were no individual artifacts that point to a Jewish way of life. Practically, this makes sense; any item of religious significance such as a Seder plate, mezuzah, menorah, or Kiddush cup would have likely held significance for the family. In the event that these items were damaged they would have made every effort at repair or curated the item in its damaged state as an heirloom. Even more secular goods such as adornment or dishes with Hebrew script or Judaic iconography would probably never make its way into the archaeological record.

Despite Abraham's public record as a Jew there is no indication of Fanny's faith, this is due in part to women's roles in the 19th century being relegated to the private sphere. It is possible given her orphaned upbringing that she never received formal religious training (Kwas 2009a). If this were the case it would explain the children's departure from the faith. In the 19th century women were solely responsible for the religious training of children due in large part to their domestic roles. Paula Hyman, in her study on gender and religious assimilation in modern Jewish history, states:

In my study of the nineteenth century Jewish press of England, France, German and the United States and of public pronouncements, I have found no references specifically to fathers' responsibilities for the education of their children or for the inoculation of a Jewish identity nor blame of fathers for the defection of their children from the Jewish community. In the gendered project of assimilation the female sex was at the center (Hyman 1997:47).

From this it can be assumed that Fanny was responsible for the training and rearing of children whereas Abraham's role would have been to ensure the childrens', specifically, boys' training in the family business. Given that the majority of his sons enter into the business of mercantilism these gender roles seem to fit. To further the idea that, if anything, the Block household was run in Fanny's Sephardic tradition is the fact that both she and Abraham are buried in the Sephardic Cemetery at Dispersed of Judah Synagogue, of which the Blocks were not members.

There is a single artifact class that may point tangentially to a religious Jewish identity: purple transfer printed wares. Purple transfer prints are found in high numbers in all three of the excavations at the Abraham Block House and comprise 12.7% of the total decorated ceramic assemblage from the most recent excavation. Of transfer prints alone purple makes up 22.1%, which seems to be quite high (Markus 2011:52; Markus 2012). Typically three colors, blue, red and purple, are referenced in the Torah and the Talmud. Blue is generally seen as representative of God or a higher power and red as life or human beings. Purple therefore is the intersection between the two (Dennis 2007:55). As a result of this, rabbinical scholars have interpreted purple as a means of interacting with God. The scripture itself makes reference to purple being used as a vessel to absolve people of unintentional sin (Lev. xvi. 10). If the Blocks were using purple for this purpose then the sin of consuming non-kosher foods such as pork and catfish would have been absolved (Markus 2012).

Artifactual Evidence of Slavery in the Block Household

While archaeology has not been able to give support to the idea that the Blocks held a religiously Jewish home there is clear evidence, both archival and archaeological that they enslaved African Americans. The location of the slave quarters in the backyard of the house lot and its location in relation to the porch of the main house and porch of the kitchen create an interesting social dynamic. A shared courtyard between the three structures meant that neither slave nor master could separate themselves from the other portion of the household. The commonality between the assemblages of the quarters and kitchen excavation seems to support this concept. The quarters have roughly the same ceramic types as the kitchen (Markus 2011:54) and both include a faunal assemblage that has many of the same animals with similar frequency (Markus et al. 2012; Winburn and Markus 2012).

The assemblage includes a number of personal effects that indicate children lived in the household, specifically in the slave quarters items such as clay marbles, porcelain doll parts, and ceramic toy tea set fragments (Markus 2011:54–55). This evidence fits with the increase in the number of slaves noted on the 1850 census, and there would also have still been some Block children in the house at the time. Additionally, there is some evidence to suggest that members of the Block household (presumably children) were learning to read and write. The presence of slate pencils and two sherds from a brown transfer printed alphabet plate indicate that someone in the Block household was receiving an education in reading and writing.

The clothing in the assemblage points to a low status of those enslaved. Of the 55 buttons in the collection only two were brass coat buttons. Furthermore, despite the presence of pants buttons there are no cuff or collar studs that would indicate the use of detachable cuff and collars (Markus 2011:56). This suggests that the slaves in the Block household were wearing work shirts rather than a higher cost, more formal wear.

In such a confined area it is difficult to differentiate material related to the Block family from those that they enslaved. This speaks to the active role that domestic slaves played on the frontier (see Stewart-Abernathy 2004). Not separated, as they would be on a plantation, domestic slaves were involved in all aspects of daily life of those that they were enslaved by.

Conclusion

This chapter has attempted to answer additional questions regarding the Block family "urban farmstead" (cf. Stewart-Abernathy 1986). Through archaeological evidence from excavations, building upon previous research, the identity and use of an additional structure on the Block property was determined to be a dwelling for enslaved persons within the household. As with previous excavations, no direct markers of religious identity were found in the assemblage but information regarding the daily lives of the Blocks and those they enslaved has come to light.

The archaeological excavations at the Block Family House conducted over the past thirty years have formed a solid base for our understanding of Jewish life on the Cotton Frontier in the antebellum period. In providing this base the entirety of the Block backyard has been tested creating a vast assemblage that has been used to examine different aspects of the Blocks' lives: foodways (i.e. Stewart-Abernathy and Ruff 1989), mercantilism (i.e. Stewart-Abernathy 1988), and slave ownership (i.e. Markus 2011; this text), all the while framing the findings around the Blocks' identity as Jews.

What has become apparent through the work conducted at the Block House is there are very few markers of religious identity, if any. This trend holds true for the other Jewish Diaspora household sites excavated in the United States. Outside of those that can be identified during the course of analysis, research questions should not include the search for religion, as it will likely not yield results. Rather investigation going forward should be undertaken to study an ethnic population that has, thus far, been underrepresented in archaeological research. The daily lives of subtly marginalized population can help to provide a more holistic understanding of the conditions in the 19th century (Spencer-Wood 1994). This household archaeology and study of intimate conditions can also provide insight into the gender roles of a population that has had a large impact on American life. The study of Jewish life archaeologically going forward should address the adaptations of an immigrant population to conditions in the diaspora. As the identification of religious material in domestic settings has proved challenging, a shift in focus to the secular and folk traditions of Jews should be undertaken.

African Diaspora archaeology can also benefit from the development of a Jewish Diaspora archaeology. The interaction between a marginalized population that is subjugating an even further marginalized group serves as an interesting case study. Historically, Diaspora studies rise out of the Jewish Diaspora and yet for its part historical archaeology has largely ignored Jews as a group. Further studies such as those undertaken at the Abraham Block House can potentially contribute to the development of a field of Jewish Diaspora Archaeology.

REFERENCES

Acly, Elizabeth
2011   *New England Hebrew Farmers of the Emmanuel Society Archeological Site-Structural Investigation Report.* Prepared for the NEHFES by Cirrus Structural Engineering, LLC, Columbia, CT.
Albert, Lillian Smith and Jane Ford Adams
1970   *Essential Data Concerning China Buttons.* Bound with Guidelines for Collecting China Buttons by Ruth Lamm, Beatrice Lorah, and Helen W. Schuler. The National Button Society of America, Boyertown, PA.
Allsworth-Jones, Philip, D. Gray, and S. Walter
1998   Excavations at the Neveh Shalom Synagogue Site in Spanish Town, January 1998. *Jamaican Historical Society Bulletin* 11(1):17–18.
2000   Neveh Shalom, An Ancient Jewish Synagogue in Spanish Town Jamaica. *Archaeology Jamaica* 12(NS):4–7.

2003   The Neveh Shalom Synagogue Site in Spanish Town Jamaica. In *Toward an Archaeology of Buildings* edited by G. Malm, pp. 77–88. BAR International Series 1186, Oxford: Archaeopress.

Anonymous

1857a   [Death Notice of Abraham Block]. *Arkansas Gazette*, April 4, 1857.

1857b   Obituary [of Abraham Block]. *The Occident* 15(1). Reprinted in *The American Jewish Archives*, October 1956.

1887   Obituary [of Hester Block]. *Arkansas Gazette*, September 13, 1887.

Applegate, Ashley and David M. Markus

2011   Preliminary Results of Historic Washington State Park Field School-Summer 2010. *Arkansas Archeological Society Field Notes* 360(May/June):6–8

Bhabha, Homi K.

2007   Of Mimicry and Man. In *The Performance Studies Reader*, second edition edited by Henry Bial. pp. 337–44. New York: Routledge.

Barka, Norman F.

1985   *Archaeology of St. Eustatius, Netherlands Antillies: An Interim Report on the 1981–1984 Seasons*. St. Eustatius Archaeological Research Series No. 1. Williamsburg, V.A.: Department of Anthropology, College of William and Mary. (see pp. 47–51)

1987   *Archaeological Investigation of the Princess Estate, St. Eustatius, Netherlands Antilles: an Interim Report on the Supposed Jewish Mikve*. St. Eustatius Archaeological Research Series No. 3. Williamsburg, V.A.: Department of Anthropology, College of William and Mary.

1988   *Archaeology of the Jewish Synagogue Honen Dalim, St. Eustatius, N.A.: An Interim Report*. St. Eustatius Archaeological Research Series No. 4. Williamsburg, V.A.: Department of Anthropology, College of William and Mary.

Bergoffen, Celia

1997   *The Proprietary Baths and Possible Mikvah at 5 Allen Street, Borough of Manhattan, New York, Phase IA Archaeological Assessment Report*. Prepared for the Eldridge Street Project, Inc. On file at the New York City Landmarks Preservation Commission.

Baugher, Sherene, Judith Baragli and Louise DeCesare

1985   *The Archaeological Investigation of the Voorlezer House Site Staten Island, New York*. New York: New York Landscape Preservation Council.

CITY/SCAPE

2003   *Stage 2 Archaeological Investigation: Congregation Moshcisker Chevrah Gur Arye Mikvah, 308 East Third Street (Block 372, Lot 27), Borough of Manhattan, New York County, New York*. Prepared for UJA Federation of New York, New York, NY by CITY/SCAPE, Brooklyn, NY.

Clouette, Bruce and Ross Harper

2007   *State Archaeological Preserve Documentation Form for the New England Hebrew Farmers of the Emanuel Society Synagogue and Creamery Archaeological Site*. Storrs, CT: PAST, Inc. Revised 2008.

Davidson, James M.

2006   Material Culture, Chronology, and Socioeconomics. In *Two Historic Cemeteries in Crawford County, Arkansas*, edited by Robert C. Mainfort and James M. Davidson, Arkansas Archeological Survey research series; no. 62. Arkansas Archeological Survey, Fayetteville, pp. 97–218.

Dennis, Geoff W.
2007   The Encyclopedia of Jewish Myth, Magic and Mysticism. Woodbury, MN:
        Llewellyn Publications.

Diner, Hasia R.
1992   A Time for Gathering: The Second Migration, 1820–1880. Baltimore:
        Johns Hopkins University Press
2005   Entering the Mainstream of Modern Jewish History: Peddlers and the
        American Jewish South. Southern Jewish History 8(2005):1–30

Ecker, Frederick H., II and Amanda L. Jackson
2000   Lloyd Street Synagogue, Historic evaluation report of the basement area
        including the mikvehs and the matzoh oven. Fredericksburg, VA: Tidewater
        Preservation, Inc.

Ezekiel, Herbert T., and Gaston Liechtenstein
1917   The History of the Jews of Richmond from 1769 to 1910. Richmond:
        Herbert T. Ezekiel, printer and publisher.

Gilmore, R. Grant
2006   Recovering the Jewish Heritage on St. Eustatius, Netherlands Antilles.
        Archaeobrief: Vakblad voor de Nederlandse archaeologie 9(1):7–10.

Gradwohl, David Mayer
1993a   Intra-Group Diversity in Midwest American Jewish Cemeteries: An
        Ethnoarchaeological Perspective. In Archaeology of Eastern North
        America Papers in Honor of Stephen Williams edited by James B. Stoltman,
        Archaeological Report No. 25, Mississippi Department of Archives and
        History, Jackson, MS.
1993b   The Jewish Cemeteries of Louisville, Kentucky: Mirrors of Historical
        Processes and Theological Diversity through 150 Years. Markers X:117–150.

Gradwohl, David Mayer, and Hanna Rosenberg Gradwohl
1988   That is the Pillar of Rachel's Grave Unto This Day: An Ethno-archaeological
        Comparison of Two Jewish Cemeteries in Lincoln, Nebraska. In Persistence
        and Flexibility: Anthropological Perspective on the American Jewish
        Experience, edited by Walter P. Zenner, 223–259. State University of New
        York Press, Albany, NY.

Guendling, Randall L., Mary L. Kwas, and Jamie C. Brandon
1999   Archeological Investigations at Old Washington Historic State Park,
        Arkansas: The 1836 Courthouse Block (3HE236–) and the Block-Catts
        House Block (3HE236–19). Submitted to Arkansas Department of Parks and
        Tourism, Little Rock.

Guendling, Randall L., Kathleen. H. Cande, Maria Tavaszi, Leslie C. Stewart-
        Abernathy, and Barbara Ruff
2002   The Archeological Investigations of the Block Detached Kitchen: The 1982
        and 1983 Arkansas Archeological Society Digs, Old Washington Historic State
        Park. ANCRC Grant 02–02, Arkansas Archeological Survey. Submitted to the
        Arkansas Natural and Cultural Resources Council, Little Rock, Arkansas.

Guthrie, Ann and Charles Witsell, Jr.
1985   Masterplan for Old Washington Historic State Park. Manuscript prepared
        by Witsell, Evans, & Rasco P.A., Historic Planners and Arkansas State Parks.
        Arkansas Archeological Survey, Fayetteville, Arkansas.

Harper, Ross
2008   *Phase I Archaeological Reconnaissance Survey of the New England Farmers of the Emanuel Society Synagogue Creamery Site, Route 85 Safety Improvements, Montville, CT.* Prepared for Purcell Associates, Inc. Archaeological and Historical Services, Inc., Storrs, CT.

Hart, John Fraser
1975   *The Look of the Land.* Prentice-Hall Inc., Eaglewood Cliffs.

Heldman, D. P.
1986   Michigan's First Jewish Settlers: A View from the Solomon-Levy Trading House at Fort Michilimackinac, 1765–1781. *Journal of New World Archaeology* 6(4):21–34.

Historical Perspectives, Inc.
2011   *Memo on Phase IB Archaeological Investigations, New England Hebrew Farmers of the Emanuel Society, Connecticut State Archaeological Preserve 24: Synagogue and Mikvah.* Chesterfield, Montville, Connecticut. Prepared for the NEHFES.

2012   *National Register of Historic Places Registration Form for the New England Hebrew Farmers of the Emanuel Society Synagogue and Creamery Site.* Report prepared for U.S Department of the Interior.

Horn, Julie Abell, Faline Schneiderman-Fox, Cece Saunders
2012   King David in a Connecticut Yankee's Court: Archaeology and History of an Orthodox Jewish Synagogue, Mikvah, and Creamery Site in Rural Connecticut. Paper presented at the Society for Historical Archaeology 2012 Conference on Historical and Underwater Archaeology, Baltimore, MD.

Hyman, Paula E.
1997   *Gender and Assimilation in Modern Jewish History: The Roles and Representation of Women.* Seattle: University of Washington Press.

Isaacs, Isaiah
1971   Will of Isaiah Isaacs of Charlottesville, Virginia, Aug. 30, 1803, and Codicil Jan. 8, 1806. In *A Documentary History of the Jews in the United States 1654–1875,* edited by Morris U. Schappes, 3rd ed., pp. 100–101. Schocken Books, New York.

Korn, Bertram Wallace
1969   *The Early Jews of New Orleans* (American Jewish Communal Histories No. 5). Waltham, Ma: American Jewish Historical Society

Kowalsky, Arnold A. and Dorothy E. Kowalsky
1999   *Encyclopedia of Marks on American, English, and European Earthenware, Ironstone, and Stoneware 1780–1980: Marker's Marks, and Patterns in Blue and White, Historic Blue, Flow Blue, Mulberry, Romantic Transferware, Tea Leaf, and White Ironstone.* Surry, England: Schiffer Publishing Ltd.

Kwas, Mary L.
2009a   "Two Generations of the Abraham and Fanny Block Family: Internal Migration, Economics, Family and the Jewish Frontier" *Southern Jewish History* 12:39–114.

2009b   *Digging for History at Old Washington.* Fayetteville: University of Arkansas Press.

LeMaster, Carolyn Gray
1994   A Corner of the Tapestry: A History of the Jewish Experience in Arkansas,
          1820s–1990s. University of Arkansas Press, Fayetteville, AR
Markus, David M.
2011   "Of the House of Israel in America": Judaism, Slavery and Assimilation on
          the Arkansas Frontier. Master's thesis, University of Arkansas; Fayetteville,
          Arkansas.
2012   Where God and Man Meet: The Color Purple in a 19th Century Jewish
          Household. Paper presented in "Beneath the Surface, Beyond the Stereotype"
          General Session at the Society for Historical Archaeology 2012 Conference
          on Historical and Underwater Archaeology, Baltimore, Maryland.
Markus, David M. and Jamie C. Brandon
2010   Recent Excavations at the Abraham Block House, Historic Washington
          State Park. Arkansas Archeological Society Field Notes 357(November/
          December):7–10.
Markus, David M., Allysha P. Winburn, and Lane Wallett
2012   Zooarchaeological Analysis from the Block House (3HE236-19) Slave
          Quarters, Washington, Arkansas. Arkansas Archeological Society Field Notes
          369(November/December):6–9.
McDowell, Linda
2000   Black Slaves and Early Freedmen of Hempstead County, Arkansas,
          1819–1850. Jubilee, Inc., Little Rock, AR.
Miller, Derek
2010   The Bridgetown Synagogue Pathway Archaeological Project: A Preliminary
          Report. The Journal of the Barbados Museum and Historical Society
          56:87–104.
2011   Scattered Synagogues: An Archaeological Exploration of Diasporic
          Community Creation. Post-Medieval Archeology 45(2):357–362.
2012a   The Jewish Diaspora on Barbados: A Preliminary Analysis. Presented at the
          Society for American Archaeology annual conference, Memphis, TN.
2012b   Homelands and Diasporas: the Relationships of the Jews in Colonial
          Barbados with their Homeland(s). Presented at the society for Historical
          Archaeology 2012 Conference on Historical and Underwater Archaeology,
          Baltimore, MD
Milne, Claudia, and Pam J. Crabtree
1998   Revealing Meals: Ethnicity, Economic Status, and Diet at Five Points. In
          Tales of Five Points, Working Class Life in Nineteenth-Century New York,
          Volume II, Rebecca Yamin, editor. John Milner Associates, West Chester, PA.
2001   Prostitutes, a Rabbi, and a Carpenter–Dinner at the Five Points in the 1830s.
          Historical Archaeology 35(3):31–48.
Praetzellis Adrian
1991   The Archaeology of a Victorian City: Sacramento, California. Doctoral
          dissertation, University of California at Berkeley, Berkeley, CA.
2004   Becoming Jewish Americans. In Putting the "There" There: Historical
          Archaeologies of West Oakland, edited by Adrian Praetzellis and Mary
          Praetzellis. Anthropological Studies Center, Sonoma State University, Rohnert
          Park, CA, pp. 68–71.

2009   Ethnicity and Socioeconomic Status. In *South of Market: Historical Archaeology of 3 San Francisco Neighborhoods. The San Francisco-Oakland Bay Bridge West Approach Project*, edited by Mary Praetzellis and Adrian Praetzellis. Two Volumes. Anthropological Studies Center, Sonoma State University, Rohnert Park California. Prepared for California Department of Transportation, District 4, Oakland, pp. 303–322.

Read, Esther D.

2012   The Lloyd Street Synagogue Mikveh: Ritual and Community in Nineteenth-Century Baltimore. Paper presented at the Society for Historical Archaeology 2012 Conference on Historical and Underwater Archaeology, Baltimore, MD.

Ross, Don

1997   The Benjamin House (3CR585). *The Arkansas Archeologist* 36:1–34.

Ruff, Barbara L.

1985   *Analysis of the Vertebrate Fauna from Feature 14 (3HE236–19), Washington, Arkansas.* Report submitted to the Arkansas Archeological Survey, Fayetteville, Arkansas.

Scott, Elizabeth. M.

1991   *"Such Diet as Befitted his Station as Clerk": The Archaeology of Subsistence and Cultural Diversity at Fort Michilimackinac, 1761–1781.* Unpublished PhD dissertation, Department of Anthropology, University of Minnesota.

1992   At Home They "Commonly Ate No Pork": Observance of Jewish Dietary Restrictions at the Solomon-Levy Trading House at Fort Michilimackinac, 1761–1781, paper presented at the 15th Annual Conference of the Society for Ethnobiology, Washington, DC.

2008   Who Ate What? Archaeological Food Remains and Cultural Diversity. In *Case Studies in Environmental Archaeology* edited by Elizabeth J. Reitz, Sylvia J. Scudder, C. Margaret Scarry, pp. 357–374. New York: Springer.

Spencer-Wood, Suzanne M.

1994   Diversity and Nineteenth-Century Domestic Reform: Relationship Among Classes and Ethnic Groups. In *Those of Little Note: Gender, Race and Class in Historical Archaeology*, edited by Elizabeth Scott, pp. 175–208. Tucson: University of Arizona Press.

1999   The Formation of Ethnic-American Identities: Jewish Communities in Boston. In *Historical Archaeology: Back from the Edge*, edited by Pedro Paulo A. Funari, Martin Hall and Sian Jones, pp. 284–307. London: Routledge.

2010   Gendered Power Dynamics Between Religious Sects, Ethnic Groups and Classes in Jewish Communities on Boston's Landscape, 1840–1936. In S.B. Baugher and S. Spencer-Wood (Eds.), *The Archaeology and Preservation of Gendered Landscapes* (pp. 189–230), New York: Springer.

Sprague, Roderick

2002   China or Prosser Button Identification and Dating. *Historical Archaeology* 36(2):111–127.

Stewart-Abernathy, Leslie C.

1982a   *Research Plan for Block-Catts Property for the 1982 Arkansas Archeological Society Training Program.* Arkansas Archeological Survey, Fayetteville, Arkansas.

1982b   1982 Society Historical Excavations: Block-Catts Kitchen Ell (3HE236–19). *Arkansas Archeological Society Field Notes* 185:7–7.

1984   *Block House Piers: a Contribution to the Archeological Underpinning of Historic Preservation in Washington, Arkansas.* Arkansas Archeological Survey, Fayetteville, Arkansas. Submitted to Department of State Parks, Little Rock, Arkansas.

1985   The Block House Cellar. *Arkansas Archeological Society Field Notes* 203:9–11.

1986   Urban Farmsteads: Household Responsibilities in the City. *Historical Archaeology* 20(2):5–15.

1988   *Queensware in a Southern Store: Perspectives on the Antebellum Ceramics Trade from a Merchant Family's Trash in Washington, Arkansas.* A six-panel poster session with paper presented at annual meeting of the Society for Historical Archaeology, Reno, NV.

Stewart-Abernathy, Leslie C. and Barbara Ruff

1989   A Good Man in Israel: Zooarchaeology and Assimilation in Antebellum Washington, Arkansas. *Historical Archaeology* 23(2):96–112.

2004   Separate Kitchens and Intimate Archaeology: Constructing Urban Slavery on the Antebellum Cotton Frontier in Washington, Arkansas. In *Household Chores, Household Choices: Theorizing the Domestic Sphere in Historical Archaeology*, edited by Kerri S. Barile and Jamie C. Brandon, University of Alabama Press, Tuscaloosa.

Terrell, Michelle M.

2000   *The Historical Archaeology of the 17th and 18th Century Jewish Community of Nevis, British West Indies.* Doctoral dissertation, Boston University, Boston, MA.

2005   *The Jewish Community of Early Colonial Nevis: A Historical Archaeological Study.* University Press of Florida, Gainesville, FL.

Wesler, Kit W.

2002   Formula Dating in Historical Archaeology: Examples from Neveh Shalom, Jamaica. Paper presented to the Archaeological Society of Jamaica Symposium on Current Research in Jamaican Archaeology, Mona, Jamaica.

2012   Archaeology of Judaism. In *An Archaeology of Religion*, by K. Wesler, pp.182–210. Lanham, MD: University Press of America

Winburn, Allysha P. and David M. Markus

2012   Zooarchaeological Analysis from the Block House Slave Quarters in Washington, Arkansas. Paper presented at the 2012 Southeastern Archaeological Conference, Baton Rouge, Louisiana.

Yentsch, Anne E.

2009   Tracing Immigrant Women and their Household Possessions in 19th-Century San Francisco. In *South of Market: Historical Archaeology of 3 San Francisco Neighborhoods. The San Francisco-Oakland Bay Bridge West Approach Project*, edited by Mary Praetzellis and Adrian Praetzellis. Two Volumes. Anthropological Studies Center, Sonoma State University, Rohnert Park California. Prepared for California Department of Transportation, District 4, Oakland, pp. 137–187.

CONTRIBUTORS

Jamie Brandon is the Arkansas Archeological Survey's Research Station Archaeologist for Northwest Arkansas and a Research Associate Professor at the University of Arkansas at Fayetteville. In this dual position, Brandon works with graduate students and teaches anthropology courses for University of Arkansas's Anthropology Department. Additionally, he is responsible for public outreach and research using the archaeological resources in his station territory, which includes 12 counties in Northwest Arkansas and the Arkansas Ozarks. Brandon serves as the Vice-Chairman of the Arkansas Civil War Sesquicentennial Commission and on the Arkansas State Review Board for Historic Preservation. He has served on the boards of the Arkansas Historical Association and the Historic Preservation Alliance of Arkansas. Brandon is an associate editor for *Historical Archaeology* and formerly served as the associate editor of historical archaeology for *The SAA Archaeological Record*.

Mary Z. Brennan is an archaeologist with the Ozark-St. Francis National Forests in northwest Arkansas. She holds a doctorate in anthropology from the University of Arkansas. Her research interests include the archaeology of the Ozarks and Upland South, constructions of kinship, community, identity and memory, and public interpretation of place and memory.

C. Andrew Buchner has 25 years experience as a cultural resource management archaeologist and is an owner-partner of Panamerican Consultants, Inc., currently managing the firm's Memphis office. He has a master's degree in anthropology from the University of Memphis and a bachelor's degree in anthropology and sociology from Westminster College. A native Arkansan, he is certified by the Register of Professional Archaeologists and is a member of various professional organizations including the Society for American Archaeology, the Southeastern Archaeological Conference, the Caddo Conference, the Society for Historical Archaeology, and the Society for Industrial Archaeology. Additionally, he is a Life Member of the Arkansas Archeological Society. He has participated in dozens of historical archaeology projects in rural and urban contexts within Arkansas and the Mid-South. Buchner has written over 600 technical reports and is published in various peer reviewed journals, as well as the Arkansas Archeological Survey's *Research Series*.

Carl G. Drexler is the Archeological Survey's Station Archeologist for southwest Arkansas and a Research Assistant Professor with the University of Arkansas, specializing in conflict archaeology, historical archaeology, and spatial analysis within archaeology. He has worked for the United States Army, National Park Service, and Colonial Williamsburg Foundation during his career, conducting research in the Southeast, Southwest, Mid-Atlantic, Midwest, and Caribbean. He earned a bachelor's degree at Grinnell College, his master's degree at the University of Nebraska, and his doctorate at the College of William and Mary in Virginia.

Jerry Hilliard has been active in archaeology for over 40 years, the last 35 working for the Arkansas Archeological Survey. He received his master's degree from the University of Arkansas in 1979. Since 1994, he has been the UAF station assistant, participating in a variety of research involving both prehistoric and historic archaeological projects. His areas of interest include rock art, Civil War archaeology, and bluff shelter and cave research.

David M. Markus is a doctoral candidate in the Department of Anthropology at the University of Florida, where he also manages the University of Florida Historical Archaeology Laboratory. His research interests include historical archaeology, Jewish and African Diasporas, and folklore studies.

Duncan P. McKinnon is an anthropology faculty member at the University of Central Arkansas and a Research Associate at the Center for American Archeology. He received his bachelor's degree in anthropology from Texas State University and his master's degree and doctorate in anthropology from the University of Arkansas. His research is focused on settlement landscapes and distributional studies with interests in environmental and humanistic geography, archaeogeophysics, prehistoric architecture, Caddo ceramics, Native American ritual and religion, and southeastern iconography and cosmology. His work has appeared in *American Antiquity, Southeastern Archaeology, Arkansas Archeologist, Caddo Archaeology Journal,* and *The Archaeology of the Caddo.* He is the geophysical specialist on the PBS television show *Time Team America.*

Eric Proebsting is the Senior Research Archaeologist at Thomas Jefferson's Poplar Forest in Forest, Virginia. He holds a master's degree in historical archaeology from the University of Massachusetts Boston and a doctorate in environmental dynamics from the University of Arkansas, Fayetteville. His areas of interest include landscape archaeology, historical ecology, plantation studies, and agricultural communities.

Leslie C. "Skip" Stewart-Abernathy has been a Station Archaeologist with the Arkansas Archeological Survey since 1977. For a much of this time, he was the de facto historical archaeologist for the state. Consequently, he has conducted projects or consulted in all 75 counties in the state. He has worked on 18th-, 19th-, and 20th-century sites in towns, cities, and in the countryside. He has also been pretty much the state's riverine archaeologist, leading documentation of boat wrecks exposed at low water on the Arkansas side of the Mississippi at Memphis and in the White River. He earned his bachelor's degree in history at Arkansas State University and his master's and doctoral degrees in anthropology and historical archaeology from Brown University.

Alicia Valentino received her doctorate from the University of Arkansas in 2007, and her master's in industrial archaeology from Michigan Technological University in 2003. She has worked in cultural resource management in the Pacific Northwest for the past eight years, and her work has appeared in *IA: The Journal of the Society for Industrial Archeology.* She currently works for Environmental Science Associates in Seattle.

INDEX

Adams, Samuel Hopkins, 124
Allen Township, 25
Annales School, 2
Antebellum Period, 132, 153n4, 192, 194
archaeological investigations, 28–29
archaeological sites, 30–33; by kin group
  26
Arkadelphia, 170, 194
Arkansas: centrality of in American
  history, xi; public perception of, x,
  xxxi–xxxii
Arkansas Archeological Society, xi, xviii,
  xxi–xxiii, xxviii, 202
Arkansas Archeological Survey, x, xiii,
  xviii, xxi–xxiii, 202; Sponsored
  Research Program, xxvii, xxx; State
  Plan, xxxi
Arkansas Gazette, 201
Arkansas Highway and Transportation
  Department, 57–59
Arkansas Post, xiii, xv, xvi–xvii, xviii, xix,
  xxv, xxxiv, 5, 142, 164, 166; Battle
  of, xvii–xviii. *See also* Bright's Tavern, Fort Carlos III, Fort Esteban,
  Montgomery's Tavern, Osotouy
Arkansas potteries: Bird Kiln (3DA12),
  60, 78; Camark, 75; Dixie Stoneware, 62; Eagle, 59, 62, 69, 75,
  81; Eagle/Niloak (3SA307), 75;
  Henderson/Benton Jug Factory, 66,
  71, 79; Herrick-Atchison (3SA339),
  64; Howe (3SA340), 57–83, 58,
  68, 69; Hyten Bros., 62; Interstate,
  75; McConnell-Osborn or Cumbie

(3SB596), 59, 75, 78; Nathaniel
  Culberson (3DA21), 60; Niloak,
  59–60, 63, 75, 79, 83; Original
  Hyten Kiln/Eagle (3SA341), 59, 68,
  75, 78; Ouachita, 75; Peebles Place
  Kiln (3SH15), 77; Welch's Kiln
  #2 (3DA8), 60, 78; Welch Pottery
  Works (3DA9), 60, 78; Wilbur, J.D.
  Pottery (3WA208), 77; Wilbur, Alfred,
  62; Winburn Tile Company, 63
Arkansas River, 112, 115
Arkansas State Parks, xiii, xxxvi
Arkansas Stoneware Manufacturer's
  Marks, 80–82
Arkansas Territory, 131–32, 135
artillery/ammunition, 177
Ashley Mansion (Little Rock), xxxii;
  cistern, 10; home of Chester and
  Mary Ashley, 9–10; site, 10–13;
  slave quarter, 11–13

Bar Mitzvah, 200
Benjamin House, 194
Bent, George, 182–83
Benton clay pits, 61–62, 64, 75–76
Benton Stoneware Association, 62
Benton Stoneware: archaeological cor-
  relates, 77–78; conclusions, 82–83;
  consumer behavior, 79–80; historic
  sequence, 59–63; pottery layout and
  patterns, 78–79; site types, 75–77
Big Lick Community, 25
Bird-in-Hand Tavern, 196
Bizzell, Oliver, xvi

Blanton Estate, xxv
Blaylock, Sandra, xxviii
Block, Abraham, 191, 192, 195, 196, 197,
    198, 200, 201, 202, 205, 208, 211
Block, Augustus, 196, 197, 201
Block family businesses, 197; Block and
    Son, 197; Block and Sons, 197;
    Block Brothers Co., 197; Block, Jett
    and Co., 197
Block, David, 196, 197, 202
Block, Frances (Fanny), 195, 196, 198,
    200, 202, 208
Block, Henry, 196
Block, Hester, 196, 202
Block, Isaac, 196, 202
Block, Juliet, 202
Block, Laura, 202
Block, Rosina, 196
Block, Simon, 196, 197, 202
Block, Virginius, 197
Block House (Washington, AR); home
    of Abraham and Fanny Block, 3, 7;
    kitchen, 7; locus of significant
    deposit in a root cellar, 3
Bohemia, 195, 199; Schwihau, 195
Bois D'Arc Creek, 193
Bonath, Shawn, xxvi, xxviii
Boston Mountains, 133
Bowers, Robin, xxxvi
Bowie, James (Jim), 193
Brandon, Jamie, xxvi, xxxvi, xxxvii
Bright's Tavern, xxv
Brust, Deacon Ray, 111
Buena Vista, Battle of, 114
Byrne, Bishop Andrew, 114–15, 126

Cadron Settlement site (Faulkner County,
    AR), xxxvi, 6
Cairo & Fulton Railroad, 61
Camp Babcock, 169
Camp Belknap, 111, 114, 115, 126
Camp Benjamin, xxxvii, 169
Camp Monticello, 169
Cande, Kathleen, xxxvii
Cane Hill (Washington County): archeo-
    logical work, 5; stoneware potters,
    9; canning jars, 3; college, 49

Carter, Claude, 37
Catholic Diocese of Little Rock, 114
Cedar Grove site, xxviii
cemeteries, 29
Chenault, Fletcher, xvii
Cherokee Old Settlers in the Arkansas
    River Valley, 6, 14
Cherokee, xvi, xxxiii
Civil War, 114, 163, 192
Cleland, Charles, xxvi
Cohen, Jacob, 198
Coleman, Roger, xxxiv
color, 207, 209, 2010; Black, 207; blue,
    207, 209; brown, 207, 2010; green,
    207; purple, 207, 209; red, 207, 209
columns on mansion porches in Little
    Rock, 10
Conference on Historic Sites Archaeology,
    xviii
conflict archaeology, 165
contextual archaeology, 130–31
Conway Water System, xxvii
corn, 135–36, 154n6
corncrib, 138
cotton, 193
Crockett, Davy, 193

Dallas County potteries, 1, 9
Dardanelle Reservoir, xvi
Davenport, John: ceramics factory and
    marks, 3
Davidson, James, xxvi
Davidsonville, AR, 5, 11, 13–14, 136
Davis, Hester, xxii, xxiii
Deetz, James, 6, 131
dendrochronology, 137–38, 143
dollar exchange, xix–xxi
Dollar, Clyde, xviii, 6, 166; effect on his-
    torical archaeology xix–xxi.
    See Dollar Exchange
Dooley's Ferry xxxviii, 167, 169
Dr. J. Hostetter's Stomach Bitters, 124
Drennen-Scott House (Van Buren, AR), 5
Duwali (Cherokee), xxxiii
Dwight Mission, xvi

Etchieson, Meeks, xxxiv

farming community, 132–33
farmsteads, 130–31: Lewis farmstead, 137–49; Moser farmstead, 142
Fayetteville, 11, 44, 54, 134–36
Federal Style (architecture), 7
Felsenthal Region, xxx
Fields, Anna Page, 28, 40
Folk Art and Technology Students, 28
Fooy, Benjamin, 6
Ford, James, xvii
Fort Carlos III, xvii
Fort Curtis, 166, 168
Fort Esteban, xvii
Fort Harrison, 113
Fort Jessup, 113
Fort Michilimackinac, xxv
Fort Smith, xviii–xxi, xxv, 5, 111–26, 164, 166
France, xvi, xxxiv
Freeman, Lazarus and Levi, 33
Freeman, William Riley, 35
Fritz, Gayle, xxvi
Fulton, AR, 192
fur trade, xvi

Gann Museum, 80
Georgian Style (architecture), 148
Gerstäcker, Friedrich, xv
GIS modeling, 29–30
Glassie, Henry, 145, 153n1
Greek Revival Style (architecture), 7, 11
ground-penetrating radar, 51, 52
Gunter, Louis and Norma Ross, 32

Harrington, J.C., xv, xvii
Hays, Hetty, 199
Helena, AR, 166, 167, 168
Hempstead County, 137, 193, 199
Henderson and Gaines (importers), 3–4
Heritage, production of, 130, 149–51
hillbilly stereotype, 142, 154n7
Historic Washington State Park, xiii, xxvi, xxviii–xxx, xxxi–xxxii, xxxvii, 164
historical archaeology: and marginalized populations xi; definitions of xii; origins of field, xv; growth of, xxvii–xxviii

Hobbes State Park, ix–x
Hodges, T.L. and Charlotte, xv, xvii
Hoffman, Michael, xxv
hogs, 136, 154n6
Holder, Preston, xvii
Hot Springs National Park, xxxvi
Houston, Sam, 193
Howard family, 37
Howard, George, 37–38
Howe Pottery: archaeology, 57–85; kiln construction details, 66–69, 70; methods, 66; stoneware decoration techniques, 71–75; vessel types, 73–74
Hull, David, 32
Hume, Ivor Noël, 167
Hunt, William, xxxvi
Hyman, Paula, 208

Immaculate Conception Church, 111–12, 114–16, 118–19, 125
Indian Creek, 24; families along, 25
Indian Territory, 113–14, 125
infirmary, 116, 119
Isaacs, Isaiah, 195–96, 198, 199
isolation, 13

JD Wilbur Pottery, xxv
Jeane, David, xxxiv
Jewish, 191, 193, 194, 195, 197, 198, 199, 200, 201, 202, 208, 209, 2011; and archaeology, 193, 194, 202, 208; in Baltimore, MD, 194; in Barbados, 193; in Boston, MA, 194; businessmen, 192, 197; in Chesterfield, CT, 194; diaspora, 193, 194, 211; Five Points, 194; in Jamaica, 193; in Manhattan, 194; in Michilimackinac, MI, 194; in Nevis, 193; in New York, 194; in Sacramento, CA, 194; in San Francisco, CA, 194; in Staten Island, 194; Sephardic, 192, 201, 208, 209; in St. Eustatius, 193; Oakland, CA, 194
Jones, Shaderick, 35
Judaism. See Jewish
Jurney, David, xxv

Kashrut. See Kosher
kiln furniture, 66–71, 74; typology, 73–74
kin-based settlement, 27, 29
kinship, 134
kitchens: Block, 7; Sanders, 14
Korn, Bertram Wallace, 197–98
Kosher, 203–4
Knudsen, Gary, xxxiv
Kwas, Mary, xii–xiii, xxxvii, 199

Lafferty, Robert, xxxv
Lake Dumond, xxxiv
Lakeport (Lake Village, AR), 5; archaeo-
    logical work, 8; "Quarters," 8
Land use, 33–38
Landis's Missouri Battery, 180–84
Latham, Cledyth Page, 31
Lawrence County, 136
LeMaster, Caroline, 191, 195 (ff)
Leonard's Valley, 24, 25
Lewis, Hugh, 136–40
Lincoln, Abraham, 130, 151
Liquizone, 124
Little Bighorn, Battle of, 167, 172
Little Rock, 9–11, 14, 114–15, 137.
    See Ashley Mansion
log architecture: cabins, 130, 145;
    construction, 144–48; floor plans,
    147–49; Lewis Home, 129, 137–49;
    origins of, 129
Log Cabin Campaign, 129
log cabins. *See* log architecture
Louisiana, 192
Lovely, Maj. William L., 112
Lower Mississippi Valley Survey, xvi

Madison County, AR, 146
maritime archaeology, xxxii
Markus, David, xxx, xxxvii
Martin, Patrick, xxv
Martin, William, xxvii
material culture, 131
Mathis, Jewell Page, 31, 39
McAlexander, William, xxxii
McClurkan, Burney, xxxvi, 166
McCrocklin, Claude, xxxiii
McDowell, Linda, 199
McGimsey, Charles R. xxii

McGowan Cemetery, 29, 35
memories, historical, 129, 149–51
memoryscape, 39–41
Menard (Menard-Hodges) site, xvii, xviii,
    xxxiv
Mercy Hospital, 119, 125
Mexican-American War, 111, 114
mid-South (region), xii
Mikvah, 194
Military Road, 57–59, 58, 61, 63–64, 66,
    75–77
Miller, John, xxxiv
Minyan, 201
Mississippi River, 6, 9
Missouri Compromise, 192
Missouri Territory, 193
Moccasin Creek, 24; families along, 25;
    folk culture, 28
Mohel, 200
Montell, Lynwood, 27, 32, 34, 36, 39–41
Monterrey, Battle of, 114
Montgomery's Tavern, xxv
Moser Farmstead, xxxi
Mount Comfort Church, xxxvi–xxxvii,
    169
myths, historical, 129–30, 149–51

National Historic Preservation Act, xviii,
    xxiii–xxiv; creating increase in
    research xxiv
National Park Service, xiii, xvii, xviii, xxv,
    xxxv; and Midwest Archeological
    Center, xvi, xxxv. *See also* Arkansas
    Post, Fort Smith, Hot Springs, Pea
    Ridge National Military Park
National Register of Historic Places, 44
Native Americans, xv, xvi, xxxiii–xxxiv,
    163; Cherokee 132; Osage 132
New Orleans, 4, 192, 196, 201
New York, 192, 199
Nuttall, Thomas, 113

Oakleaf Hotel. *See* Ashley Mansion
Occident and American Jewish Advocate,
    201
Old Davidsonville State Park, xiii, xxvi,
    xxviii–xxix, xxxvii
Osotouy, xvii

Overland Mail Company, 135
Ozark Mountains, AR, 3
Ozark National Forest, 23–24
Ozarks (region), 130–52; perception of,
    142

Page and Montell collections, 27
Page family farmsteads, 37
Page, Bill, 38–39
Page, Earl, 39
Page, John, 28, 32, 35
Page, Lottie, 38
Page, Mart and Mattie, 32
Page, Nehemiah Scott, 28–31, 33, 36–38
Page, Nora, 37
Page, Quinn, 38
Page, Robert, 35
Page, Steve, 28
Page, Tate, 27, 32–34, 36, 39–41
Page, Thomas G., 32
Pain, Samuel H., 35
Palmer, Edward, xiv, xvi, 5
Panamerican Consultants, Inc., 58
Parker, Isaac, 126
Parkin Lumber Company, xxiii
Pea Ridge, Battle of, 45, 48, 172–74
Pea Ridge National Military Park, xviii,
    xxxv–xxxvi, 164, 167–68; archaeol-
    ogy at, 174–77; significance of, xix.
    See also Wilson, Rex
Pfeiffer, Michael, xxxiv
Phillips, Clara Howard, 38
Phillips, Phillip, xvii
Pioneer Washington Cemetery, 202
population counts: Allen Township, 25
Poteau River, 112–13
Prairie Grove, 45, 47, 48; Battle of, 168

Quapaw, xvii
quarters for enslaved persons; at Ashley
    Mansion, 9, 12–13; at Lakeport
    Plantation, 9; at Sanders House,
    14–15

refined earthenware: edged, 141–42;
    painted, 141; printed, 141
remote sensing, 51, 54
Reservoir Salvage Act, xxiii

Ridge House (Fayetteville), 5
Riggs, John, xxxiv
ritual bath. See *Mikvah*
River Basin Survey, xv
Ross Community, 25
Ross families, 37
Ross, Martin C., 31
Rowe, Moss, 205–6
Ruff, Barbara, 203

S.S. Homer, xxxii
S.S. Sultana, xxxii
Sabo, George xxvi, xxxiii
saddlebag-style house, 148
Sanborn Fire Insurance maps, 116,
    118–19, 122
Sanders House (Washington, AR): home
    of Simon Sanders's family, 14;
    kitchen, 15–16; Sarah Virginia
    Sanders Garland, 15–16
Santeford, Lawrence, xxvii
Sawdust Hill Community, xxx
sawmills, 143–44
Schambach, Frank xxviii
Scott, Douglas, xxxv
Section 106 compliance, 57
self-sufficiency: myth of, 144
settlement, 27, 29, 33–38
settlers, 131–34, 153n3
Shannon Cemetery, 29, 35
Sharp County potteries, 9
Shiloh Museum of Ozark History, 130,
    149–52
Sisters of Mercy, 111–12, 114–16,
    118–23, 125–26
slavery, 132, 192, 194, 198, 199, 205,
    207, 209, 2010; quarters, 205
Small Business Set Aside Program, xxx
Smith, Sam xxvi
Smith, Gen. Thomas A., 112
smokehouse, 138
Society for Historical Archaeology, xix
South, Stanley, xviii
Southern Memorial Association, 44, 45,
    47, 48, 51, 55
Southwest Trail, 193
Spadra site (Johnson County), xvi, xxv, 6
Spears, Carol, xxxv

St. Anne's Academy, 111, 116, 118–20, 125–26
St. Edward's, 116, 119, 125
Stahle, David, xxv
steamboats, xxxii, 135, 142
Stevenson, William, xiv, 193
Stewart-Abernathy, Leslie C. "Skip," xii, xxvi, xxxii, xxxviii–xxxix, 28, 142
Stone, Lyle, xxvi
stoneware dealers: Caldwell, Henry T., 65, 82
stoneware potters: Bird/Byrd brothers, 60, 81; Davis, Lee, 62; Dovey, Arthur, 63; Glass, Lafayette, 60, 81–82; Henderson, Samuel, 62; Herrick, Amos L., 64–65; Herrick, E.L., 64; Howe, James H., 64–65, 72, 79, 82; Hyten, C.D. "Bullet," 62–63, 75, 85; Leech, J.J., 64, 73, 81–82; Roark & Wilbur, 81; Warren, A.W., 65; Welch, John, 60, 81; Wilburn J.D., 81; Womack, David, 62
stoneware: in Dallas County, AR, 1, 9; in Saline County, AR, 9; in Sharp County, AR, 9; in Washington County, AR, 9
subsistence, 135–36, 154n6
synagogue, 192, 194, 199–200, 201, 209; Dispersed of Judah (*Nefutze Judah*), 201, 209; Gates of Mercy, 192, 200; Shearith Israel, 199

Tara sites, xxxiii
Taylor, Zachary, 111–26
Tennessee Valley Authority, xv
Texas, 192; Dallas, 192; Houston, 192
thematic mapping, 29–30, 33
Thomas, Jerry, xxviii
Threemile Creek, xxvi
townships, 153n5

Treat, 24–25
Treat Cemetery, 29
tree-ring dating. *See* dendrochronology
Trubowitz, Neil, xxviii

University of Arkansas, 52
urban farmsteads, xxx, 205
urban renewal, 10
Utley, Robert, xix

Valentino, Alicia, xxxvi
Van Buren, 135, 142
Van Winkle Mill (Washington County), ix–x, xxxvi, 5, 143–44
Van Winkle, Peter, x
Virginia, 195, 198; Charlottesville, 195; Richmond, 195, 196, 199, 200

Walker-Stone House, xxvi
Wallace Bottom, xxxiv
Wallace's Ferry, action at, 168
War of 1812, 113, 196
Washington County, AR, 132–37, 142, 146
Washington, AR, 3, 6–7, 11, 14, 137, 191, 192, 193, 194, 196, 199, 201, 202, 205
waster sherds: piles, 58, 59, 66, 69–71
Waterman, Dave, 32
Watkins, Beverly xxx, xxxi
West, Elliott, ix, x
Westbury, William, xxv
Western Kentucky University, 27–28
White River Township, 133–40
White River, 133
Wilson, Rex, xviii
Works Progress Administration (WPA), xv; Early Settlers' Personal Histories, 146
World War II, 163